Taking Conspiracy Theories Seriously

COLLECTIVE STUDIES IN KNOWLEDGE AND SOCIETY

Series Editor: James H. Collier is Associate Professor of Science and Technology in Society at Virginia Tech.

This is an interdisciplinary series published in collaboration with the Social Epistemology Review and Reply Collective. It addresses questions arising from understanding knowledge as constituted by, and constitutive of, existing, dynamic and governable social relations.

The Future of Social Epistemology: A Collective Vision, edited by James H. Collier

Social Epistemology and Technology: Toward Public Self-Awareness Regarding Technological Mediation, edited by Frank Scalambrino

Socrates Tenured: The Institutions of 21st Century Philosophy, Adam Briggle and Robert Frodeman

Social Epistemology and Epistemic Agency, edited by Patrick J. Reider

Democratic Problem-Solving: Dialogues in Social Epistemology, Justin Cruickshank and Raphael Sassower

The Kuhnian Image of Science: Time for a Decisive Transformation?, edited by Moti Mizrahi

Taking Conspiracy Theories Seriously, edited by M R. X. Dentith

Overcoming Epistemic Injustice: Social and Psychological Perspectives, edited by Benjamin R. Sherman and Stacey Goguen (forthcoming)

Taking Conspiracy Theories Seriously

Edited by
M R. X. Dentith

ROWMAN &
LITTLEFIELD
INTERNATIONAL

Lanham • Boulder • New York • London

Published by Rowman & Littlefield International Ltd
6 Tinworth Street, London SE11 5AL, United Kingdom
www.rowmaninternational.com

Rowman & Littlefield International Ltd. is an affiliate of Rowman & Littlefield
4501 Forbes Boulevard, Suite 200, Lanham, Maryland 20706, USA
With additional offices in Boulder, New York, Toronto (Canada), and Plymouth (UK)
www.rowman.com

British Library Cataloguing in Publication Data
A catalogue record for this book is available from the British Library

ISBN: HB 978-1-7866-0828-4
    PB: 978-1-7866-0829-1

Library of Congress Cataloging-in-Publication Data
Names: Dentith, Matthew R. X., 1977- editor.
Title: Taking conspiracy theories seriously / edited by Matthew R. X. Dentith.
Description: Lanham : Rowman & Littlefield International, [2018] | Series: Collective
studies in knowledge and society | Includes bibliographical references and index.
Identifiers: LCCN 2018035886 (print) | LCCN 2018038022 (ebook) | ISBN
9781786608307 (electronic) | ISBN 9781786608284 (cloth : alk. paper) | ISBN
9781786608291 (pbk. : alk. paper)
Subjects: LCSH: Conspiracy theories—Philosophy.
Classification: LCC HV6275 (ebook) | LCC HV6275 .T35 2018 (print) | DDC
001.9—dc23
LC record available at https://lccn.loc.gov/2018035886

Contents

Acknowledgments

This book principally owes itself to James Collier, former editor of the *Social Epistemology Review and Reply Collective* (SERRC), who suggested that the fruitful exchanges about conspiracy theory and conspiracy theory theory, which appeared in the pages of the SERRC, would make for a good volume on the topic. Of course, it also goes without saying that the book also owes itself to the contributors to that set of exchanges—Kurtis Hagen, Lee Basham, Martin Orr, and Patrick Stokes—and the new contributors—Charles Pigden, David Coady, Ginna Husting, and Marius Hans Raab—without whom this book would be an empty vessel.

This book is also the by-product of a project I undertook at the Institute for Research in the Humanities (ICUB-IRH) at the University of Bucharest (Romania), and thus that institution can be held partially to blame or praise for the text. Much of the substance of my contributions to this volume was developed while I was in Bucharest from September 2016 to September 2017. Especial thanks, then, to Mihnea Dobre and Iulia Nitescu for their support for my work there. I also cannot stress how much help and support I received from my fellow Fellow Timothy Tambassi (even if his greatest creation—the pita pizza—made me think that there was something deeply wrong in the world that even my theory of conspiracy theory could not possibly explain) and Giulia Lasagni (who shared with me the horror of Timothy's attempt to rewrite the nature of pizza itself).

For my own part I want to dedicate this book to my Aunt Dorothy, who would have thought this book was fabulous and, who as the literal red-headed stepchild of the family, taught me the secret of naughty-naughty time. I think my getting to write on both conspiracy theory and conspiracy theory theory would have made her very chuffed. I also cannot help but mention my partner-in-crime, H. O. Ransome: you are one hoopy frood who really knows where his towel is.

Introduction

M R. X. Dentith

This book began as a series of productive exchanges in the pages of the *Social Epistemology Review and Reply Collective*, where a number of contributors grappled with some of the more interesting aspects of conspiracy theory theory (the *theory* of conspiracy theory). I say "more interesting" because conspiracy theory and conspiracy theory theory are, I would argue, interesting in their own right. After all, whether you think we live in an age of conspiracy theories, or that they are a problem in search of a cure, conspiracy theories and the study of such theories has been, and is, a fertile playground for philosophers, sociologists, and psychologists (as the contributors to this volume admirably attest to). However this volume takes conspiracy theory seriously in a way that much of the recent literature has not; we are advocating not just that we take conspiracy theory seriously as a *topic of study*, but also that conspiracy theories themselves should not be dismissed just because they have been pejoratively labeled as "conspiracy theories."

This volume consists of both adapted and new material. Some of the chapters—by Kurtis Hagen, Lee Basham, Martin Orr, Patrick Stokes,[1] and, of course, myself—further the arguments and themes originally published in the journal of the *Social Epistemology Review and Reply Collective*. Others—by Charles Pigden, David Coady, Marius Hans Raab, and Ginna Husting—are unique to this volume.

The volume also consists of two parts, the first of which may well come across as a little vainglorious. Section One begins with a reprint of my article "When Inferring to a Conspiracy Might Be the Best Explanation," which was first published in *Social Epistemology* (2016b). This led James Collier, then editor of the *Social Epistemology Review and Reply Collective,* to commission a series of reply pieces from Lee Basham and Patrick Stokes. Their dueling replies ended up focusing on a specific question in conspiracy theory theory: just what does the particularist position in the field of conspiracy theory theories entail?

The term *particularism* is a term of art we owe to Joel Buenting and Jason Taylor, who—in their paper "Conspiracy Theories and Fortuitous Data"— carved at the conceptual joint two approaches to talk of conspiracy theory in the existing academic literature: *particularism* and *generalism* (2010).[2] The generalist position advocates a *general* approach to talk of conspiracy theory, choosing to treat such theories as a class and judging them accordingly. Generalist positions treat belief in conspiracy theories as problematic *generally*. That is, generalists treat the label "conspiracy theory" and "conspiracy theorist" as a pejorative.

The particularist, however, argues that we have to treat conspiracy theories like we would any other theory, and evaluate them on their merits. That is, we cannot generalize about the class of conspiracy theories in order to judge particular instances of them. Rather, we must treat each and every conspiracy theory according to the evidence.

The position I argued for in "When Inferring to a Conspiracy Might Be the Best Explanation" is a particularist one: given that conspiracy theories can satisfy the requirements of the inference to the best explanation, then we ought to assess such theories like we would any other theory. However, in the second chapter, "Conspiracy Theory and the Perils of Pure Particularism," Stokes argues that no matter the epistemic merits of being a particularist, there are ethical considerations we must take into account when engaging in the *social practice* of conspiracy theorizing. Stokes advocates the adoption of a kind of *reluctant* particularism, where the social practice of theorizing about conspiracies turns out to be something we should be reluctant to engage in.

Basham, however, disagrees. In chapter 3, "Conspiracy Theory Particularism, both Epistemic and Moral, Versus Generalism," his argument is that particularism is just that: particularism, and a *reluctant* or *defeasible* particularism is just generalism under another name. This is a point I reiterate in chapter 4, "What Particularism about Conspiracy Theories Entails." I argue that what motivates Stokes' reluctant particularism is not so much a problem with particularism but, rather, the foibles of people theorizing on their own time. As such, we do not need to restrict or become reluctant about particularism. Rather, we need to embrace it while also educating others about it.[3]

The second section of this volume, "Diagnosing Conspiracy Theory Theorists," is inspired by an opinion piece that appeared in the June 6, 2016 edition of the French newspaper *Le Monde*. In the *Le Monde* piece, "Luttons Efficacement Contre Les Théories Du Complot," a collection of French social scientists and one UK-based Australian social psychologist—Gérald Bronner (Sociology, Université Paris-Diderot), Véronique Campion-Vincent (Sociology, Maison des Sciences de l'Homme), Sylvain Delouvée (Social

Psychology, Université Rennes), Sebastian Dieguez (Neuro-psychology, Université de Fribourg), Karen Douglas (Social Psychology, University of Kent), Nicolas Gauvrit (Cognitive Psychology, École Pratique des Hautes Études), Anthony Lantian (Social Psychology, Université de Reims), and Pascal Wagner-Egger (Social Psychology, Université de Fribourg)—argued that the reaction by the French State to (apparent) conspiracist tendencies among the French public has, thus far, been too hasty, and taken time and money away from the more methodical studies of conspiracy theories which they engage in (2016). These works are briefly glossed and discussed in chapter 5.

The appearance of this piece led Lee Basham and myself to author a response, which was co-signed by a number of contributors to this volume (2016). We argued that their prescription was a solution in search of a problem. This, in turn, led to a response by the authors of the *Le Monde* piece (sans Karen Douglas), in which they criticized our take on their own work, and said that they were simply "asking questions" (Dieguez et al. 2016).

We offered the co-authors of the *Le Monde* piece the opportunity to contribute to this volume, but they—as a group—decided neither to contribute, nor let us reprint their work. This puts them at a disadvantage, but does not present any great challenge to us: the chapters in the second section deal broadly with issues having to do with the social scientific discussion of conspiracy theories *generally*, of which the authors of the original *Le Monde* opinion piece (and its associated reply) are merely representative.

In chapter 6, "The Psychologists' Conspiracy Panic: They Seek to Cure Everyone," Lee Basham and I relate the general project espoused by Bronner et al. to the concerns of the social scientific study of conspiracy theory as a whole. We argue that the danger of condemning both conspiracy theorists and their conspiracy theories inherent to this kind of research program has grave consequences both epistemically and politically.

In chapter 7, "Social Scientists and Pathologizing Conspiracy Theorizing," Lee Basham argues that a conspiracy theory phobia distorts and pathologizes the social scientific evaluation of conspiracy theories and conspiracy theorizing. This notion of a conspiracy theory phobia is also addressed in chapter 8, "Governing with Feeling: Conspiracy Theories, Contempt, and Affective Governmentality," where Ginna Husting, using Arendt's theory of political action, argues that a "conspiracy panic" polices the boundaries of what is able to be said, known, thought, or felt, placing the purported conspiracy theorist outside the bounds of "reasonable politics."

In chapter 9, "Conspiracy Theorists and Social Scientists," Kurtis Hagen argues some epistemic humility on the part of the social scientists who study conspiracy theories and conspiracy theorists would benefit their research programs, given that their studies inappropriately pathologize conspiracy theorists, which in turn makes them as critics as guilty as their putative charges.

In chapter 10, "Clearing Up Some Conceptual Confusions about Conspiracy Theory Theorizing," Martin Orr and I argue that a recurrent problem in much of the wider academic literature on conspiracy theories is either a conceptual confusion or a refusal to put theory before practice, either of which is at odds not just with the philosophical literature but also the general tenor of the social sciences over the latter part of the twentieth century and beyond.

In chapter 11, "To Measure or Not to Measure? Psychometrics and Conspiracy Theories," Marius Hans Raab discusses the various benefits and costs of how psychologists measure belief in conspiracy theories. Used reasonably, such measurements can enrich philosophical discussions with empirical findings. However, the approaches we currently find in psychology suggest an accuracy in measurement that is impossible given the fuzziness of the construct being measured.

In chapter 12, "Anti-Rumor Campaigns and Conspiracy-Baiting as Propaganda," David Coady compares rumors and conspiracy theories, arguing that neither deserve their bad reputations, reputations which are the result of a certain kind of anti-democratic propaganda.

In chapter 13, "On Some Moral Costs of Conspiracy Theory," Stokes returns to his argument about the moral costs of conspiracy theory and conspiracy theorizing, arguing that the tendency to generate and expand accusations in order to defend the core thesis of the conspiracy theory abuses important ethical norms. Responding to Stokes, in chapter 14, "Conspiracy Theories, Deplorables and Defectibility: A Reply to Patrick Stokes," Charles Pigden argues that the kind of conspiracy theories which motivate Stokes' reluctant particularism can be appraised on purely particularist grounds if we consider the cost or benefit of defection by conspirators.

Finally, in chapter 15, "Taking Conspiracy Theories Seriously and Investigating Them," I have the unenviable task (in that trying to keep to the standard of the preceding chapters is a Herculean task) of tying this volume together. Reflecting on previous work, I argue that we should not only treat conspiracy theories seriously, but we should investigate them, using Deweyan communities of inquiry as a model. Treating conspiracy theories seriously requires we engage in a systemic investigation of them, foregoing generalism of any kind. Rather, we must investigate the particulars of each and every theory.

It is our hope that these contributions will lead to even more fruitful work in conspiracy theory theory. Collectively these chapters argue that we need to take the study of conspiracy theories seriously, but also take particular conspiracy theories seriously too. Once we dispense with a generalist take on conspiracy theory and conspiracy theorizing, our only option is to embrace particularism and, of course, conspiracy theory.

NOTES

1. Stokes also provides us with a new piece unique to this volume in Section Two.

2. It is fair to say that analyses of conspiracy theory through the lens of particularism and generalism predate Buenting and Taylor, but the labels themselves appear to be theirs.

3. A point Charles Pigden also presses in chapter 14 of this volume.

Section One

THE PARTICULARIST TURN IN THE PHILOSOPHY OF CONSPIRACY THEORIES

Chapter 1

When Inferring to a Conspiracy Might Be the Best Explanation[1]

M R. X. Dentith

1. INTRODUCTION

While philosophers have been late in coming to the analysis of these things we call "conspiracy theories," it seems that—as a discipline—many of us analyze them with much more sympathy than our peers in the social sciences. In a raft of papers and books, starting with Charles Pigden's "Popper Revisited, or What Is Wrong with Conspiracy Theories?" (1995), philosophers like Brian L. Keeley (1999), Juha Räikkä (2009a), Joel Buenting and Jason Taylor (2010), Lee Basham (2011), David Coady (2012), and myself (2014) have argued that as conspiracies occur—and that theories about conspiracies sometimes turn out to be warranted—conspiracy theories cannot automatically be dismissed just because they are called "conspiracy theories."[2]

This does not mean that philosophers consider belief in conspiracy theories to be the exemplar of rational thinking; the current findings in the Philosophy of Conspiracy Theories (to coin a new discipline) simply show that belief in conspiracy theories is not prima facie irrational. Rather, the kind of issues often held up as being a problem for belief in conspiracy theories tend to also be examples of issues common to a great many other beliefs that we do not typically think of as prima facie suspicious.

However, there still remains the view among some philosophers—and a great many thinkers in other disciplines—that even if explanations of events citing conspiracies can be warranted, conspiracy theories themselves are still unlikely. For sure, many of the complaints such conspiracy theory theorists (to coin another name) have about belief in conspiracy theories get phrased in terms of conspiracy theorists seeing conspiracies where none exist, or being prone to making bad inferences. Yet at the heart of these complaints— as we will see—are claims either about the unlikeliness of conspiracies or conspiracy theories. These claims of unlikeliness are then meant to explain why most ordinary people (and a large number of academics) are justified in treating conspiracy theories as a kind of suspicious belief. Yet, as we shall see, it is not obvious that conspiracy theories are unlikely. Indeed, when we understand what this supposed unlikeliness means, it throws an interesting light on how we sometimes avoid talking about just how much conspiratorial activity might be going on around us. Not just that: as we will also see, our judgments about the likeliness of conspiracies and conspiracy theories, in turn, affect our judgments as to when some theory about a conspiracy might just qualify as an inference to the best explanation.

1.1 Philosophers and the Unlikeliness of Conspiracy Theories

Let us start with the philosophers. Karl Popper, in *The Open Society and Its Enemies*, considers conspiracy theories to be unlikely. Why? Because such theories take it that history is largely the result of a succession of successful conspiracies. However, Popper believes that as most of us accept conspiracies are both rare and seldom successful, conspiracy theories are just unlikely (1969). While Popper accepts that conspiracies occur, belief in what he calls the "conspiracy theory of society" is irrational because conspiracy theories are rarely warranted. Popper's most modern echo is Quassim Cassam, who argues that conspiracy theorists suffer from the epistemic vice of gullibility.[3] As such, while he—like Popper before him—admits conspiracies occur, conspiracy theories—being the kind of thing *gullible* conspiracy theorists believe—simply turn out to be so unlikely as to be untrue (2015).

Neil Levy argues that conspiracy theories which conflict with official theories—theories that have been endorsed by some authority—are prima facie unwarranted. As such, they turn out to be unlikely compared to their non-conspiratorial rivals (2007).

Pete Mandik takes a slightly different tack, and argues that when there is conflict between an official theory of the type "shit happens"[4] and a conspiracy theory, then we have no good reason to *prefer* the conspiracy theory (2007). Conspiracy theories are, for Mandik, no more likely than their non-conspiratorial rivals. Indeed, because conspiracy theories often portray a world of complex causation—which might be better understood as the result of the law of unintended consequences—we are justified in thinking conspiracy theories are prima facie unlikely. This, in turn, justifies our preference for the hypothesis that "shit just happens."

Mandik's view echoes an argument put forward by Steve Clarke. Clarke argues that conspiracy theories are examples of dispositional explanations (explanations which rely on some central claim of someone *intending* for an event to happen). He argues that we should prefer situational explanations

(explanations which rely on some central claim about the context or situation under which a series of events occurred), because situational explanations are better than claiming some event was the result of intentional activity. Given that most of the rival explanations to conspiracy theories—so Clarke claims—are situational in character, we should think conspiracy theories—as dispositional explanations—are unlikely, at least compared to their situational rivals (2002).[5]

Peter Lipton—in what is admittedly only a passing reference in his book *Inference to the Best Explanation*—thinks that conspiracy theories may very well be unlikely, using such theories to illustrate how to disambiguate what it is we mean by "best" when parsing talk of inference to the best explanation.

> By showing that many apparently unrelated events flow from a single source and many apparent coincidences are really related, such a [conspiracy] theory may have considerable explanatory power. If only it were true, it would provide a very good explanation. That is, it is lovely. At the same time, such an explanation may be very unlikely, accepted only by those whose ability to weigh evidence has been compromised by paranoia. (2004, 59–60)

Lipton distinguishes two notions of "best": the most likely explanation, and the one that provides the most understanding (with respect to some account of the explanatory virtues), which he calls the "loveliest explanation." Lipton considers conspiracy theories to be problematic because, while they have some lovely features (if they were true they really would provide a very good explanation as to why some event occurred) they are unlikely compared to their rivals. This is because Lipton assumes that conspiracy theories *only seem likely* because conspiracy theorists suffer from paranoia.[6] For Lipton, it is evidence (or the lack thereof) that makes conspiracy theories unlikely because conspiracy theorists are paranoid, and thus see evidence of conspiracies where none exist.

1.2 Non-philosophers and the Unlikeliness of Conspiracy Theories

These philosophers who think that conspiracy theories are unlikely are in good company. For example, Cass Sunstein and Adrian Vermeule (foreshadowing Cassam) claim conspiracy theorists suffer from a "crippled epistemology." Conspiracy theories are unlikely because the:

> [A]cceptance of such [conspiracy] theories may not be irrational or unjustified from the standpoint of those who adhere to them within epistemologically isolated groups or networks, although they are unjustified relative to the information available in the wider society[.] (2009, 204)

Which is to say that conspiracy theories look likely to conspiracy theorists, but only because they typically consort with, and gain information from, other like-minded individuals.

Similarly, Michael J. Wood and Karen M. Douglas argue that conspiracy theorists are, typically, more interested in disputing rival and official theories than they are promoting their own conspiracy theories. They characterize conspiracy theories as a kind of "negative belief," one which calls into question another explanation, and is indicative of a worldview in which most of what we are told is a lie. They consign belief in such theories to something akin to paranoia (Wood and Douglas 2013).

Jovan Byford differentiates conspiracy theories from "legitimate analyses of secrecy,"[7] arguing—like Popper before him—that as conspiracy theorists see the world as the product of successive and successful conspiracies, conspiracy theories are unlikely. This is because they do not reflect the way in which the world actually works (2011).

Meanwhile, Robert Brotherton and Christopher C. French build into their definition of what counts as a "conspiracy theory" that such theories are "an unverified and relatively implausible allegation of conspiracy, claiming that significant events are the result of a secret plot carried out by a preternaturally sinister and powerful group of people." As such, they take it as a given that conspiracy theories are going to be unlikely (2014).

Much of this kind of work accepts that conspiracies occur, but holds that conspiracy theorizing—the generation of, or coming up with, conspiracy theories—is a suspicious kind of activity to engage in. As Sander van der Linden writes:

> Clearly, people and governments have conspired against each other, throughout human history. Healthy skepticism lies at the very heart of the scientific endeavor. Yet there is something fundamentally dangerous and unscientific about the nature of conspiracy theorizing. (2015)

There is something chilling about this kind of sentiment. "Yes," the proponent of this view agrees, "conspiracies occur. Just don't go around suspecting people of conspiring; that's unhealthy!" While often this suspicion of conspiracy theorizing is couched in terms of conspiracy theorists suffering from some ominous and psychological pathology, a failure by said theorists to think critically about their conspiracy theories, or the inability for adherents of conspiracy theories to contemplate non-conspiratorial alternatives, at root this suspicion stems from some variety of the claim "Look, conspiracies are unlikely, or even if they do occur, conspiracy theories are unlikely, right?" Yet this latter claim—no matter what we believe about the psychology of conspiracy theorists—is not something we should accept without further examination. This is particularly important because while many of us might reasonably think claims about conspiracies should be evaluated according to the evidence, many theorists—as we have seen—argue that we can dismiss such claims out of hand *merely* because they are conspiracy theories.

2. UNLIKELY COMPARED TO WHAT?

If we are told something is unlikely, we need to ask "In relation to what?" Likeliness is a relative thing. One argument for the relative unlikeliness of conspiracy theories is to claim that conspiracies are unlikely, say, because conspiratorial activity is taken to be rare or, if not rare, seldom successful. Popper—echoed by Byford—argues that conspiracy theorists see the world as the product of successive and successful conspiracies, a position many conspiracy theory theorists take to be obviously false; conspiracies are either unlikely, or, when they do occur, seldom successful. Brotherton and French—in a similar vein—posit that conspiracy theories are unlikely because they are based upon unverified and relatively implausible claims of conspiracy. For theorists of this ilk, conspiracy theories turn out to be unlikely, because of the unlikeliness of conspiracies.

Another argument for the relative unlikeliness of conspiracy theories is that they are unlikely because even if we accept that conspiracies occur, given a choice between a conspiracy and a non-conspiracy theory, the non-conspiratorial explanation will just be more likely, all things considered. This kind of view can be found in the works of Cassam, who takes it conspiracy theorists are gullible (and thus treat conspiracy theories as more likely than they really are); Sunstein and Vermeule (whose argument is a more sophisticated take on Cassam's), who argue conspiracy theorists only see conspiracy theories as likely because they suffer from a "crippled epistemology," born out of existing in isolated epistemic communities; and Levy (as well as Mandik) who claims we have no good reason to *think* conspiracy theories will ever be more likely than their rivals.[8]

Yet it is not clear that conspiracies or conspiracy theories are *relatively* unlikely. For example, Kathryn S. Olmsted's book *Real Enemies: Conspiracy Theories and American Democracy, World War I to 9/11*—in which Olmsted covers topics such as the secrecy behind the United States's entry into the First World War, the ills of the McCarthy Era, and the way in which the official theory of 9/11 was sometimes misrepresented by the authorities for political point-scoring—reads as a litany of US government–run conspiracies. Her calm and dispassionate historical analysis of a century of US political practice presents conspiracies not so much as deviation from the norm, but, rather, as standard operating practice (2009). We can add to this numerous other examples; the Gulf of Tonkin Incident in 1964[9]; the Ford Pinto Scandal of 1977[10]; the Snowden revelations of 2013, concerning the National Security Administration (NSA) in the United States covering up the existence of a mass surveillance program; and the Volkswagen Emissions Scandal of 2015.[11] In each of these cases the idea that the perpetrators were up to no good was labeled as a "conspiracy theory." These examples are but the tip of an iceberg.

So, if, there really is anything to the claim conspiracy theories are *relatively* unlikely, then the debate about said likeliness depends on:

(a) how you define what counts as conspiratorial, and
(b) whether you accept the claim that any official theory which cites a conspiracy as a salient cause is no longer considered to be a conspiracy theory.

Understanding how our definitions of these key terms rules in or out certain kinds of activities or theories as conspiratorial ends up being important not just for our understanding of these things called conspiracy theories, but also for working out whether some claim about a conspiracy can ever qualify as being part of the best explanation for some event.

2.1 What Counts as a Conspiracy?

Conspiracy theories posit the existence of a conspiracy, where the conspiracy is the salient cause of some event. The most minimal conception of what counts as a conspiracy, then, must satisfy the following three conditions:

The Conspirators Condition: There exists (or existed) some set of agents with a plan.[12]
The Secrecy Condition: Steps have been taken by the agents to minimize public awareness of what they are up to.[13]
The Goal Condition: Some end is, or was desired, by the agents.[14]

These conditions are individually necessary and jointly sufficient for some activity to be classified as conspiratorial, and it is fair to say that some beliefs about the likeliness or unlikeliness of conspiracy theories hinge on finessing or questioning such a minimal definition of what counts as a conspiracy.

For example, Mandik argues that theories about *known* conspiracies— citing such examples as the official theories of 9/11, the Watergate Affair, and the Iran-Contra deal—fail to be proper conspiracy *theories*. Why? Because the aforementioned conspiracies were not kept secret; they were not conspiracies in the sense that we typically talk about when discussing conspiracy theories (2007). Yet the view that a conspiracy is not a *proper* conspiracy unless the conspirators keep their activities *properly* secret is incredibly idiosyncratic. If that were the case, how could we have *any* belief in the existence of conspiracies? Indeed, if we accept Mandik's view, then it is not even clear that conspirators could believe in the existence of their own conspiracies. After all, the fact *someone* knows about the conspiracy means it is not being kept *properly* secret. Not just that, but if someone blows the whistle on a conspiracy, does that mean—under Mandik's view—that the conspiracy is no longer a conspiracy because it is no longer secret?

Mandik challenges the idea of known conspiracies being the kind of thing we mean when people talk about conspiracy theories. However, when it comes to the secrecy condition of conspiratorial activity, all we need say is that some conspirators will be more successful at keeping their existence and activities secret than others. If we restrict talk of what counts as conspiratorial to cases of *proper* secrecy, then not only are we using a restrictive definition (with some strange corollaries), but it just follows from said definition that conspiracy theories will be unlikely. After all, if a conspiracy must be kept *properly* secret, then the associated conspiracy theory turns out be irrational to believe. This is because it will not be based upon any good evidence of a conspiracy.[15]

The problem with Mandik's view—and this applies to Popper's as well (who runs a similar argument)—is that what he means by "conspiratorial" does not match what we know of actual conspiratorial activity. A lot hinges on what is captured by the term "conspiracy." If we stick to the minimal definition of conspiracy, then objectors might say that it rules in seemingly non-conspiratorial activities, like that of organizing a surprise party. If this is a bullet we have to bite with regard to the definition of what counts as a conspiracy, then so be it. Surprise parties—like conspiracies—are organized by agents who work in secret, and desire some end. While the minimal definition of what counts as conspiratorial makes conspiracies appear to be either commonplace or, at least, more common than we would typically think, this should not worry us.

After all, if we want to truly appraise whether conspiracies are really unlikely, we need to look at the wider and more general class of conspiratorial activity, one that is ruled in by the minimal definition. If we rule out certain kinds of conspiratorial activity for either not being secret enough, or not being of interest, then that affects our estimates as to how likely or unlikely conspiracies are. After all, one of the key features of the debate over the likeliness and warrant of conspiracy theories is how to account for cases of known historic and contemporary conspiratorial activity. Mandik—like Popper—has to explain away how known conspiratorial activity—and theories about that activity—are either not the subject of warranted conspiracy theories, or not really conspiracies in the first place. Popper, for example, claims that the Holocaust—a massive plot to secretly wipe out the Jewish people in Europe—does not qualify as a conspiracy theory because it is both known and was unsuccessful (1972). As such, defining away certain cases of known conspiracies as *not conspiratorial enough* moves the problem of assessing the likelihood of conspiracy theories away from talk about the evidence to simply making it a definitional issue instead.

2.2 What Counts as a Conspiracy Theory?

No matter what we believe about the likeliness of conspiracies, surely we are justified in thinking that conspiracy *theories* are unlikely? After all, there are an awful lot of conspiracy theories, and many—if not most of them—turn out to be unwarranted. This kind of argument is commonly put forward as one reason for being suspicious about conspiracy theories *generally*, but it, too, relies on us defining what gets ruled in—and what is ruled out—by the term *conspiracy theory*.

Take, for example, official theories or official stories (as they are often interchangeably called). Some official theories—theories which have been endorsed by some authority—are theories about conspiracies, but they are not typically taken to be examples of *conspiracy* theories. One reason for making such a distinction is the idea that conspiracy theories are never official. An endorsed explanation *which cites a conspiracy as a salient cause of some event* cannot be called a "conspiracy theory" because conspiracy theories are—by their very nature—unofficial. Thus, official theories—like the examples of 9/11, Watergate, and the Iran-Contra deal that Mandik offers—might well cite conspiracies as salient causes of those events, but their officialness means that while they are technically theories about conspiracies, they are not conspiracy theories.

One philosopher who argues along these lines is David Coady. However, he does not think conspiracies are unlikely, or that conspiracy theories are prima facie unwarranted. Rather, he merely respects the intuition that such theories are—in some sense—unofficial. In *Conspiracy Theories and Official Stories*, he includes in the definition of a conspiracy theory that:

> Finally, the proposed explanation must conflict with an "official" explanation of the same historical event. (2006b, 117)

and notes:

The last part of this definition rules out the possibility of an official explanation of an event qualifying as a conspiracy theory, no matter how conspiratorial it is. (2006b, 117)

However, Coady does not buy into any claim that theories which are *official* are more warranted or rational to believe, noting that "quite often the official version of events is just as conspiratorial as its rivals." (2006b, 125) More recently Coady has argued for a more conditional view, claiming that if you are the kind of person who thinks conspiracy theories are unofficial, then:

[T]he relationship between conspiracy theories and officialdom is like the relationship between rumors and officialdom, with the difference that rumors are defined as merely lacking official endorsement, whereas conspiracy theories, on this way of understanding them, must actually contradict some official version of events. (2012, 122)

and:

[T]o say that a conspiracy theory by definition contradicts an official version of events is to say nothing about whether it is true, or whether a person who believes it is justified in doing so. (2012, 123)

Coady, then, is not committed to thinking that conspiracy theories will be unlikely compared to official theories. This is because—in a range of cases—some official theories will simply turn out to be unlikely compared to their rival conspiracy theories.

It is useful, then, to contrast Coady's view with that of Levy. Levy stipulates that:

A conspiracy theory that conflicts with the official story, where the official story is the explanation offered by the (relevant) *epistemic authorities*, is prima facie unwarranted. (2007, 182)

Levy builds into the definition of a conspiracy theory the claim that conspiracy theories which are in conflict with some official theory will be unwarranted, and thus automatically so unlikely as to be false.[16] Yet there are many different kinds of official theories, and the officialness of these various kinds is conferred on them in a variety of different ways. Sometimes theories are official because they have been endorsed sincerely by field-relevant experts, and sometimes theories are official because someone has either insincerely endorsed them, or because they have no relevant expertise (and so their endorsement means nothing).

Take, for example, the official theory as to why it was necessary for the United States and the United Kingdom to invade Iraq in order to dismantle a purported Weapons of Mass Destruction (WMD) program. These days it is well accepted that what seemed to be a relevant authority with respect to claims about whether Iraq was keeping secret the existence of a WMD program—the Central Intelligence Agency (CIA)—either insincerely endorsed the official theory for reasons not to do with epistemology but, rather, politics, or mistook the official credentials of certain members of the Intelligence community as being based upon merit, rather than just stature.

It turns out that even relevant authorities can be insincere or duplicitous, and so we cannot simply prefer official theories over conspiracy theories. It is a problem, then, if we build such a stipulation into our definition of such theories. Levy's view restricts what it is we mean by the term *conspiracy theory*. After all, conspiracy theories are just going to be unlikely relative to non-conspiracy theories, if we stipulate that conspiracy theories can never be official, well-accepted explanations; we are, in such cases, restricting the class of things we are comparing the likelihoods of, seemingly in order to ensure that conspiracy theories come off badly, and thus end up being *prima facie* unlikely.

Then there is Clarke. Clarke's argument about the unlikeliness of conspiracy theories hinges on them being the wrong kind of explanation; he builds into the definition of what a conspiracy theory is that they are dispositional explanations—in this case, explanations which cite the intention to conspire as a salient cause—and that we should prefer rival, situational explanations instead (2002). However, there is no obvious case for conspiracy theories being largely dispositional. Indeed, any explanation—conspiracy theory or not—might be an example of both. For example, the official theory about the assassination of President John Fitzgerald Kennedy invokes both the intentions of the lone assassin, and situational factors. Conspiracy theories almost certainly do invoke dispositions, but, then again, so do official theories. It is not even clear that conspiracy theories are any more dispositional than their rivals, or that their rivals are any more situational.

To be fair, Clarke now considers his view about the overly dispositional nature of conspiracy theories to be in error (2006). Instead, he argues that the apparent dispositionality of conspiracy theories is a problem to do with the *psychology of belief in conspiracy theories*, rather than a problem with conspiracy theories as explanations. What is interesting about this is that Cassam echoes Clarke on both the psychology of belief in conspiracy theories, and the situational nature of such conspiracy theories, without picking up on the subsequent critiques of Clarke's work. As Lee Basham and I have argued, the problem for Cassam's version of Clarke's argument[17] is that he characterizes belief in conspiracy theories along the lines of theories *which have already been classified as unlikely* (2015). Cassam gets to his conclusion that con-spiracy theorists suffer from the intellectual vice of gullibility by restricting belief in conspiracy theories to those which he takes it are irrational to believe in the first place. As such, Cassam restricts the scope of what counts as a "conspiracy theory" in order to make belief in such theories prima facie unlikely.

Restricting the definition of what counts as a conspiracy theory ends up making conspiracy theories relatively unlikely, because the interesting cases of warranted conspiracy theories get defined away as not being *proper* conspiracy theories. However, if we keep to a general definition, then we can analyze conspiracy theories with respect to the evidence which either warrants or does not warrant them, rather than dismissing conspiracy theories out of hand for just being conspiracy theories.

3. A CASE FOR TREATING CONSPIRACY THEORIES ON THEIR INDIVIDUAL MERITS

An obvious objection to the preceding arguments is to say something like: "This simply shows that conspiracies and conspiracy theories are more likely than previously thought, but it does not show that such activity and theories are as likely as non-conspiratorial equivalents, let alone more likely." This is an understandable response, but all we need argue is that it is not clear that conspiracies and conspiracy theories are unlikely compared to their rivals. As a consequence, we should take a particularist approach to dealing with claims about conspiracy theories, rather than trying to make general claims about them.

The notion of particularist versus generalist views about conspiracy the-ories comes out of the work of Joel Buenting and Jason Taylor. They argue that when we look at the range of views about conspiracy theories we find there are two opposing positions: generalism and particularism (2010).

According to the generalists, conspiracy theories can be assessed *without considering the particulars of individual conspiracy theories*. It is the view that conspiracy theories are typically irrational.[18] The pejorative definition of what counts as a "conspiracy theory"—which says such theories are unlikely—falls under the rubric of the generalist view.

Particularists, however, argue that the rationality of belief in conspiracy theories can only be assessed by considering the evidence for and against *individual* conspiracy theories. Particularists—particularly Charles Pigden, David Coady, and Lee Basham—have recently gone on the offensive. They have argued not only is particularism a defensible position, but that the generalist strategy has a number of unfortunate consequences. For one, the generalist approach rests upon a naïve understanding of both the appeal to authority, and what role officialness plays in theories which have been endorsed, a point David Coady has stressed (2007). For another, generalists—like Cassam when it comes to the conspiracy and official theories of 9/11—end up looking confused. The generalist has to principally accommodate the conspiracy theories they take to be irrational, as well as the theories *that cite conspiracies as salient causes* which they happen to endorse as warranted. Lee Basham has taken such confusions to task in his work (2011).

Then there is the social cost of generalism. As Charles Pigden has forcefully argued:

> [T]he idea that conspiracy theories *as such* are intellectually suspect helps conspirators, quite literally, to get away with murder (of which killing people in an unjust war is an instance). (in press)

Pigden's point here is worth reiterating: a general skepticism of these things called "conspiracy theories" makes it all the easier for conspirators to get away with their conspiracies. After all, it is easy enough for them to respond to any claim about their activity as being *merely* a conspiracy theory. Yet we need to remember that it is uncontroversial to say conspiracies occur. So why, then, is it controversial to say conspiracy theories are irrational to believe?

As such, the preceding argument as to why we should treat conspiracy theories on their individual merits is designed to bolster the particularist case; given many of the attempts to show that conspiracy theories are unlikely come out of problematic generalizing strategies, should we not assess particular conspiracy theories on their individual merits? If we accept that conspiracies are not unlikely (or, at least, not as unlikely as some conspiracy theory theorists have made out), surely they can—in a range of cases—feature in our best explanations.

3.1 Showing That a Conspiracy Theory is Likely

Particularism requires we assess conspiracy theories on their own merits, and if the evidence shows that both a conspiracy occurred, and said conspiracy is the probable cause of some event, then we should accept some conspiracy theory as both likely, and as the best explanation. So, how might we show that some conspiracy theory is a good explanation? How do we work out whether some explanatory hypothesis *which cites a conspiracy as a salient cause* is the one we want to say is the best explanation of why some event occurred? Well, when we infer to an explanation, we typically consider:

The *posterior* probability: The extent to which the available evidence renders some hypothesis probable.

The *prior* probability: The degree to which the hypothesis is independently likely.

The *relative* probability: The likelihood of the hypothesis, relative to the other hypotheses being considered.

Of course, there is also the possibility that some other, worthwhile hypotheses might not have been considered. Even if we end up accurately appraising the probability of rival hypotheses, it is still possible that some worthwhile candidate might not have been considered, because of a lack of knowledge about them, or because we have a disposition to ignore certain possibilities. Our choice of plausible hypotheses can also be restricted to what we have been told about. Even if we can give an account as to how we satisfy the first three probabilities when inferring to an explanation, it is always possible we have ignored other plausible hypotheses for reasons beyond our control.

For example, Lipton's worry about conspiracy theories comes out of his view that such theories are lovely *but unlikely*. He takes it that one sense of inferring to the best explanation is appealing to the *likeliest explanation*. That is to say, we appeal to the way in which the available evidence renders the hypothesis in question probable. Likely explanations, then, are explanations that are probable in the posterior sense. He contrasts such likely explanations to another conception of the inference to the best explanation, the inference to the *loveliest* explanation. Lovely explanations emphasize not just how the available evidence renders some hypothesis probable, but also include considerations such as the various explanatory virtues. Lipton takes it that lovely explanations include aspects of both prior and relative probability, such as how the explanatory hypothesis is consistent with what else we know, has explanatory power, predicts new and novel observations, applies to a large number of related phenomena, and is simple (2004).

Lipton's worry about conspiracy theories—one that he shares with Cassam, Clarke, Levy, and Mandik—ends up being centered on the idea that either conspiracies or conspiracy theories are generally unlikely; either conspiracies just are independently unlikely, or even if conspiracies do occur, conspiracy theories are rarely warranted. As such, they are unlikely compared to their rivals. Yet, as we have seen, neither of these positions is obvious or warranted; such claims about said independent likeliness typically depend on the definitions of "conspiracy" or "conspiracy theory" we are using. So, while Lipton accepts that conspiracy theories can be lovely, it is not clear that they turn out to be unlikely. That is, unless we define them as such.

3.2 The Independent Likeliness of Conspiracies

Our estimates as to how independently likely conspiracies are vary over time. Certainly, post the revelations of the NSA's mass surveillance program by Edward Snowden in 2013, claims of large-scale, political conspiracy have been treated much more sympathetically, and considered more likely by ordinary reasoners; it appears people *underestimated* how independently likely it was that a major, political conspiracy was happening here-and-now.

Working out the true prior probability or independent likeliness of claims of conspiracy being in among the pool of credible explanatory hypotheses will be, of course, difficult. However, it is fair to say that people either underestimate or underplay both historical and contemporary accounts of events which cite conspiracies as salient causes.

Take, for example, the extraordinary death of Alexander Litvinenko. He was poisoned with the rare, expensive, and highly radioactive radionuclide, polonium-210. Litvinenko, a former Russian Federal Security Bureau (FSB) agent, was living in exile in London at the time of his death, and was a vocal detractor of Russian Federation president Vladimir Putin. On November 1, 2001, he met with two of his former FSB colleagues, and one of them surreptitiously slipped the polonium-210 into Litvinenko's teapot.

Litvinenko's death was long and protracted, and so it looked as if he had been poisoned in a truly unusual way—polonium-210 is prohibitively expensive to buy,[19] and very difficult to refine—in order to send a message. The way in which Litvinenko was killed looked very much like an assassination, and given that there were easier and faster—and certainly cheaper—ways to dispose of Litvinenko, his death had all the hallmarks of being a state-sponsored hit. So, given what we know about the death of Alexander Litvinenko, it seems certain that his death was the result of a conspiracy; his death had to be plotted by agents who acted in secret. Any account of the death of Litvinenko turns out to be a conspiracy theory. The big question about Litvinenko's death is who was behind the conspiracy?

Now, we could claim—like Mandik and Popper—that this is not a proper conspiracy because it is not sufficiently secret. All this does, however, is rule out cases which raise the prior probability a conspiracy could be considered in the pool of candidate explanatory hypotheses for certain kinds of events. Mandik and Popper rule out known conspiracies as being properly conspiratorial, and thus end up thinking that conspiracies are independently *unlikely*. Yet in the Litvinenko case this seems absurd; the available evidence renders some hypothesis about a conspiracy as quite probable indeed. The big question should be which theory about a conspiracy is going to be the best explanation?

In this particular case, there are at least two major, rival conspiracy theories. The first is that Litvinenko was killed at the behest of the Russian State, as both a punishment, and a warning for those who would side against Putin. The other hypothesis is that Litvinenko was killed by Russian dissidents, in a manner which made it look as if it were ordered by Putin; Litvinenko in this version of the story was either a willing sacrifice, or a patsy. Both hypotheses explain who the poisoners were, and where the poison was sourced; they differ only with respect as to the real motive of the poisonous conspirators.[20]

So, with this in mind, when we consider which conspiracy theory is the best in this case—if we assume all the relevant alternative explanatory hypotheses have been covered[21]—then we should expect there to be some argument about how probable one of the particular claims of conspiracy is. That is, if we are to think of it as *the* salient cause of the event, and thus part of the best explanation. Such an argument would show that the explanatory hypothesis is probable in the posterior sense—Lipton's *likeliest explanation*—as well as the prior and relative sense.

3.2.1 Evidence and Prior Probabilities

When judging any putative explanation with respect to prior and posterior probabilities, there is a tension between our judgments about the independent likeliness of certain hypotheses being in the pool of credible explanations, and the evidence required to show that one of those hypotheses is the most likely.

For example, in a world where 99 percent of people cheat on their partners, you only need a little evidence to justify your suspicions that your partner is cheating on you. After all, the prior probability they are being unfaithful is very high—it is just independently likely they are cheaters[22]—and so the evidence required to justify your suspicions is low.

Conversely, in a world where 99 percent of people are faithful to their partners, the idea your partner is cheating on you would be so preposterous that you would require a lot of evidence to even suspect them of such a thing. There is, then, a tension between the independent likeliness of some explanatory hypothesis, and the evidence required to support it. A high prior probability reduces the evidential requirement associated with the posterior probability. After all, if some hypothesis is independently likely, then this reduces the evidential burden on showing that it is at least a contender for being in the set of credible explanatory hypotheses for some event.[23]

So, how independently likely are conspiracies? On one level this is not an easy question to answer, because we do not know. That is an empirical question. On another level, however, we can say that we typically and artificially lower the independent likeliness of conspiracies by our choice of definition as to what counts as *properly* conspiratorial. A lot of the aforementioned theorists who claim conspiracies are unlikely get to that conclusion by simply defining particular examples of conspiracies as being out-of-court. This, at the very least, suggests that conspiracies are more independently likely than most of us typically think.

Of course, claiming we typically underestimate the independent likeliness of conspiracies does not mean that we should consider conspiracies independently likely as salient causes *for all kinds of events*. We still need to judge explanatory hypotheses with respect to the kind of events we are seeking to explain. It may make sense to consider a conspiracy as a salient cause, say, in a political scandal, while also thinking that the extreme weather event in Otago last August is most likely explained by a change in climate (rather than, say, covert, US-sponsored weather manipulation). After all, conspiracies might be more common than we think, but only relatively likely when it comes to explanations for certain kinds of events (say, political scandals), and relatively unlikely in others (say, why the courier always delivers packages when I am not at home).

3.3 Connecting Prior, Posterior, and Relative Probabilities

As we have seen, the independent likeliness or prior probability of conspiracies being a salient cause for particular kinds of events depends both on how we estimate how likely conspiracies really are (which sometimes turns on how we define conspiratorial activity) as well as the kind of events we are trying to explain. However, when we consider any claim of conspiracy which is embedded in a conspiracy theory—to wit, an explanation citing a conspiracy as a salient cause—we have to demonstrate that there is a link between the conspiracy *and* the event in question. After all, in many cases a conspiracy might well be shown to exist, and yet turn out not to be the salient cause of some event. However, demonstrating there is a connection between a conspiracy and the occurrence of some event—such that the conspiracy is the salient cause of that event—shows that the conspiracy theory is probable in the prior, posterior, and relative sense. By showing a conspiracy was both likely and a salient cause, the existence of said conspiracy will feature in the best explanation of the event in question.

None of this says that conspiracy theories are *prima facie* likely. That would be a generalist claim, one which would be as problematic as the generalist skepticism typically associated with conspiracy theories. Rather, this is an argument in favor of particularism about conspiracy theories. When we hear some conspiracy theory we should, at the very least, treat the claim of conspiracy seriously, and look at the evidence. This is not an arduous burden: when inferring to any explanation we have to look at the evidence before we can accept or dismiss it. Conspiracy theories are no different.

What is interesting and striking, then, about much of the current literature on belief in conspiracy theories, is that people want to be able to generalize about such theories in a way which marks them out as special or different. By defining both conspiracies and conspiracy theories as *prima facie* unlikely, such theorists shift the burden of proof. However, if we consider that conspiracies are more independently likely than most of us think, or have been told, then the burden of proof on the conspiracy theorist will—in a range of cases—turn out to be not so extraordinary. In a world in which we admit not just that conspiracies occur, but there are more of them than maybe we would like to think, if someone claims there is a conspiracy in existence *here-and-now*, then should we not investigate said claim? That is, we should not just dismiss it. No; we should treat the allegation seriously enough to ask what is the evidence, and how well does that evidence stack up compared to other, rival explanatory hypotheses. Could this particular conspiracy theory prove to be the best explanation of some event? If the answer is no, then the conspiracy theory is unwarranted, and we have learnt that some other explanation will be the best. However, if the answer is yes, then we have on our hands a case where inferring to a conspiracy turned out to be the best explanation. As such, people who put forward conspiracy theories should not be seen as facing a higher burden of proof than those who offer explanations of similar, complex social processes. If someone alleges a conspiracy was a factor in some event, we should ask for evidence, and see if that evidence renders that hypothesis probable.

This prescription for a sensible treatment of claims of conspiracy flies in the face of much of the current literature on conspiracy theories. For example, conspiracy theories are bad according to social psychologists because conspiracy theories are unlikely, and belief in them has negative social consequences. Brotherton and French—as previously mentioned—claim conspiracy theories are unlikely, and from this they go on to argue that conspiracy theorists are particularly prone to suffering from the conjunction fallacy (where people overestimate the likelihood of two things being connected) (2014).

Jan-Willem van Prooijen and Michele Acker claim that:

> Furthermore, accumulating research findings reveal a range of detrimental perceptions and behaviors that are associated with conspiracy beliefs, including health problems, decreased civic virtue, hostility, and radicalization. (2015, 1)

Yet they take it that these behaviors are not the result of people judging the merit of conspiracy theories, but, rather, because conspiracy theorists lack some sense of control over their lives and the world in which they live. Then there is Preston R. Bost and Stephen G. Prunier's claim that conspiracy theories are often inherently implausible, and that belief in such theories is often predicated on people overstating the motives of suspected conspirators (2013).

Yet if it turns out we are wrong about the supposed unlikeliness of conspiracies here-and-now, those negative social consequences—distrust in authority; apathy with respect to engaging in the political process; and the like—might very well be appropriate responses to talk of conspiracy theories. It is, then, important to understand this issue of just how probable conspiracies really are, and what this says about how we go about inferring that a conspiracy theory is the best explanation. This is of serious import, because it very much looks like we typically and artificially underestimate the prior probability of conspiracies. With that in mind, then, our condemnation of conspiracy theorists—those who believe conspiracy theories—needs to be similarly examined.

4. CONCLUSION

As we have seen, much of the reasoning behind thinking both conspiracies and conspiracy theories are unlikely comes out of defining them as such, rather than asking what prevents them from featuring in the set of best explanations. If we claim conspiracies are only conspiracies *if they are kept perfectly secret*, or that conspiracy theories which have been endorsed are no longer *proper conspiracy theories*, then we run the risk of defining away some truly interesting questions which are at the root of whether or not conspiracy theories really are irrational to believe, unwarranted, and the like. It seems that by defining away conspiracies and conspiracy theories as *prima facie* unlikely, then we not only do the analysis of inferring what gets ruled in by our best inferences a disservice, but we unfairly shift the burden of proof onto those who might well have good reason to infer that a conspiracy really is occurring here-and-now. This matter is of import to the academic discussion of these things we call "conspiracy theories" because—once again as we have seen—there are a plethora of views—both inside and outside of Philosophy—which adopt question-begging definitions in order to come to the conclusion such theories are bunk.

NOTES

1. Original published in *Social Epistemology* 30, no. 5–6 (2016): 572–91, doi: 10.1080/02691728.2016.1172362. Reprinted with permission.

2. The aforementioned philosophers all agree that some version of the following captures the definition of a conspiracy theory: it is an explanation of an event which cites a conspiracy as a salient cause of said event.

This definition—being perfectly general—does not build in that belief in conspiracy theories is irrational, and thus the philosophical debate has shifted to an analysis of the *purported* problems with belief in such theories, and whether our commonplace suspicion—that such theories are bunk—is itself justified.

3. A view held by many other academics. Cassam's argument echoes that of Susan Feldman, for example, who writes:

Conspiracy theorizing does not point to possession of an incommensurable world view, but does suggest possession of defective epistemic character. (2011)

4. "Shit happens" is Mandik's playful term for what are commonly called "coincidence theories" or "cock-up theories." Such theories explain away the occurrence of an event as being the result of often unpredictable, complex, and intersecting causes; while such theories might look conspiratorial, they are, in fact, better explained as the product of happenstance.

5. Clarke, in a more recent paper, worries that conspiracy theories are typically examples of degenerating (Lakatosian) research programs, and so he takes it that conspiracy theories are unlikely because, among other things, they tend not to make successful or novel predictions (2007).

6. In this respect Lipton is echoing the work of Richard Hofstadter, who claimed that belief in conspiracy theories is similar to (but not exactly like) clinical paranoia (1965).

7. Byford's work here echoes that of Lance deHaven-Smith, who would rather we talk about "state crimes against democracy" than pejoratively-labeled "conspiracy theories" (2013).

8. Wood and Douglas offer a variation on this kind of argument: Even if we accept that conspiracies occur, given a choice between a conspiracy and a non-conspiracy theory, we should prefer the non-conspiratorial explanation, rather than give into a pathological worldview in which rival, non-conspiracy theories are a lie.

9. The Johnson Administration in the United States claimed, at the time, that the North Vietnamese navy attacked the USS *Maddox*. This story turned out to be disinformation, which is to say it was a story which later turned out to be a lie. It has been claimed that said lie was designed to provide a pretext for an escalation of US involvement in Vietnam.

10. The Ford Motor Company knowingly manufactured a car, the Ford Pinto, with a serious design fault, where the fuel tank could be punctured in a rear-end collision, which could subsequently result in fatalities due to fires from the spilt fuel.

11. It was discovered that diesel cars produced by Volkswagen were not only passing environmental tests through the use of sophisticated cheating devices, but senior personnel at Volkswagen were covering up their cheating by falsely blaming the people running the tests.

12. Conspiracies are a kind of group activity: people conspire *together*, and so it is a necessary condition for the existence of a conspiracy that there exists some set of agents who have a plan. Defining a "conspiracy" as being the product of a set of conspirators is circular (since it builds into the definition of a conspiracy that it is a conspiracy), but for the purposes of this analysis it is easier to refer to "conspirators" than, say, "planning agents"; the latter locution does not exactly roll off of the tongue.

13. Conspirators operate—at least for a time—in secret. Such secrecy sometimes explains why the evidence which would satisfy this condition might be vague. However, if it turns out the conspirators have even some success in keeping their plot a secret, this would explain why details remain unknown.

14. There could be a mismatch between what the conspirators desired and the outcome of their activity, but this should not be considered a problem with determining whether there is a conspiracy. After all, the conspiracy theory should—if it is an adequate explanation—explain away said difference. As long as the work the conspirators undertook is in some way responsible for the actual outcome, this should not be a concern.

15. This notion of "perfect secrecy" can also be found in the work of Juha Räikkä (2009b). Räikkä explores the idea that we can rule out known conspiratorial activity as being properly described as a "conspiracy theory"—like the involvement of the Nazis in the Holocaust, or the CIA in acts of rendition—because a "genuine conspiracy" is one where the conspirators maintain perfect secrecy. Given that we know about the CIA's rendition program, and the Holocaust, these are not genuine conspiracies. Rather, they are part-and-parcel of everyday history.

However, in a more recent paper (co-authored with Lee Basham) Räikkä argues that the explanation of known conspiracies falls under the rubric of these things we call "conspiracy theories," and that our distaste to call them as such is evidence of a "conspiracy theory phobia" (in press).

16. Susan Feldman also takes it that conspiracy theories, similarly, cannot be official theories (2011).

17. Although, given the lack of references in *Bad Thinkers*, it is not clear that Cassam has read much, if any, of the philosophical material on conspiracy theories, and so Cassam may well have just reinvented Clarke's position without realizing it.

18. There may well exist generalists who believe that conspiracy theories are typically rational, but such figures do not seem to exist in the academic discussion concerning conspiracy theories; philosophers who have defended conspiracy theorizing have not committed to the notion all or most such theories are good, but, rather, that the commonplace suspicion of conspiracy theories is itself not justified.

19. The official findings of eminent UK judge Sir Robert Owen, who chaired the public inquiry into the death of Alexander Litvinenko, estimated that the cost of the polonium-210 used to poison Litvinenko was somewhere between \$US20,000 and tens of millions of dollars (the discrepancy between the two values is the

result of experts in 2015 disagreeing about the cost of obtaining the radionuclide in 2006) (2016, 226).

20. According to Sir Robert Owen, the assassination of Alexander Litvinenko was ordered by elements within the FSB, and it was very likely that Vladimir Putin signed off on the kill order (2016, 241–44). The official story, then, of Litvinenko's death is that of a conspiracy by the Russian State to kill a defector. Putin and the Russian government, however, claim this is just yet another anti-Russian conspiracy theory, designed by enemies of the Russian State to cause it embarrassment.

21. For the sake of this example we shall, although the Litvinenko story is a lot messier than the presentation of it here. Litvinenko was an informant for British Intelligence, and it is claimed he had begun working for the Spanish Intelligence services; Litvinenko likely had many enemies, some of whom would have had access to assets of their particular states.

22. You are also likely a cheater, at least with respect to this possible world. This might reduce the evidential threshold even further, since you would likely know (a) what cheating looks like and (b) what evidence of hiding cheating also looks like.

23. The caveat here is "Somewhat . . ." since even in a world where cheating is very likely indeed, you still need some evidence to support the claim your *particular* partner is cheating on you. After all, it might be unlikely they are faithful, but it is still a possibility that should be considered seriously.

Chapter 2

Conspiracy Theory and the Perils of Pure Particularism

Patrick Stokes[1]

It's hard to think of any other phenomenon as widespread and salient in contemporary society that has been so roundly ignored by philosophers as conspiracy theory. Why this neglect has happened isn't clear, but perhaps part of the problem is simply that belief in conspiracy theories is seen as so thoroughly disreputable that few philosophers feel the need to think about them. Nonetheless, a small but illuminating literature has emerged over the last decade, focusing almost entirely on the status of conspiracy theory as an epistemic problem and attempting to determine whether and under what conditions conspiracy beliefs might be warranted. Quite astonishingly, something like a broad consensus has emerged: regarded simply as explanations, conspiracy theories are not *intrinsically* irrational, and believing in conspiracy explanations is not necessarily unwarranted. After all, there are conspiracies we all agree happened—Watergate, Iran-Contra, etc.—and the search for a (non-question-begging) definition of "conspiracy theory" that would exclude beliefs about these accepted conspiracies, but include those wacky theories we want to dismiss, appears doomed to failure. There is, as Brian Keeley puts it, "no principled way of distinguishing, *a priori*, the two classes from one another" (2007, 137).

Accordingly, philosophers like M R. X. Dentith and Lee Basham have argued, *generalism* about conspiracy theory—the view that conspiracy theories as a class of explanation are intrinsically suspect—is unsustainable, and should be rejected in favor of a *particularism* whereby we only judge individual conspiracy theories on their merits, rather than judging them based on their membership of that class (Dentith 2016b). Particularists differ about the, well, particulars, but they agree that conspiracy theories should each be taken on their own merits and not simply dismissed out-of-hand.

It seems clear that a return to blithe generalism is unsustainable—and this is indeed a problem in terms of public discourse, given the way generalism about conspiracy theories is sometimes used to provide cover for political actors who don't want the true nature of their actions scrutinized too closely. Charles Pigden draws a line from Karl Popper's denunciation of the "conspiracy view of society" (Popper 2012, 306–8) to Tony Blair's attempts to deflect awkward questions about the motive for the invasion of Iraq by dismissing these questions as based on "conspiracy theories." Pigden pulls no punches here: "the idea that there *is* something suspect about conspiracy theories is one of the most dangerous and idiotic superstitions to disgrace our political culture" (2006, 139). David Coady is no less strident, declaring that "The contemporary treatment of those accused of being conspiracy theorists is an intellectual witch hunt," even if some conspiracy theorists do in fact deserve to be criticized (2012, 111).

Yet if there are good reasons, both epistemically and politically, to reject generalism, does that thereby commit us to particularism—or might there be reasons to reject particularism as well? In considering this question it is important to bear in mind two things: firstly, that conspiracy theorizing is not merely a formal category of explanation but also a concrete, historically and socially conditioned practice (and as such open to ethical evaluation), and secondly, that epistemology is never undertaken in a vacuum, but always by human beings in a world already freighted with moral obligations and historically conditioned meanings. In what follows I want to gesture toward some respects in which particularism may involve us in ethically problematic practices. The very act of entertaining a conspiracy theory as a *worthwhile hypothesis for investigation* may come at a serious moral cost, both in licensing socially harmful practices and in violating the attitude of trust that is, I argue, a precondition of ethical life. The position I advocate then is somewhere in the messy middle: a "defeasible generalism" or "reluctant particularism."

1. CONSPIRACY AS A FORMAL CLASS OF EXPLANATION

A central plank of the argument for particularism is the philosophical literature's very basic, and accordingly very capacious, definition of what a "conspiracy theory" actually is. Dentith, for instance, asserts three individually necessary and jointly sufficient conditions for classifying some activity as conspiratorial:

1. The conspirators condition: There exists (or existed) some set of agents with a plan.

2. The secrecy condition: Steps have been taken by the agents to minimize public awareness of what they are up to.
3. The goal condition: Some end is, or was desired, by the agents. (2016b, 6)

For the most part, philosophers have been reluctant to expand much on this minimal definition, and indeed even Dentith has subsequently moved away from the secrecy condition (Dentith and Orr 2017). Coady initially offers a definition that embeds a narrower version of condition 3 ("the conspiracy postulated by the proposed explanation must be a conspiracy to bring about the historical event which it purports to explain" rather than just that the conspirators desired *some* goal) and adds that "the proposed explanation must conflict with an 'official' explanation of the same historical event" (2006b, 117). In later work Coady argues that conspiracies also require active deception, not just secrecy (2012, 114), though presumably this condition could be tweaked to say that conspirators *would* engage in deception *if* required (in some cases deception may never become necessary).

Once we define "conspiracy" in this very formal and minimal way, it is relatively straightforward to show that there is nothing intrinsically irrational, or even unreasonable, about explanations of that form. Indeed, once we've taken that definition on board, as several writers have noted, it turns out we're *all* conspiracy theorists: we all believe that conspiracies are the best explanation of many historical events, from the murder of Julius Caesar to Stalin's show trials to Watergate. Conspiratorial activity is at least sometimes, perhaps even often, the best available explanation to which to infer (Dentith 2016b).

Philosophers acknowledge this definition clashes with the ways we *generally* talk about conspiracy theory. They like to remind us that, according to this definition, the "official" explanation for the 9/11 attacks is itself a conspiracy theory; that is, it explains the attacks as the outcome of a conspiracy on the part of al-Qaeda. Yet when we think of "conspiracy theories" we don't generally think of such "accepted" explanations as falling under that heading.[2] We don't typically group officially sanctioned beliefs about al-Qaeda flying planes into buildings or Russian FSB agents murdering opponents of the Kremlin with polonium-laced tea with beliefs about the New World Order or the "Clinton Body Count." Yet if there is a formal difference between "Putin murdered Alexander Litvinenko" and "Bill Clinton murdered Vince Foster" it is hard to see what it might be. Appeals to the official status of one story but not the other don't work, because an officially sanctioned story in one society might be considered a conspiracy theory in another. If we attempt to force that sort of solution we end up, as Pigden points out, with a blatantly gerrymandered and chauvinistic definition according to which a conspiracy theory is "a theory which posits a secret and morally suspect plan *on the part of Western governments or government agencies* to influence events by partly covert means" (2006, 164). We have obvious reasons to look askance at any definition of conspiracy theory that entails that conspiracies are something only *other* societies do.

2. CONSPIRACY THEORY AS TRADITION AND PRACTICE

There are, undeniably, risks involved in a naïve generalism that reflexively dismisses any explanation in terms of conspiratorial activity. But there is also a corresponding risk of severing conspiracy theories from the social contexts in which they arise, as well as focusing on conspiracy *theory* as a propositional entity rather than conspiracy *theorizing* as an action. Conspiracy theories, as the term is popularly used at least, do not simply appear on paper and in the abstract. They are constructed by real people, and consist of speech acts that accuse other, real or allegedly real,[3] people of doing secret and (typically) immoral things. That locutionary function of conspiracy theories is thus unavoidably social, and their utterance *qua* speech acts is thereby subject to ethical evaluation.

As Clarke notes, "Although individuals may generate their own conspiracy theories and may choose to keep these to themselves, the construction of the vast majority of conspiracy theories is a social enterprise" (2007, 169). Indeed, conspiracy theories are rarely created *ex nihilo*, but instead tend to be cobbled together and adapted from a set of pre-existing templates. They are typically offered by conspiracy theorists—that is, not simply "a person who is unusually willing to investigate conspiracy" (2007, 195) but someone who antecedently accepts that observed events are at least not infrequently best explained by conspiracies. Conspiracy theorists are participating in a recognizable "tradition of explanation" (Byford 2011) or within the language and concerns of a recognizable "style" (Hofstadter 1965), one that brings with it its own historically conditioned recurring tropes and causal narratives. This broader epistemological stance toward society, and practices that stance licenses, are lost sight of if we simply analyze conspiracy theories in formal terms.

Witness, for instance, the speed with which the "false flag with crisis actors" narrative is deployed now in the wake of any mass casualty event in the United States.[4] The fact this accusation is made within hours, even minutes of such events, suggests these accusations are not being offered as *sui generis* hypotheses suggested by specific features of observed events, but as expressing a prior commitment to a particular explanatory framework—roughly, one that stipulates that mass-casualty events are at least very likely to be orchestrated by undeclared forces for manipulative ends, and their "official" explanations are likely to be cover-stories. To use a line from Jane and Fleming (2014, 96), "one cannot avoid the impression that the theories involved have been formulated well in advance of the assembling of evidence; these are conclusions lying in wait for friendly 'facts.'" That, of course, is also true of many other explanations that can be offered: consider how quickly after such events "mainstream" media and political figures prematurely assume them to be the work of Islamist terrorists, for example. (It's to the false flag theorist's credit that he or she at least *looks* for confirmatory evidence.) But what is common in *both* cases is a reflexive explanation in terms of which data is then interpreted. The similarity in these explanations, coupled with the speed with which they're deployed, suggests we're not talking about wholly self-contained explanations either, but with specific explanatory tropes deployed across different events.[5] And that opens up the possibility of assessments that go beyond the epistemic. There may be no a priori epistemic reason not to believe in a given conspiracy theory simply *because* it is a conspiracy theory. But nonetheless we can ask whether we have ethical reasons to avoid participating in the practice of conspiracy theorizing, in which we explain events using the resources and assumptions of the conspiracy theory tradition.

The boundaries of such a tradition or style of explanation are, naturally enough, fuzzy and ill-defined. Nonetheless, any critique of conspiracy theorizing as a real-world practice needs to resist an artificial simplicity that would strip it of its distinctive content (including its aetiology). Viewed thus, both generalism *and* particularism turn out to take us further away from the concrete contexts in which we consider conspiracy theories. The generalist occludes the historical and cultural context in which conspiracy explanations have often turned out to be correct. The particularist, by insisting on viewing each conspiracy theory solely on its own merits, requires a certain indifference to the contingent cultural, historical, and rhetorical explanatory repertoires from which conspiracy theorists typically draw their hypotheses. The generalist will refuse to even consider that the U.S. government knowingly presented unreliable intelligence to justify invading Iraq, while the particularist will refuse to even acknowledge that "climate change is a hoax perpetuated by the UN and 'international bankers' to bring about a socialist one-world government" is not a self-standing hypothesis but a recrudescence of various long-standing conspiracy tropes, including old anti-Semitic ones.

3. ARGUMENTS FOR PARTICULARISM

Particularists can agree that conspiracy theories often have problematic origins and results. They simply insist that this tendency alone doesn't entitle us to reject any conspiracy theory simply *because* it is a conspiracy theory.

Individual conspiracy theories may be ludicrous, hateful, or destructive, but, as philosophers working in this area have demonstrated, that doesn't entail that *any* conspiracy theory is just thereby necessarily wrong. That in turn would seem to suggest we should not denounce conspiracy theorizing as a practice or conspiracy theory as a tradition, because the theories offered by that practice and tradition may well turn out to be true. Certainly a number of high-profile conspiracies have occurred. Watergate is often invoked here by default, but there are many relatively recent examples from the Gulf of Tonkin Incident through to the Volkswagen emissions scandal. Even the 2017 release of documents around the JFK assassination *did* evidence a conspiracy, just not the particular conspiracy theory that those conspiracy theorists tend to offer—namely, a conspiracy by the CIA and FBI to hide the extent of their prior knowledge of Oswald and so their negligence in not stopping him.

But what's noticeable in all these cases is that exposure, when it came, was driven by the usual, more or less "official" knowledge-generating organs of "free" societies, such as journalism, universities, and even government itself—albeit with sometimes agonistic relationships between these organs (e.g., journalists vs. government) or even within them. That's fine, the particularist might insist: insofar as Woodward and Bernstein, for instance, were pursuing a conspiratorial explanation of the Watergate break-in and its aftermath, they were conspiracy theorists. (Indeed, as Dentith [2017b] notes, we may find forms of *recognized* if not *accredited* expertise on particular conspiracy theories among journalists and the like.) So too are historians who assume Julius Caesar was murdered as a result of a conspiracy rather than some bizarre spontaneous, highly localized fit of homicidal pique among his coincidentally armed contemporaries. But this again just brings home the extent to which a formal, epistemological understanding of conspiracy theory takes us away from the recognizable social *practice* of conspiracy theorizing, from its explanatory styles and tropes.

Apart from exposing genuine conspiracies, a corresponding negative argument for particularism about conspiracy theory is that it is only by investigating conspiracy theories that we can dispose of the untrue ones. It may well be the case that most of what we usually call conspiracy theories fall apart under scrutiny, but given we cannot know ahead of time that they will, or *which* ones will, we still need to apply that scrutiny. Again, that holds on the level of formal epistemology: I cannot *disprove* an empirical claim without at least some sort of investigation, however cursory. But if we are to consider conspiracy theory as a social practice, other considerations come into play when deciding what we should and should not investigate.

For one thing, while serious investigation might disprove many conspiracy theories, the confident assertion that "Poorly evidenced conspiracy theories will be quickly set aside" (Basham and Dentith 2016, 14) thereafter simply isn't borne out by experience. It may well be true that, as Basham claims, "Many of the tenets of the 9/11 truth movement have been abandoned by its own members" (Basham 2016, 8–9), but that movement has hardly vanished; as Alex Jones has demonstrated, you can still go on TV and publicly call 9/11 an inside job and Sandy Hook a hoax and still have the president-elect of the United States call you to thank you and your viewers for their support.[6] It will likewise come as cold comfort to CDC employees harassed by anti-vaccination activists outside their workplace, for instance, to hear that "The anti-vaccination movement has been profoundly undermined" (Basham 2016, 8) and even less comfort to parents in the Northern Rivers region of New South Wales, where vaccination levels, thanks to denialism, remain dangerously low. If this is a movement that has been profoundly undermined, one shudders to think what it looks like in rude health. If trust in democratic institutions is, in Basham's phrase, a "political piety," then the idea that weak conspiracy theories are quickly defeated by rational scrutiny is an "epistemic piety" that falls sadly short of reality.

4. REASONS FOR RELUCTANCE

Of course, it's hardly the fault of hard-working epistemologists if, in practice, conspiracy theorists don't abandon debunked or discredited conspiracy theories. Plenty of false beliefs persist, and this is clearly no demerit of those who seek to expose their falsity; nor is it necessarily a reason not to expose them. So, while the fact conspiracy theories persist despite debunkings does deprive particularism of at least one argument in its favor, it is far from decisive, and offers no support for generalism either. But other problems arise for particularism—not epistemically, but ethically.

First, let's put ourselves in the shoes of a would-be conspiracy theory investigator. Dentith thinks of conspiracy theorizing not simply as an activity for individual investigators, but for Deweyan communities of inquiry with the epistemic burden of assessing conspiracy theories distributed across that community (Dentith, 2018b). Such a community will not be wholly innocent of conspiracy theory tropes. That might already raise the suspicion that when such inquirers resort to a conspiracy theory, they are already drawing on and reconfiguring existing narratives rather than creating genuinely new explanations in response to the evidence. Nonetheless, insists Dentith, "members of the community of inquiry will surely know about certain conspiracy narratives (or the social practices associated with some cases of conspiracy theorising) without necessarily having to in any way endorse or engage with them" (Dentith 2017a, 6).

Dentith argues that some of my worries about conspiracy theory as a practice are really concerns about certain types of conspiracy *narrative*. The problem is not the simple act of forming (or asserting) explanations of observed events that involve two or more actors conspiring in secret, but the deployment of particular narratives about specific conspiracies; for instance, the "Jewish World Conspiracy" narrative (or overlapping narratives, perhaps) promulgated by figures as diverse as the Tsarist Okhrana, Henry Ford, Nesta Webster, Adolf Hitler, and David Duke. "To theorise about a conspiracy—to wit, to engage in conspiracy theorising—is a different task from hooking into an existing conspiracy narrative to press a point" (Dentith 2016a, 31), and accordingly, the two should be evaluated separately.

Yet if the particularist is committed to not ruling out *any* conspiracy theory ahead of time, then it's not clear that she *can* in fact avoid having to engage with particular conspiracy narratives, including the deeply problematic ones. Say Dentith's investigator (or a community thereof) sees reports of a mass shooting event, and wonders: "Perhaps this shooting is a false flag designed to create conditions in which the government can disarm the population." That is not a stand-alone explanation, but one embedded in a tradition of anti-government anxieties. It sits within a long, ongoing, evolving, recogniz-able history of interpretation. As noted above, these days it re-emerges, fully formed, within minutes of any major mass shooting, regardless of context or location. Just through asking the question of whether this story *might be true*, our investigator(s) is already engaging—even unwillingly, perhaps—with an existing cultural practice of explanation.

Much here will of course hang on precisely what "engagement" means. Endorsement, denunciation, reflexive dismissal, and agnosticism are all ways of engaging with a theory, after all. But particularism requires a fairly par-ticular sort of engagement: namely, an openness, at least to some degree, to the possibility that any given conspiracy theory might turn out to be true. To the extent that they are committed to not dismissing any conspiracy theory ahead of time, the particularist will regard any conspiracy theory as *prima facie* a candidate for further investigation. Such further investigation may well be shut down *almost* immediately if a conspiracy theory is simply absurd on its face. Such absurdity can't consist *merely* in the fact the conspiracy theory *is* a conspiracy theory, however, but only in something such as an obvious logical contradiction or physical impossibility.

Dentith's particularism *does* allow us to dismiss conspiracy narratives that are discredited or problematic. But their particularism still requires at least *some* investigation in these cases, and the motivation here remains, on their telling, fundamentally epistemological rather than ethical:

After all, if the evidence is "This looks like a redressed version of a Jewish banking conspiracy narrative," then the appropriate evidential response is to ask "Hasn't this been debunked?" Because if it has, then we will have evidence to mount against the new version. If it has not, then we need to investigate the claim further. (2016a, 31–32)

Asking "hasn't this been debunked?" is already an investigation, albeit a very cursory one. If the answer is "yes," we may regard the investigation as concluded. If the answer is "no," then, Dentith says, further investigation is needed.

However, as noted above, we do not apply our evidential reasoning in a vacuum, but do so from within historically conditioned and epistemically finite situations. We also do so not as disembodied loci of disinterested reason, but as ethically embedded and emplaced agents. Our speculations and investigations are actions, and so are ethically as well as rationally evaluable. And on Dentith's telling, our community of inquiry is, as noted, not innocent of the history and social meanings of conspiracy theories. Faced with something that looks like a variant of a Jewish banking conspiracy narrative, the question that confronts that community is not just "has this been debunked?" but "is the offering of this theory recognizably part of an anti-Semitic social practice?" If the latter, and given the supremacy of the ethical over other kinds of normativity,[7] we do in fact have a reason *prior to* investigation to simply reject this theory: treating it as possibly true by investigating it would be taking part in an ethically risible practice. Basham claims it is a virtue of particularism that it "directly confronts theories that are unwarranted (Jews are trying to destroy Western civilization)" (2016, 11–12), but as he presents particularism here, it doesn't look like *this* is the sort of confrontation he has in mind. It remains *logically* possible such a theory is true. But not only are we not morally or rationally obliged to entertain every theory, we are morally obliged to reject some theories even at the risk of occasionally being wrong.

Of course, not all conspiracy theories are anti-Semitic or emerge from ethically or politically problematic practices or narratives. They can just as easily emerge from a raw history of colonial oppression as from a playful engagement with pop culture. It's hard to see how wondering if Paul McCartney is dead or Elvis is alive could possibly be ethically objectionable in anything like the way "international banking families" conspiracy theories are.

Attention to conspiracy theory as a social practice will, however, reveal a range of other harms associated with the practice. These harms can be quite horrific: the belief that the Sub-Saharan AIDS epidemic is a conspiracy on the part of Western governments and pharmaceutical companies led to an estimated more than 330,000 preventable deaths (Chigwedere, Seage, Gruskin, Lee, and Essex 2008). However, it could be objected here that there is nothing *intrinsic* to conspiracy theory that leads to these consequences. False belief systems that don't integrally posit a conspiracy—for instance, quack cancer treatments pursued instead of conventional treatment—could just as easily yield similar consequences.

Other harms are more tightly connected to the structure of conspiracy ideation, however. A conspiracy theory requires conspirators, and this sometimes leads conspiracy theorists to confront those they believe to be in on the conspiracy. Such confrontations can be merely annoying or faintly absurd, as when moon landing denialist Bart Sibrel accosted Apollo 11 astronaut Buzz Aldrin and received a punch in the jaw for his trouble. Yet they can also be deeply sinister and traumatic. A conspiracy theory of the "false flag with crisis actors" type formed around the Sandy Hook Elementary Shooting of 2012. This theory posited that the shooting never happened, and that those being presented by the media as eyewitnesses and the parents of victims were actors in the employ of the U.S. government. A local man, Gene Rosen, was visibly distressed as he spoke to the media after the shooting about how he had helped children fleeing the massacre. Shortly thereafter Rosen started getting phone calls and emails from "Sandy Hook Truthers" accusing him of being a crisis actor: "How are all those little students doing? You know, the ones that showed up at your house after the 'shooting.' What is the going rate for getting involved in a gov't sponsored hoax anyway?" (Seitz-Wald 2013). A "truther" named Andrew Truelove stole signs from memorials dedicated to seven-year-old Sandy Hook victims Grace McDonnell and Chase Kowalski, then phoned their parents to insist their dead children had never existed (Goldstein 2014). A professor of communication, James Tracy, harassed Sandy Hook parents Lenny and Veronique Pozner, demanding they prove their murdered son Noah had existed (McPhate 2015). In a similar vein, anti-vaccination activists have been known to accuse the parents of children who have died from diseases like pertussis of being "shills" for pharmaceutical companies for speaking out about the need for vaccination, and even questioning whether the deaths occurred at all (Tierney 2015, 2016).

Again, one might reply that conspiracy theory belief is neither necessary nor sufficient for indulging in abusive behavior of this sort. No doubt a great many conspiracy theorists are utterly horrified by such actions, and would rightly bristle at being tarred with the same brush. Yet while these are not necessary features of conspiracy theory as a practice, they are undeniably enabled by it. It takes a fairly remarkable degree of self-confidence, to put it politely, to accuse someone of only pretending to be a grieving parent. That confidence is considerably easier to muster, however, from within a community of inquiry that is predisposed to explaining events in terms of organized malfeasance, and that posits conspiracy as frequently being a reasonable best explanation to infer to. It is also much easier when grieving parents have become a piece of disconfirmatory data to a theory to which you're antecedently committed. I'll have more to say about this in a later chapter. I will also discuss the more fundamental problem that conspiracy theory requires accusation, and that to participate in practices of accusation has an unavoidable moral cost. For the moment, it is enough to have shown that there are reasons to think *pure* particularism won't be any more of an option than pure generalism: namely, that unqualified particularism about conspiracy theory will end up with our taking offensive or harmful theories more seriously than we ought to, and participating in traditions we ought to spurn.

5. CONCLUSION

What, then, might lie between, or beyond, generalism and particularism? Perhaps something that might be described as "defeasible generalism" or "reluctant particularism." Such an attitude would not begin from the premise that conspiracy theories are always false. It would not foreclose the possibility of ever investigating any conspiracy theory. It would, however, approach such theories with a certain reticence, given the social practice within which those theories are embedded and the moral costs associated with taking part in the conspiracy theory tradition. We would approach any claim that borrowed tropes or argumentative patterns from the conspiracy theory tradition with a particular suspicion, albeit a suspicion that could be countervailed in certain circumstances—namely where the growth of evidence passes a certain point (which, no doubt, cannot be specified ahead of time). We would apply an ethical heuristic in judging whether conspiracy claims are worth entertaining, much as we do when, for instance, we refuse to think badly of people until compelled by evidence to do so. Such a heuristic is not simply prudential—indeed it's not hard to imagine how someone might take default suspicion to be more prudent—but rather reflects the need to avoid being caught up in patterns of thought that lose sight of the moral gravity of accusation.

Basham (2016) claims that my "reluctant particularism" or "defeasible generalism" is an unstable binary: it either collapses into generalism (given that generalists preserve some sliver of defeasibility) or is simply particularism. On the first, this amounts to saying there effectively is no such thing as generalism to begin with. But I assume rather that Basham thinks generalists incoherently both avow that we can reject any conspiracy theory simply because it *is* a conspiracy theory and maintain that sometimes we should accept conspiracy theories as true. My reluctant particularist, by contrast, holds that we should be reticent to indulge conspiracy theories enough to investigate them, given the troubling aspects of conspiracy theory as a social practice. Reticence, crucially, is not blanket refusal, and reluctant particularism is not simply an algorithm for deciding which theories to dismiss or endorse; it is, rather, an epistemic stance formed from a commitment to not engaging in harmful practices and to interpreting others in the most charitable way possible. That stance will not rule out complex accusatory explanations, but it will assume, ahead of time, that such explanations are exceptional. They will be dispreferred, but not ruled out.

It is decisive here that the reasons for reluctance are ethical rather than "purely" epistemic. Hence reluctant particularism is not simply on a par with scientific skepticism, as Basham seems to think:

> If "reluctant" means we will not immediately embrace a theory, but seek significant evidence for or against, then this is simply the particularist position. We have the same "reluctance" towards any scientific theory. This reluctance doesn't view the theory as *prima facie* false. Saying a theory is not yet warranted is not to say it probably never will be, just because of the sort of theory it is. (2016, 6)

Quite right. But the comparison with science only goes so far, for we do not stand in a *moral* relation to the objects of scientific inquiry, at least as regards the purely scientific questions we pose of them; we do not harm subatomic particles or besmirch nebulae by postulating hypotheses about them that turn out to be false. Leveling a false accusation has a moral cost to it that proposing a flawed hypothesis in physics or chemistry, in itself at least, does not. That generates a very different form of reluctance. The scientist is reluctant from fear of getting the facts wrong. The moral agent is reluctant from fear of wronging the other.

It could be objected here that such an attitude would make us more vulnerable to becoming victims of conspiracies. A standing vigilance toward power (in all forms, including state power) is essential to any healthy society and polity, and maintaining such vigilance may seem incompatible with a standing reluctance to accept conspiratorial explanations. But equally we might note that a refusal to fall back on conspiracist tropes and patterns of thought may also help in such vigilance, by making it easier to avoid seeing patterns that aren't really there. Either way, we would do well to remember that conspiracy theories don't exist merely on paper. They're something we *do*—and that makes us responsible for how we do so.

NOTES

1. Elements of this chapter first appeared in (Stokes 2016, 2017a). Thanks to Matthew Dentith and Lee Basham for their helpful replies in that discussion, and to

Lee for comments on further material included here. Full disclosure: I am an administrator of Stop the AVN, a group that campaigns against anti-vaccination activism. Stop the AVN receives no funding from any source.

2. Though as Wood (2016) found, people don't necessarily judge a theory as less believable even if it is labeled a conspiracy theory.

3. I include "allegedly real" to cover instances where the conspiracy theory posits an otherwise-unattested class of conspirators rather than imputing conspiratorial action to persons whose existence is generally accepted.

4. On false flags, see Dentith (2017b).

5. Again, a conspiracy theorist might insist that each of these conspiracy theories is an inference to best explanation given a set of background conditions that stipulate "governments routinely falsify events." It's not clear however that this putative fact alone would account for the stylistic similarities between different conspiracy theories, and at a certain level of generality it simply fades into an unfalsifiable claim about how conspired the world is. (It might also be the case that conspiracy theories resemble one another because conspirators have a limited repertoire of ways of conspiring and so a recognizable *modus operandi*.)

6. http://www.politico.com/story/2016/11/trump-thanked-alex-jones-231329.

7. Of course, some moral philosophers don't accept that ethical normativity trumps other forms. Williams (2015) is the *locus classicus* here. But as MacIntyre (2016) has recently noted, part of what makes Williams so striking on this topic is precisely how unusual that position is.

Chapter 3

Conspiracy Theory Particularism, both Epistemic and Moral, Versus Generalism

Lee Basham

1. INTRODUCTION

Particularism is the view that explanatory theories, including those referring to a conspiracy, should be evaluated on their evidential merits. When confronted with social and moral panics concerning the legitimating of conspiracy theories, particularism is also the view that evaluation on evidential merit is the most moral thing to do. Generalists see conspiracy explanations as suspect *because* they are conspiracy theories.[1] They show scant interest, even preemptive contempt, for evidence that any particular conspiracy theory is warranted or evidentially indeterminate. In Patrick Stokes' wide-ranging "Between Generalism and Particularism about Conspiracy Theory: A Response to Basham and Dentith," (2016) he gazes back in time, encountering issues that have caught the attention of social epistemologists for the last twenty years, Charles Pigden (2016), Brian L. Keeley (1999), David Coady (2012), Kurtis Hagen (2011), and M R. X. Dentith (2014) among them. I am happy to be in the mix. The first issue before these epistemologists is simple: Are conspiracy theories discredited by being conspiracy theories? The answer quickly emerges: no.

Some still want the answer to be yes. Political piety and moral anxiety appear to be primary motives. Panics are not necessarily irrational or always destructive. Stokes' attention to this critical subject has proven quite valuable, even when we fundamentally disagree. He impugns the efforts of epistemologists as toxic to superior values: Faith in and fidelity to our traditional information hierarchy to morality as he sees it, and the state. In the end, Stokes argues we should resuscitate the censorial, "That's just a conspiracy theory." That is, epistemic generalism, in concert with pathologizing and silencing that inevitably follows like a shadow. He seems surprised anyone would ever criticize this, writing:

> Quite astonishingly, something like a broad consensus has emerged [in epistemology]: regarded simply as explanations, conspiracy theories are not *intrinsically* irrational, and believing in conspiracy explanations is not necessarily unwarranted.[2]

Why this might strike some as "astonishing" is, if not quite astonishing, surprising to the historically literate. Conspiracy, both political and economic, is rather normal in human affairs, even within Western-style democracies. Examples are legion.

This basic insight is not welcome by some. It is routinely pathologized as the expression of a mental disease. In the H. G. Wells morality tale, *Country of the Blind*, we learn that "[f]or a week before the operation that was to raise him from his servitude and inferiority to the level of a blind citizen Nunez knew nothing of sleep, and all through the warm, sunlit hours . . . [for] the blind insisted, these orbs you call 'eyes' are actually a defect and should be removed."[3] Wells understood reactionary pathologizing, the tactic of medicalizing alternative conclusions, and the frequent evidence and reasonable inferences supporting these. In the present case, conspiracy theorizing: It is not an infectious pathogen, an ability in need of active dismissal and removal. In a kingdom of the blind, the one eyed become far more effective citizens.

By now, the hope that the public will think of conspiracy theory as intellectually illegitimate is like chasing a train that long left the station. If the culture's understanding of conspiracy theory, not epistemology's, is our focus, this is the key: They merge. Conspiracy theory is now culturally and intellectually legitimate and will stay that way. Fighting back is like denying HIV: futile. "Conspiracy denialism" is over.[4] The pejorative power of labeling an explanation as "conspiracy theory" is rapidly diminishing.

This is good news for public reason. As sophisticated social primates, humans are frequent conspirators and for that reason, also ought to be conspiracy theorists. This isn't going away. A large study by social psychologist Michael Wood shows what we already know; "conspiracy theory" possesses no negative connotation except as residue among certain academic, media, and political elites (2016). There has been a sea-change: Well-evidenced conspiracy explanations are now widely available to the public. But it seems now we are discussing openly what has always been there and ought to have been: Conspiracy explanation, both personal and political, has always thrived in close social groups, but groups heretofore isolated from each other. The collapse of isolation has produced a shockwave of panic and reaction among elites. Before this, academic historians deployed and disseminated momentous conspiracy explanations only to the most limited and educationally well-placed, well-groomed audiences. For instance, those who are reading this text. Now the world is the audience.

Social epistemologists are glad to help midwife this social sea-change. Theorists like Peter Knight (2000), Jodi Dean (1998), Jack Z. Bratich (2008), Brian Martin (2015), and Ginna Husting and Martin Orr (2007) have also shown us how to grow beyond any pejorative connation to "conspiracy theory." The "furious agreement" Stokes focuses on concerning conspiracy theory's logical, evidential, and political legitimacy is not particularly furious. It is well justified by a review of history, analysis of political rhetoric, and the application of mainstream epistemology. It is liberating. Conspiracy theories cannot generally be dismissed anymore. Even our new friends, social psychologists, increasingly acknowledge the pitfall of any general dismissal of conspiracy theory. The moral accusation of "pathologizers" of intelligent, informed, and rational citizens stung a number in the academic community. Some responded quite positively, seeing the wisdom in this critique. Others responded with anger, umbrage and mockery.[5] We are now seeing a more nuanced approach among many thinkers. But for guards of the *Ancien Régime* a marked bewilderment at all this lingers, as in much academic, mainstream media, and government discourse. Being denizens of the primary institutions of our social hierarchies, this should hardly surprise. Domestic information control is the first resort of the powerful.

2. SOCIAL EPISTEMOLOGY AND CONSPIRACY

Adopting a negotiator stance, Stokes offers to seek a halfway house between the opposites of particularism and generalism: "What, then, might lie between, or beyond, generalism and particularism? Perhaps something that might be described as 'defeasible generalism' or 'reluctant particularism'" (2017a, 38). In itself, that sounds encouraging, given the dangers of generalism to democracies or ordinary life.

But it is a mistake to think particularism is the opposite of generalism, a mirror image. The opposite would be *anti-generalism*: conspiracy theories are prima facie true. Both appear equally irrational in manner and measure. Generalists and anti-generalists tend to end up in similar places. Generalists are usually found as lower-level, true-believing functionaries in political parties, corporations, and within sullen cubicles in academic departments, while anti-generalists are often found in mental asylums or in the company of stolen shopping carts. Neither have much to recommend them as lifestyles or epistemic positions. Particularism is the better place, a common-sense halfway house between either extreme—the real halfway house.

Stokes often implies conspiracy theories are the product of irrational processes, based on presupposed, presumably evidentially vacuous narratives, traditions and paranoid prejudices on the verge of superstition, and so on. This is the tired, standard pathologizing tactic that is used to support generalism concerning these theories. Generously, at several points, he concedes, "That there is nothing prima facie *epistemically* false about conspiracy explanations *simply as such* is, to reiterate, now well established" (2017a, 48). But then he argues that we should dismiss them without evidential consideration, even when they are politically momentous, "likewise it is far from clear why I *should* speculate whether mass shooting events were hoaxed by the government" (2017a, 49).[6]

The answer is easy enough: Because epistemology determines ethical response in these cases, not the other way around. Imagine we are told that we, the rational, have to be dragged, kicking and screaming, by overwhelming evidence, to accepting the conclusions of this superstitious "tradition," evidence increasingly *overwhelming* in proportion to the *offensiveness* of these conclusions. A quagmire. Conspiracy theory is not the only one with a tradition in play. This is the basis of the entire *tradition* of generalism; difficult, potentially politically disruptive theories must be rejected for those very reasons and none other. Evidence need not apply. We can do this in the twinkling of an eye. This is what Stokes offers us. If he replies that we should evidentially evaluate "offensive" momentous conspiracy theories on salience, then he is invoking particularism. At one point he actually does this, prefacing his purely analytical advice with "Given what passes for 'evidence' for a Sandy Hook hoax" (2016, 38). We can't have it both ways. We will return to this issue below.

Particularism and generalism have social consequences. Generalism functions as a stabilizing, silencing tactic concerning conspiracy explanations and as a bridge to the pathologizing approach to those who explore conspiracy explanations. Particularism takes a cautious view of institutions that can gain much by public deception: governments, mass media, and corporations. For particularism, the salvation of the state lies in watchfulness of the citizen. The way a paranoid anti-generalism embraces all conspiracy theories, generalism postures an equally paranoid stance to the very idea of conspiracy theorizing.

Presented with a dilemma argument with a conclusion one dislikes, one escape is to deny the disjuncts are exhaustive. Pronounce a new halfway house. The trick is to have this halfway house be distinct from the original disjuncts. Stokes labels his halfway house between particularism and generalism as (a) "defeasible generalism" or alternatively, (b) "reluctant particularism." The reference is the same.

About (a): *All* generalists have a "defeasible" caveat because all grudgingly recognize that some conspiracy theories have proven well warranted and true.

But they require "overwhelming" evidence be presented before a conspiracy theory is to be considered as plausible. That places Stokes' position squarely within the generalist camp. It does not distinguish Stokes' position from traditional generalism. Yet Stokes labors on, under the guise of a halfway house he never builds and nor occupies. This is garden-variety generalism.

About (b), "reluctant particularism": It means "defeasible generalism." Stokes treats the phrases as interchangeable, alternative labels: the same rose by another name. Conspiracy theories are prima facie false, but if presented with "overwhelming evidence" in their favor, but overwhelming what, exactly, except political piety?

If "reluctant" means we will not immediately embrace a theory, but seek significant evidence for or against, then this is simply the particularist position. We have the same "reluctance" toward any scientific or other theory. This reluctance does not view the theory as prima facie false or even suspect prior to examination: no mal-biasing, which is a less severe but nevertheless prejudicial attitude. Saying a theory is not yet warranted is not to say it probably never will be, just because of the sort of theory it is. However Stokes' view, as we will see, is just standard generalism. It need not be, but at this point of development certainly appears to be.

3. MEET THE PUBLIC TRUST
APPROACH (ONE MORE TIME)

Why then is conspiracy theory the subject of so much attention? The role of *prior probability* is often ignored in the debate between generalist dismissal and particularist legitimation of conspiracy theorizing. Some still seem uninterested in the idea that conspiracy theory is not merely a cultural artifact but a rational practice. Stokes prefaces his remarks by resurrecting an element of Keeley's argument in "Of Conspiracy Theories" (1999), but amplifies it into a broadside as Keeley would not, writing:

> I'd suggest we have reasons to be wary of conspiracy theorizing as a practice simply because the internal logic of conspiracy explanation disconnects the morally serious act of accusation from the force of evidence. To defend a conspiracy theory over any length of time typically requires the conspiracy theorist to recruit more and more people to the conspiracy. Conspiracy theory as a practice does not simply trade in suspicion, but in *accusation without warrant* [emphasis added]. (2016, 37)[7]

Of course. Just like trade in warrantless accusation defines lipstick and cologne. All three points in this passage are mistaken.

First, the "internal logic" of conspiracy theory is the normal evidential logic of all credible histories and projections of human affairs. People are not long attracted to conspiracy theories *sans* any evidence. The de-rationalizing and pathologizing political tactic is no longer an option, that is, the view that conspiracy theory is born of an irrational disposition to believe conspiracy theories and, saints deliver us, evidence only comes later. So we need to nip conspiracy theory in the bud. Two points about this tactic suffice. First, it is irrelevant how some suspicions or beliefs *initiate* their existence. At bottom, many reasonable suspicions and beliefs are initiated by mechanisms we have little or no conscious access to and control over. Gifted mathematicians and researchers of all walks call it "intuition" and "insight." Such reasoners should be set aside? Second, what if we have, on the basis of evidence, a prior pattern established, and evidence does come later, and takes hold of the investigation? Typically, we do: The pattern in conspiracy theory, criminal investigation, jurisprudence, and science is the same: (1) A reasonable explanatory template based on *prior* success, here, the historically established *prior probability* of conspiracy in societies like our own (even including faked events and false flag operations); (2) application of an explanatory template to a new scenario and consideration of evidence show a good fit; and (3) conclusion: The new scenario bears the relevant and sufficient marks of the old. This is all of law, science, and life. If we are intellectually honest, we can only intervene at step 2.

Next, evidence morally justifies public challenge and accusation.[8] Evidence often makes accusation morally obligatory. Democracy, if functional, is day-by-day, morality work. This is the price of the freedom to live in such a society. A nice thing about Western-style democracy is, if you don't want to directly participate in the issues of the day, you will not be stopped. If you do want to, and we hope you do, you ought not allow establishmentarians to filter you out.

Finally, well-placed conspirators, economic and/or political, can recruit vast numbers and powers to their purposes without any of these knowing the real goal of their actions.[9] In the recent past they have, on any objective account of the recent. Once these elementary points are grasped, epistemic particularism follows. The unleashing of a conspiratorial project, any project, does not require proselytization of entire bureaucratic populations. It typically requires rather the opposite. History shows this is easily achieved.

For instance, that the public was intentionally deceived into supporting the 2003 Iraq invasion is now widely recognized.[10] No mass of bureaucrats was required. With only a few well-placed operators, spectacular effects can be achieved. We have long seen the mainstream media is easily beguiled into believing it is breaking the big story about a new international menace on the basis of anonymous but seemingly sincere and authoritative sources. That is why it succeeded. The result was catastrophic. Even early on, the death toll was astonishing (Iraq Family Health Survey Study Group 2008). Now it is arguably a million or more if we factor in the consequent regional wars. Given the political leadership's commitment to the invasion, only the publicly widespread and well-evidenced conspiracy theory stood in their way. If properly politically empowered, it could have saved these lives. But because it was a conspiracy theory, it was widely dismissed and pathologized by the mainstream media in the United States and elsewhere.[11] A noble formula for our future? We might have our doubts.

This is a serious challenge to "reluctant particularists" like Stokes. To support his faith in the honest intentions of the U.K. and US governments, he cites a British government document, the Chilcot Report:

> The Chilcot Report, for instance, is *comprehensively* [emphasis added] damning about the UK Government's decision to go to war, yet even it stops short of alleging a conspiracy. . . . Of course, it may yet emerge someday that there *was* a conspiracy: a phone transcript might yet surface of Bush telling Blair "Let's milk this 9/11 thing by pretending Iraq has WMD and then invading to take their oil." But I'd be willing to bet that if that does happen, it won't emerge from the ranks of those now popularly referred to as conspiracy theorists. It will come, as it usually does, from whistleblowers and journalists. (2017a, 54)[12]

But in hundreds of pages Chilcot *never* mentions the allegation of an orchestrated conspiracy to deceive the public, an allegation front and center in the media and in common conversation—as if it never existed. As epistemologists we should not lean on such thin reeds. To Stokes' credit, he concedes this *lacuna* in correspondence. As for whistleblowers and investigative journalists, what are these but beloved conspiracy theorists seeking or armed with evidence?

From a psychological viewpoint, resorting to a document like Chilcot reveals generalists as epistemically repressed to the extreme, rejecting conspiracy theory *via* the slightest ability to evade *certainty*. Such "reluctance" distorts reasoning to a Cartesian degree.[13] Along with Juha Räikkä, I argue that this practice expresses an irrational *conspiracy theory phobia* (in press). The motivating flip side of this coin is generalists' *political piety.* But political beliefs are not a jury trial, where innocence must be conferred upon power until inescapably defeated.[14] In real life "defeasible generalism" means *Cartesian.* It is a nonstarter. It has all the marks of a civil religion. To add a wonderful, if all too human wrinkle, we witness that the deployment of generalism among its advocates is also a selective, *opportunistic* tactic: one to use or set aside according to the needs of political faction, an on/off switch, generalist hypocrisy, almost to their credit. A twenty-first century example is the accusation by political elites who typically scoff at conspiracy theories that the Trump Administration constitutes a cabal of Russian agents.

4. GENERALIST RETREAT FROM EPISTEMOLOGY TO INFORMATION-AGNOSTIC MORALISM

If we wish to argue that accusations of high-placed conspiracy are by nature almost certainly untrue, we run face first into recent history. If we wish to argue that recent history is no longer indicative of current practice, we run face first into current practice. If we wish to argue that the issues are not epistemic, but merely ones of social stability, good manners, and morality, we will have abandoned the epistemic issue.

With a Stokes-style halfway house nowhere in sight, a broad horizon of traditional generalism before us, the goal of an unbiased assessment of warrant is swept aside. We needn't be detained by the question, *is the conspiracy theory true?* We can indulge a generalism of non-epistemic nature: moral censure.[15]

To illustrate, Stokes calls this a "good start":

> Does taking this theory seriously enough to investigate it require me to dismiss grieving parents as frauds, under conditions in which there exist no compelling theory-independent reasons to think they are? If so, don't take this theory seriously enough to investigate it. (2017a, 56)

One wonders what the finish line looks like.

What might "theory-independent reasons" be? Except we're not allowed to be investigating evidence of a possible conspiracy? A silencing standard. All such evidence only exists within explanatory templates and expectations based on history. And what might be a "compelling reason" for investigation? Seriousness of accusation plus motive, ability, and opportunity? As is the norm? Or something *much* more? What lofty standard might this be? In its vagueness, "no compelling" disguises the silencing tactic as epistemic, when it is prohibition: Do not investigate.

We might try this "good start" on law enforcement: "You have no theory-independent reasons and no compelling evidence. You're being rude. Stop asking questions." Law enforcement officers would not be impressed, nor should they. Nor does law enforcement start with a badge. It starts and must with a watchful citizenry. These laws are our laws, after all. Evidential evaluation simply requires an honest inventory of the evidence for and against a hypothesis when that hypothesis is salient and possible. One need not believe a hypothesis to examine its evidential situation. Dismissal of grieving parents? That's question begging. The issue is: Are they? Claims concerning momentous political events cannot simply be declared. But they can be evidentially defended. To decide, we must return to the epistemic. And this serves well in the Tracy affair: The accusations of faked death certificates *are* poorly argued and evidenced.[16]

Particularism, like any system of accountability, is both punitive and preventive of moral abuses. As in any system of accountability lacking total powers of surveillance, there will be false positives and false negatives. When we reflect on the horrific scale those abuses can achieve, it is inescapable: If we are to maximize moral outcomes in a representational democracy like ours, we are morally *obligated* to adopt a particularist stance toward conspiracy theory.[17] *Information-agnostic moralism* only makes for fine Trojan horses.

Let's look, then, at Stokes' horses. I suspect Stokes' "reluctant particularism" is really more a *moral generalism*, one which claims we should not investigate certain conspiracy theories because they are morally offensive and the investigation would, for that reason, offend the investigated and others. Only when overwhelming evidence is thrust upon us—from somewhere or other—we should entertain and pursue them. First, Stokes challenges us by postulating the following:

> Imagine you meet someone who tells you their child has been killed. What would need to be the case for you to begin to suspect that they are lying not merely about the death of that child, but about the child's very existence? Now imagine how strong those suspicions would need to be for you to demand that the person you're talking prove, to your satisfaction, that their child had existed. The evidentiary bar here would have to be very high indeed. (2017a, 54–55)[18]

We can properly call this *moral generalism*. Moral generalism claims our fellow citizens are prima facie immoral when they create, develop, and publicly share conspiratorial possibilities and argumentations that are morally offensive in certain ways. Here the immoral is *usually* a basic consequentialism. Sharing them without rejection might do social or personal harm, so these should not be shared. While Stokes makes no attempt to show they do *more* harm than good, Stokes seems to assume this is obvious. That is easy to contest, and has been in our previous exchanges. But let's look at his particular examples, because he uses these not just as a moral critique of belief in particular conspiracy theories, but ironically, as a critique of epistemic particularism.

Conspiracy theories persist for years, even decades, in the absence of evidence, and can continue to cause harms while they do. There was never any evidence to suggest that AIDS was invented by Western drug companies and governments in an attempt to exploit and control Africa, yet this belief persisted long enough to kill over 330,000 people. (2016, 37)

But the historical record is quite clear. Conspiracy theory was not the culprit. The Thabo Mbeki administration viewed AIDS to be the product of starvation, a shocking testament to so many South Africans' poverty, one Mbeki's administration had promised to reverse.[19] The evidence for this is vast.[20] We will return to this.

This caution made, consequentialist arguments against conspiracy theorizing, like those by Stokes, follow a five-step pattern common among those who resent reasonable public skepticism. Stokes claims not to recognize this argument in his writings, but it is quite clear. If he drops his consequentialism, he has little left to invoke:

(1) Conspiracy theories sometimes cause harm.
(2) Particularism claims we should evaluate conspiracy theories on the evidential warrant of each, and select those examined on their salience to our political and personal needs.
(3) Unwarranted conspiracy theories are popularly believed for long periods of time with "never any evidence" (the "unreasoning masses" gambit).

This is mistaken. Conspiracy theories that are long lived are most always characterized by interesting, if not always decisive, evidence. Once the politically motivated mal-bias against them—in most cases, an expression of political piety, not evidential evaluation—is subtracted, the theories become more plausible, outliving even the participants of the times. One example of this pattern is that historical distance makes conspiracy theories more palatable.

For the moment, what is the case offered for (1)? Stokes offers anecdotes, HIV/AIDS in South Africa, and Australian vaccination levels.

Stokes' South African AIDS example doesn't illustrate (1). He cites 330,000 deaths but not one conspiracy theory, let alone an arguably causative one. When we finally find the "330,000 killed" paper, "Estimating the Lost Benefits of Antiretroviral Drug Use in South Africa" (Chigwedere, Seage, Gruskin, Lee, and Essex 2008) no conspiracy theory is mentioned—instead, a description of poor public policy motivated by non-conspiratorial beliefs. An extensive review of the literature shows these deaths were not caused by a warrantless popular belief in a Western anti-African conspiracy, thundering through the administration and then the cities and villages.[21] We see a Mbeki administration increasingly desperate to stem the dismal tide, uncertain and frightened. The tragedy begins with a top-down decision by the newly minted post-racist government of South Africa to reject anti-HIV drugs.[22] Motivated by scientifically interesting, if mistaken early doubts about HIV causation, a policy emerged that was racially and politically amplified by understandable desires to demonstrate independence from Western nations.[23] There was also the desire to avoid being labeled as a sexually promiscuous African nation, spreading a "monkey-virus" like fire.[24] The South African federal government rejected offers of free anti-HIV drugs. The paper's premise is that had the government accepted and distributed the drugs, most would have gladly used them and the 330,000 would have been saved.[25]

The "330,000" killed by conspiracy theory is a canard. The timing of the political change-over to Mbeki's presidency, with its commitment to *poverty* as the cause of all popular problems, could not have been worse. But when comparative research of adjacent townships showed poverty and malnutrition was the same, and anti-viral drugs made the difference, Mbeki's government quickly reoriented to anti-viral treatment, in capitulation to the moral force of the brilliant anti-Mbeki Treatment Action Campaign.[26]

But let us *pretend* that the Mbeki government *really believed* both HIV *and* anti-HIV drugs were Western stealth genocide and successfully propagated the same absurdity within the public. Is this a counter-example to particularism? It is the opposite.

What we typically observe is the success of evidence-dissemination and open debate. The anti-vaccination movement has been profoundly undermined in instances where it ought to be, but not in instances where valid questions exist. Particularism. Many of the tenants of the 9/11 Truth movement have been abandoned by its own members after lengthy, public, rational debate, some quite quickly, even within months. Particularism. Similarly, and at the cost of significant social and personal anguish, the Iraq war is now widely recognized in the West to be an act of political conspiracy on the part of the United States and other Western governments, particularly those of Bush and Blair. Particularism. The future wars particularism can prevent on the basis of past accuracy and deployment are far worthier of our moral compass.

Returning to the consequentialist moral argument, the missing premise appears to be,

(4) Because popular conspiracy theories sometimes cause harm, our default analysis of conspiracy theories should not be in terms of evidential merit, but in terms of how they promote or undermine our moral and political projects; conspiracy theories that undermine these should be rejected.

Stokes' conclusion,

(5) For both epistemic and moral reasons, we should reject particularism
    about conspiracy theories and embrace "defeasible generalism."

If Stokes says he does not recognize himself in this argument, we should be
cautious. Because he says he does, writing:

> Basham takes it that when I discuss the moral cost of conspiracy accusation in
> this way, "the 'immoral' is a simple consequentialism." Consequences matter,
> and that is why I noted them in the case of AIDs denialism in South Africa,
> but the claim is not fundamentally or solely a consequentialist one. . . . But
> let's dwell on consequences for a moment, as that is where Basham launches a
> defense of particularism. (2017a, 53)[27]

So, the consequentialist argument offered by Stokes appears fairly central to
him, but there is more:

> Basham claims that particularism about conspiracy theory, characterized by
> "evidence-dissemination and open debate," has in practice yielded various
> dividends, both in terms of confirming some conspiracy theories and refuting
> others. Two things need to be noted in response. The first is that all of the con-
> spiracy theories Basham claims to have been defeated are alive and well: it will
> come as cold comfort to CDC employees harassed by anti-vaccination activists
> outside their workplace to hear that "The anti-vaccination movement has been
> profoundly undermined" and even less comfort to parents in places like the
> Northern Rivers region of New South Wales, where vaccination levels, thanks
> to denialism, remain dangerously below herd immunity level. (2017a, 53)

We need to untwine these interwoven considerations. What are the facts?
When we review video of anti-CDC demonstrations in Atlanta, the numbers
appear to be around eighty persons.[28] These few demonstrators, at rare
occasions, hardly reflect a viewpoint not profoundly undermined.[29] I presume
we care, because the consequences of low vaccination are quite bad. So, a
consequentialist argument. We should not be tempted to hysteria, let alone
be concerned, by such meager public attentions. Nor should we resent them
in any functional democracy. If evidence swells their numbers, we should
openly and honestly address that evidence, not work to suppress it.

As for dangerous levels of non-vaccination in the Northern Rivers region
of NSW, according to the Australian government, this agricultural back-
water has approximately 86 percent full immunization,[30] far above levels
in most advanced countries and for almost any vaccination strategy, more

than sufficient for herd immunity in an urban population, let alone a widely dispersed, isolated agrarian community.

So what is the additional, *more fundamental* moral argument Stokes mentions? It invokes a handsome prince.

5. THE PRINCE DID IT: ETHICS AND BAD-THINK

Sometimes conspiracy accusations harm innocent lives, especially in the powerful hands of law enforcement and mainstream media. Stokes focuses on the theory Princess Diana was killed by Prince Philip.[31] Many are still concerned by this conspiracy theory, one based on motive, ability, and opportunity arguments, that Prince Philip, along with other members of the British royal family, played an instigating role in the violent and bizarre death of Princess Diana. The divorced princess, a media phenomenon, died a tragic death, one understandably subject to some suspicion. In a silencing tactic that eventually extends to the *minds* of others, Stokes argues,

> If I publish a blog insisting without anything like credible evidence that Prince Philip had MI6 murder Diana, I've still wronged Prince Philip even if he never finds out or doesn't care or suffers no other unwelcome effects of my accusation. (2017a, 54)

Consequences might still be in play here for the larger society, however, for instance the merit of having *any* princes wandering around. The choice of an example invoking a *prince* is wonderfully ironic in a discussion of the conduct of democracy. For an example even more shorn of consequentialist dimensions, Stokes offers, "My walking into a room and idly wondering if you're planning to kill me may not cause you much upset. . . . I've still entertained the idea you might be a murderer, and thereby done you a passing wrong" (2017a, 50). He positions this as politically relevant in powerful democracies, like the U.S. or E.U. embracing hundreds of millions of people and potentially threatening many more. In the next sentence he walks into the radical dis-analogy of this cerebral story to the world we live in: "There are of course circumstances where that's a warranted suspicion or even a necessary prudential response; but those circumstances are, precisely because they violate the background trust intrinsic to human sociality" (2017a, 50). Yes, those circumstances are situations of radically unequal power, say between the citizenry and the danger of rogue government: in short, the circumstances of all representational democracies. There is no rational trust intrinsic to such nation states, nor should there be: That's the very premise of democracy, the rational expectation of "high crimes and misdemeanors" from the extraordinarily powerful. Conspiracy theory, empowered by significant evidence, is nothing idle like "idle speculation." It is intensely existential in importance to the preservation of our world. Stokes is right, conspiracy theory as it lives and speaks is embedded in a cultural narrative; that culture is termed "democracy." More largely, survival.

But to briefly turn back to the cerebral story, I am not sure what the wrong-doing could be here. I certainly do not believe I am morally wronged if a stranger randomly, momentarily, wonders if I may wish to kill him. Who knows why he thinks that? Who cares?[32] At most, perhaps he has wronged only himself; a fleeting, self-inflicted injury of fear to his consciousness. Whatever the subtleties, I think we can get past that fleeting thought-crime if we prefer functional democracy. That this case could or should motivate public policy and public attitudes concerning conspiracy theorizing in an open society appears absurd, however interesting the case might be to some ethicists, in isolation from real world, political considerations. Any investigation must begin with a reasonable hypothesis, one based on an unbiased inventory of possibilities. Such an initial thought—"the prince did it"—is normal to all law enforcement investigations and, as evidence accrues, the development of a trial by jury. The prince *does* fulfill the criteria of the triangle of crime—motive, ability, and opportunity—so he is a reasonable suspect. Without such inventories, law enforcement is impossible. So, too, the regulation of our personal lives. We have to *form* a hypothesis to explore whether we should pursue its truth or not. The point is entirely logical. In every one of Stokes' examples, and all he might give, he of necessity must violate his "no accusation" standards to give these very examples out to the public. For instance, imagine the hypothesis, "Stokes is a self-confessed anxious person because he has done terrible things in the past." I don't believe this in the least (unless "terrible" just includes us all). But many hearing it will wonder—is that *just* a hypothetical? Within the public such things are inevitable and cannot be meaningfully regulated nor the basis for public regulation—unless, that is, like certain psychologists, we wish to attempt a rigorous program of mental hygiene. Good luck with that.

Stokes is also deeply afflicted by the Professor James Tracy affair. What are the ethical implications of seeking evidence when the accused appear to be private individuals? But this question is not about conspiracy theories or theorizing. The ethics of the Tracy affair can easily be understood as involving no conspiracy theory at all. As an insurance investigator, I might accuse a man of faking the death of a child, even though the man was involved in no conspiracy to do this. Offensive if the child really died? Deeply. Did anyone die at Sandy Hook? The question returns us to evidence, not to information-agnostic moralism. Compared to the difficulty of a mass murder, investigation is comparatively minor, difficult, but nevertheless necessary. This is the refrain of every court of wrong death enquiry in the land, be it legal or the court of public belief. My moral humanity actually prefers a crisis-actor conspiracy theory in every similar instance.[33] There is a deep decency to crisis-actor conspiracy theory. To truly try to envision the rapid execution of screaming and sobbing children trapped in a classroom is soul-shattering. But my rationality, on the basis of evidence, thought through with care, intervenes. People mass-murder. It is that kind of planet. It has been for a very long time. Worse: Children who kill children are celebrated in our morally deranged press and culture as entities of intense, universal fascination.

6. CONCLUSION

We don't need a world increasingly closed, but one more informationally open. Because there is more we need to be informed about, not less. Only horizontal transfer and evaluation of evidence can do this. This is under vast attack and will be for the foreseeable future. These are interesting times. Respect for conspiratorial possibilities is integral to this. The truth of our times, and any, is that we are frequented by conspiracies within our political and economic hierarchy. From either an epistemic or moral perspective, Stokes has not located a halfway house but a traditional generalism, epistemically and normatively; generalism doubled: "super-generalism," one commonplace among our political, economic, media, and academic elites.

It is no surprise Stokes, seeking a halfway house after rejecting particularism, must be driven to generalism. It's a logical inevitability: Like all theories, conspiracy theories are warranted, unwarranted, or evidentially indeterminate. They are clearly socially and personally relevant or irrelevant, or which currently remains unclear. We can be sure that there is no successful inductive argument against conspiracy theorizing that doesn't equally, perhaps even more successfully, mitigate against empirical science itself. This double standard is understandable, expressing a Western political piety of our times, but a piety that, to the consternation of many elites, appears to be collapsing within the general populace.

It should collapse. A censorial tactic, as we see in the "vaccination wars," and many other controversies, tempting as the tactic may be when an orthodoxy is faced with considerable, intelligent, and growing dissent, is as likely to "boomerang." Physicist and expert on political and scientific suppression and dissent Brian Martin explains,

> However, even if dissenters are completely wrong, suppressing them can be damaging in several ways. It sets up a pattern of unfair behavior that can hinder open discussion of issues even within the dominant viewpoint. It discourages

supporters from thinking for themselves about the evidence and arguments, because they encounter contrary views less frequently. Critics can keep advocates honest and alert, with their arguments well formulated. Finally, suppression can aid the cause of critics by making them feel unfairly treated: some observers may wonder why proponents cannot rely on the arguments. When the struggle is open and honest, the outcome will seem more legitimate. (2015, 144)[34]

Generalism is not a morally appropriate attitude in an open society. Sociologically, it has proven to be a slow but accelerating suicide, as witnessed by the popular embrace of conspiracy theories on general principle. It only breeds anti-generalism. It ignores the key role conspiracy theorists play in securing our democracy; frequently these people are acting in our self-defense. Today journalists can be anyone possessed of reasoning and evidence, and access to an attentive audience. This makes our Internet so terrifying to authoritarians, both non-Western or Western, and such a source of hope for advocates, like myself, that a far less hierarchical system of information discovery and dissemination is finally within our reach. Alternative newspapers of the decades past did not suffice. The Internet, if not sabotaged by generalist censorship, might.

Conspiracy theorizing is critical to social progress. In the words of sub-comandante Marcos, "*Yo no sueño con que el mundo cambie, sueño con que el pueblo tome consciencia. Si el pueblo tome consciencia no hacen falta sueños.*"[35] As Marx puts it: "To call on [people] to give up their illusions about their condition is to call on them to give up a condition that requires illusions." Citizen researchers should always be welcome. A new day of epistemic communication and honesty is at hand. Between the extremes of generalism and anti-generalism, the real halfway house of intellectual caution is particularism. Put the lights on. Let's keep them on.

If Stokes and like-minded philosophers can advance a clearer understanding of the limits to their reluctance, what it is that defines this "reluctance" as substantively more open to the evidential consideration of conspiracy theories, this could easily put Stokes on the path of an intellectually honest, politically prudent, and responsible particularism. A standard like "overwhelming evidence" is standard generalism whenever applied to any particular case. It is a standard that is irrationally biased against many conspiracy explanations, so it is inappropriate to the requirements of good epistemology. Most accepted scientific theories do not enjoy "overwhelming evidence" but merely the preponderance. And some are quite offensive at the onset: the theory of evolution's debut, to an overwhelming literalist religious society, for instance. Surely an "offensiveness" standard, premised on the narrative that Darwin was an atheist (which he was), would have counseled us all turn our backs, evidence be damned. It is also, as history shows, morally reckless given the needs of justice and democracy. Stokes with his insights about explanatory narratives and expectations, social and psychological, can develop a structure of evaluation that would help us distill down to those conspiracy theories worthy of pure evidential consideration, without us needing to first be "overwhelmed" by evidence—from where, we might wonder. Moral dimensions might successfully be enfolded into a credible particularism if this is done with great caution, lest we collapse back into a dangerous generalism.

Two standards for success come to mind. First, these moralist nuances must not shield unpalatable and unexpected political conspiracies from exploration and revelation. Second, they should be based, ultimately, on some sort of epistemic grounds: For instance, a general tradition of "trust" should be epistemically defensible and radically defeasible, not a free-floating postulate.[36] I look forward to the advances on this front that Stokes and like-minded moralists can provide.

NOTES

1. In what follows my definition of "conspiracy theory" is essentially the one followed by most all social epistemologists: Any explanation that refers to a conspiracy as a causal factor in events past, present, or future. This is now the dominant core-view in epistemology and elsewhere, as the pejorative connotation cannot credibly be held a necessary feature of conspiracy theory. For a discussion of definitional issues, see my 2011 and, especially, Dentith 2014.

2. Personal correspondence, March 2018, shared draft.

3. Text available at http://www.online-literature.com/wellshg/3/.

4. To flip a Stalin-esque locution that we should be skeptical of, "[fill in blank] denialism."

5. This is addressed in several chapters of Section Two of this volume.

6. For instance, crisis-actor theories.

7. A similar broadside can be found in philosopher Quassim Cassam's brief campaign (see (Cassam 2015, 2016)) against conspiracy theorizing, one fortunately at this writing suspended. See https://www.3quarksdaily.com/3quarksdaily/2015/08/bad-thinkers-dont-be-so-gullible.html for a critique by M R. X. Dentith and me.

8. Unless we invoke the questionable mechanisms of "toxic truths"—truths too socially damaging at the time to tell or to even investigate. See Basham (2018, 2011).

9. See Basham (2003).

10. For a typical mention of this now mainstream conclusion, see: https://www.nytimes.com/2016/07/08/opinion/iraq-war-lies-13-years-later.html.

11. For one of many academic critiques, see Kumar (2006).

12. The Chilcot report is long read indeed, which an aversion to references forces one to. It can be found at: http://webarchive.nationalarchives.gov.uk/20171123123237/http://www.iraqinquiry.org.uk/.

Contra Stokes, the report's criticisms mainly concern the military conduct of the invasion. While they largely gloss over the decision to go to war, they do suggest Blair exaggerated the danger of Iraq to the West, but with some relief, Blair notes, "What I cannot and will not do is say we took the wrong decision. . . . As this report makes clear, there were no lies, there was no deceit." (https://www.theguardian.com/uk-news/2016/jul/06/ tony-blair-deliberately-exaggerated-threat-from-iraq-chilcot-report-war-inquiry)

13. Descartes' standard for knowledge in the *Meditations on First Philosophy* appears to be, "evidence *necessitates* the truth of the conclusion." Evidential certainty in the strictest sense. This absurd standard would defeat even my belief I am typing this endnote.

14. It is of interest that major political leaders, the very same, on the run often retreat to an "absolutely prove it" stance: generalism.

15. Like Stokes, the anti-conspiracy theorizing factory at King's College, currently presided over by social psychologist Karen Douglas, has recently turned away from strictly psychological issues to focus on information-agnostic moralizing. Their (questionable) claims included that conspiracy theorists are more likely to criminally conspire (which is interesting considering almost every human is a conspiracy theorist) and suffer a seemingly suicidal attitude toward the environment. For instance see: Douglas, Sutton, and Cichocka (2017).

16. Mainly, that different fonts were used to fill in different blanks. As if one person at one computer using one font must be completing the entire form, when these blanks involve very different questions only competently answered by equally different specialists. Subsidiary arguments are also offered. Like all arguments concerning politically momentous events, they must be evaluated on evidence. See Fetzer and Palecek (2015) for a collection of these arguments. This evaluation can be done personally or by delegation to evaluators we have reason to trust. What it cannot be done by is *fiat*.

17. When during a graduate talk, explaining the idea that some conspiracy theories are too socially toxic while nevertheless true, I was asked why we should care if a true but powerfully destabilizing conspiracy theory brought down one's society. Such a society that produced such a catastrophe needs to be laid low, she argued. The tragic events in Germany come to mind. I found her conclusion excessive but hard to argue against. I will continue to reflect on it.

18. In personal correspondence, philosopher M R. X. Dentith has emphasized this understanding of Stokes' essential project.

19. For a press account of Mbeki's persistence in pursuing poverty as the primary source for AIDS, see, https://www.theguardian.com/world/2000/jul/10/sarahboseley1.

20. We should also note "never any evidence for [blank]" stamps for important political claims are almost always false. There is *some* evidence. This does not mean it is convincing. "No evidence" claims are instead rhetorical simplicities that social epistemology cannot indulge.

21. An 800-plus-page review that we are forced to undertake due to lack of references.

22. For a compendium of all remarks by the Mbeki administration concerning HIV/ AIDS, see the Mandela Centre of Memory site, https://omalley.nelsonmandela.org/

omalley/index.php/site/q/03lv03445/04lv04206/05lv04302/06lv04303/07lv04313. htm. Also see http://bmj.rethinkers.net/bmj_debate.html for a record of the HIV debate as conducted in the *British Medical Journal*. It's tragic that this debate misled Mbeki's administration. See consequentialist philosopher Peter Singer's essay, "Mbeki Ignored the Science on HIV" at https://www.theguardian.com/commentisfree/2008/ dec/17/mbeki-south-africa-aids. Singer never invokes any role for conspiracy theory in the tragedy. Bad science prevailed.

23. A mainstream media brief can be found at http://www.pbs.org/pov/stateofdenial/ the-aids-rebel/3/.

24. For an NIH-funded analysis concerning the plight of women in the Sub-Saharan AIDS catastrophe, see https://www.ncbi.nlm.nih.gov/pmc/articles/PMC3874682/. The conclusion is that *male* promiscuity is a serious factor, and female disempowerment created serious vulnerabilities. For Mbeki's umbrage concerning the allegation of SA promiscuity in spreading HIV, "Lies have short legs!" at http://www.anc.org. za/ancdocs/anctoday/2005/text/at21.txt.

25. Or the 365,000 number that often appears in the relevant literature.

26. For a concise history of TAC, http://www.tac.org.za/community/ files/10yearbook/files/tac%2010%20year%20draft5.pdf.

27. I suspect that he means "HIV denialism."

28. https://www.youtube.com/watch?v=wRUs1Qs0Gbs, for a 2016 video.

29. Stokes' argument is rather like arguing a statistically significant number of US citizens believe "God Hates Fags" because the Phelps family of thirty people in Topeka, Kansas insists God does.

30. For press release, see https://www.smh.com.au/national/nsw/child-immunisation-rates-at-record-high-but-gaps-among-sydney-s-suburbs-20180309-p4z3mv.html. The source report, *The NSW Immunisation Coverage Report, 2016* is at http://www.health.nsw.gov.au/immunisation/Documents/2016-annual-coverage-report.pdf.

31. For a typical press discussion of the theory, see http://www.dailymail.co.uk/ home/article-1004181/Not-shred-evidence-Prince-Philip-ordered-Dianas-death-says-coroner.html. The coroner, an unabashed particularist, remarked, "A belief expressed in legal proceedings which is not supported by evidence is worthless, it is not evidence."

32. I am open to the thought that certain types of involved human relations may morally entail cognitive no-go zones. I am even open to the idea I ought not secretly despise my loving, good dogs. They are *good dogs*. But Stokes' case explores the far outer limits of such intuitions, and at any rate, is politically irrelevant.

33. Aside: Perhaps some conspiracy theorists are sometimes the kindest hearted of us all, sometimes driven to misplaced and socially bizarre acts of cognitive desperation, the way some cannot accept a parent has died. Other times, they are so keenly attuned to the complexity of a situation that they prove correct in their conclusions. People are very diverse in their abilities and motives, whatever their pronouncements.

34. Also see Martin (1997) (particularly chapter 4 on "defamation").

35. Chiapas radio *Voceros* communication, Fall 1994. English translation: "I don't dream of changing the world, I dream the people gain awareness. If the people

achieve awareness they do not have to dream." I would add, religious attitudes can include the political, not just metaphysical. One such is our Western-style representative democratic systems are inherently open. They are not. History indicates rather the opposite.

36. I do not believe there is such a tradition on the political level, or that there should be, though I agree it is critical on the personal.

Chapter 4

What Particularism about Conspiracy Theories Entails

M R. X. Dentith

1. INTRODUCTION

When I wrote "When Inferring to a Conspiracy Theory Might Be the Best Explanation" (2016b, reprinted in the first chapter), I expected the debate to center around issues to do with whether conspiracy theories do indeed feature in the accounts of our best explanations. But the replies in the journal of the *Social Epistemology Review and Reply Collective* quickly turned to a discussion of just how we should model and talk about particularism, the thesis that we should judge conspiracy theories on their evidential merits. This was either gratifying (my discussion on why conspiracy theories can feature in our best explanations was obviously so self-evidently true that no further discussion was necessary[1]) or unnerving (sometimes the best response to a bad idea is, after all, to just ignore it).

This volume is rooted in the particularist tradition, although, as this section shows there are questions about just what particularism entails, and what this says about conspiracy theorizing as a practice. Stokes, as evidenced by chapter 2, is troubled by the social practice of conspiracy theorizing, claiming that:

> The very act of entertaining a conspiracy theory as a worthwhile hypothesis for investigation may come at a serious moral cost, both in licensing socially harmful practices and in violating the attitude of trust that is, I argue, a precondition of ethical life.

I will return to the issue of *investigating* conspiracy theories in chapter 15, but let me speak to Stokes' (and then Basham's) construal of particularism, and what I think they tell us about how we should treat conspiracy theories seriously.

2. THE PROBLEM OF RELUCTANT PARTICULARISM

Stokes is concerned that when we talk about conspiracy theorizing in a particularist fashion we are blithely ignoring the fact that many conspiracy theories tap into existing narratives (sometimes automatically and without much forethought). He claims to advocate particularism, but of a special type: a "defeasible" or "reluctant" particularism. He admits that a return to "blithe" generalism is untenable, but this could be seen as a bit of a warning sign, given we are now talking not just about types of particularism but also types of generalism. *Blithe* generalism suggests that there might be a proper, non-callous and indifferent generalism which would be more suitable for the analysis of conspiracy theory. Yet it is hard to see how such a non-blithe generalism would not also suffer from the faults of *blithe* generalism, given it would still be committed to assessing conspiracy theories as a class rather than dealing with them on a case-by-case basis. As I will argue, it seems Stokes might want to have it both ways: we can be non-blithe generalists in an *ethical* sense and reluctant particularists *epistemically*.

So, how does particularism deal with the fact that some conspiracy theories seem less evidence-based and more a gut reaction, or motivated by the theorist's politics?

The obvious response is that the gut reactions and politics here are the result of conspiracy theorists (i.e., those interested in particular kinds of events) just happening to be unusually (or perhaps "properly") attentive to previous examples of similar kinds of events. Thus when they tap into existing narratives they are asking, "Is this just more of the same?" That is, why can't we say that these recurrent conspiracy theories are just examples of conspiracy theorists following the evidence, suggesting the possibility of certain conclusions?

But I suspect Stokes is concerned that these reactions are not at all epistemically motivated at base. I am reminded here of Brian L. Keeley's seminal article, "Of Conspiracy Theories," in which he discusses what he calls "mature conspiracy theories," a species of *unwarranted* conspiracy theory (1999). A *mature* conspiracy theory is like a particularly mature cheese: the smell should make you—at the very least—suspicious about the quality of the cheese. Mature conspiracy theories "smell." This is not to say that they are false, but their "smell" (their maturity) justifies our suspicion of them. They are unwarranted, in the sense they are unreasonable to believe given that they have failed to gain warrant over time. So, while it might be the case that alien shape-shifting reptiles secretly control the world, the associated conspiracy theory can be unreasonable to believe if it either lacks adequate evidence (it is unwarranted) or, over time, no good evidence for the theory is ever presented (it fails to gain warrant).

I contend it is these *mature* conspiracy theories which concern Stokes, and thus drive his "reluctant particularism." In chapter 14 Charles Pigden addresses this concern with the idea of *defectibility*, pointing out that if these are the kind of theories Stokes is concerned with, then the worry can be resolved on purely particularist grounds. But maybe this is not the exact issue for Stokes, because as he puts it, his reluctant particularism is based on a certain reticence to engage in the social practice of conspiracy theorizing. In chapter 2 he writes:

> Reticence, crucially, is not blanket refusal, and reluctant particularism is not simply an algorithm for deciding which theories to dismiss or endorse; it is, rather, an epistemic stance formed from a commitment to not engaging in harmful practices and to interpreting others in the most charitable way possible.

Stokes distinguishes between conspiracy theory as a *proposition* versus conspiracy theorizing as an action or practice: this is the crux of his concern. It does not matter if a conspiracy theorist theorizing about conspiracies is acting epistemically. Rather, the issue is that the act of conspiracy theorizing is problematic because the kind of narratives conspiracy theorists tap into are sometimes, maybe often, harmful.[2]

Yet it is hard to work out how we can accept the former claim (the particularist position) if we also accept that latter (the position of reluctance). Do we want to live in a world where, if we were allowed to theorize about conspiracies, then we could investigate them, but it turns out theorizing about conspiracies is generally frowned upon?[3]

It is true that theorizing about conspiracies occurs in a social and historical context. But, as I will argue in chapter 15, I think we can theorize about conspiracies without needing to engage in it *publicly*. As such, if there is a reluctance to engage in the practice of conspiracy theorizing because it can cause harms when undertaken publicly, then we can still conspiracy theorize in private. However, it's important to note that Stokes' position is problematic for the sheer fact that theorizing generally sometimes means making extreme accusations in a public setting which, nonetheless, turn out to be justified.

Indeed, we tolerate and even encourage particularism with respect to non-conspiracy theories in certain sectors of our society. A police officer, on learning that a spouse has been murdered, will think the most likely suspect is the surviving partner, and so will then bring them in for questioning; this is considered a vital part of the healthy functioning of our police and judicial systems. Sometimes we are allowed to make accusations based upon limited evidence because that evidence is suggestive, and what it suggests is a greater harm has been, or is about to be, committed. That is, we allow a certain distrust by investigators in order to maintain public trust generally.[4]

Crucial to Stokes's argument for a reluctant particularism is his view of trust, which is informed by the work of K. E. Løgstrup (1997). In a previous work he wrote that:

> [T]rust is both conceptually and ontogenetically primary, distrust secondary; without that foundational trust the sphere of human life falls apart. (Stokes 2017a, 57)

Trust, under this view, is a pre-condition for social life; we must trust one another to form the social bonds which ultimately make up our epistemic communities. I agree that some assumption of trust in one another is necessary for communities to function both ethically and epistemically (much of our knowledge is socially constituted, after all), but the level of trust we must assume is—I argue—up to debate. While I think trust is a condition for social life, it is also conditional. Its ebb-and-flow can—depending on the kind of society in which you live—go from full-blown trust in one another to complete distrust of other persons. That is to say, we start with a conditional, not foundational, trust, and once we start, everything is up for grabs. This calculation of trust, at least with respect to conspiracy theories, is subject to our beliefs about how conspired or unconspired our societies are; it is informed by our judgments about the prior probability that conspiracies have occurred. But that calculation once again requires we are particularists about these things called "conspiracy theories."

Indeed, this story of trust affects how we talk about the exceptions to that trust we allow certain members of society to indulge in. There is a story to be told about how we establish trust in the police and the courts, which includes information about the fairly obvious discrimination in who gets arrested/ prosecuted (and who does not). We often like to think that generally our society functions even given lapses in trust precisely because we treat these as the exceptions which prove the rule.[5]

Not just that, but there are costs/harms to both sides, something which Stokes does not consider. Making an accusation can be costly to the target of the accusation, but it can also be costly to the accuser. Think, for example, of the opprobrium women still suffer if they accuse someone of rape. People accused of rape often can swat such accusations aside, but accusers typically have their lives turned upside down, with all of their life choices questioned and a fair amount of victim-blaming heaped upon them. Notably, the cost of publicly suspecting that a conspiracy might be a good explanation for a particular event (i.e., being publicly recognized as one of those "conspiracy theorists") carries with it costs and harms as well. As Douglas Adams might have said, humans are not proud of those who treat conspiracy theories seriously, and rarely invite them round to dinner.

Perhaps a more relevant problem related to this is that sometimes the accusations in particular conspiracy theories are too vague to be acted upon. In his paper "Conspiracy Theories and the Internet—Controlled Demolition and Arrested Development," Steve Clarke advances an argument to the extent that in the age of the Internet conspiracy theories have become vaguer and less precise in their claims (2007). This might be a rather pessimistic view of conspiracy theories, but it also speaks to a feature of *some* of them; they may well accuse some group, but they do not accuse particular people. That is, there are accusations, but they occur at a level of generality that seems acceptable, say, when we accuse governments of malfeasance.

Of course, someone like Stokes can reply that vaguer claims are tangibly worse. Blaming international banking cartels allows such theorists to engage in crypto anti-Semitism, for example, and vague claims may well persist where precise ones might falter. But this is where our understanding of conspiracy theories comes in handy. Though we must take each conspiracy theory seriously enough to investigate it, many conspiracy theories have already been investigated, and we can approach new iterations of them with knowledge of their past variants. That is, after all, part of the evidential pool particularists rely on in their analysis.

Which is to say that, contra Stokes, particularism is not indifferent to the social context of conspiracy theorizing. In chapter 2 Stokes writes:

> The particularist, by insisting on viewing each conspiracy theory solely on its own merits, requires a certain indifference to the contingent cultural, historical, and rhetorical explanatory repertoires from which conspiracy theorists typically draw their hypotheses.

You could talk about particularism in this way, but only if you radically restrict what counts as evidence to the particularist. But the kind of particularism which infused "When a conspiracy theory might be the best explanation" (i.e., the basis for this discussion) takes the kind of evidence Stokes thinks (strict) particularists are not attentive to ("contingent cultural, historical, and rhetorical explanatory repertoires") into account. After all, when judging the prior probability that a conspiracy exists the evidence is not just "Have people conspired in the past?" It is also "What has made people think conspiracies of this type were common?" and "How many such past accusations of these kinds of conspiracy turned out to be warranted?" When we judge the relative probability, we have to compare and contrast the conspiratorial explanation on offer with rival explanations, some of which will account for the *appearance* of conspiracy as something situated in a cultural or historical narrative.

It is true that *naive* investigators might not think this through, and thus fail to be attentive to all the kinds of evidence they should be contemplating, but that is not a problem with particularism. That is, instead, a problem with theorists, and it's hardly a unique problem to conspiracy theorists. From scientism (where scientific reasoning is inappropriately applied to situations not amenable to scientific investigation) to the notion of the "Great People of History," it turns out that people misapply theses all the time.

Stokes, I contend, is considering an interesting issue, but it is one more to do with a particular kind of conspiracy theorist than it is with conspiracy theorizing *per se*. That is, he is concerned with *mature* conspiracy theorists, those who believe *mature* conspiracy theories. It is not the social practice of conspiracy theorizing which is the problem. It is, rather, the reluctance of *mature* conspiracy theorists to give up on their *mature* conspiracy theories.

Stokes presents an interesting discussion of what he takes to be the intertwined roles of epistemology and ethics. For Stokes they are tightly linked, and it is tempting, then, to take a naive view and think that this entails—on Stokes' part—some claim that ethics curtails or blocks our epistemic duties. That is, he seems to advocate for a non-blithe moral generalism concerning conspiracy theory which trumps our epistemic duties. But it would be strange to think Stokes is not committed to some view that we must chase truths in order to quash immoral falsehoods. But reluctant particularism entails this: in his own words he says "we are morally obliged to reject some theories even at the risk of occasionally being wrong."

It is not all bad, however. Stokes concludes his chapter with this timely reminder:

> [W]e would do well to remember that conspiracy theories don't exist merely on paper. They're something we do—and that makes us responsible for how we do so.

This is true: we should be responsible as particularists.[6] But this is not grounds for reluctance.

3. THE PROBLEM OF A BLITHE PARTICULARISM

Whereas I have reservations (to put it lightly) about Stokes' so-called reluctant particularism, Basham's particularism is a heavily peated, almost raw whisky[7] in comparison. As he argues, if Stokes is really concerned about a middle ground between generalism and the treatment of conspiracy theories seriously, then he's tilting at the wrong windmill. The opposite of generalism is just anti-generalism; particularism is the middle ground, especially if—as I have argued—particularism works with the full spectrum of available evidence, cultural mores, and more.[8]

But whereas Stokes is *reluctant* to endorse pure particularism, Basham could be accused of being *blithe* about particularism. He writes in the previous chapter:

> By now, the hope that the public will think of conspiracy theory as intellectually illegitimate is like chasing a train that long left the station. If the culture's understanding of conspiracy theory, not epistemology's, is our focus, this is the key: They merge. Conspiracy theory is now culturally and intellectually legitimate and will stay that way.

If only this were true (and, indeed, it might be true somewhere but certainly not everywhere). If Stokes is reluctant to embrace particularism as particularism, Basham could be criticized for thinking that particularism (at least in the eyes of the public) has won, and that now all we need do is drag some pesky social scientists into the light. Yet I cannot help but think he sees the world as a better place than the rest of us do.

For example, I belong to a European Union (E.U.) research network, COMPACT (the **COMP**arative **A**nalysis of **C**onspiracy **T**heories) which focuses on the analysis of conspiracy theories.[9] As such, I am quite aware that generalism still is the dominant force in the academic sphere, with only faint lip service paid to particularism when people say "Well, of course *that* conspiracy theory turned out to be true, but . . ." Part-and-parcel of COMPACT's work is compiling volumes looking at conspiracy theories and attitudes toward conspiracy theory in various E.U. countries. The results seem, for a particularist, disturbing, because they suggest that people by-and-large still treat conspiracy theories as intellectually suspect.

Now, this research is filtered through the lens of the researchers, and so it is possible that the results are generalist either by design or accident. But they suggest that perhaps the political piety that conspiracy theories are bunk remains. These results can also be reinforcing, as what we are told people think about conspiracy theories can end up prescribing to members of our societies just how they should talk about these things called "conspiracy theories." Particularism is the way, but we still have much work to do in order to direct people to it.

Basham also claims that particularism has a successful track record of overturning faulty (unwarranted) conspiracy theories, but this is the very ground of the debate between Basham and Stokes. Stokes points out that some debunked conspiracy theories (those *mature* conspiracy theories) continue to persist (and, in some cases, even gain new adherents) in our epistemic communities. Basham seems blithe in response, taking Stokes to task, for example, on anti-vaccine conspiracy theories in Australia. Basham suggests that the problem cannot be all the bad given the vaccination rate is approximately 86 percent in the areas said to be worst affected by anti-vaccine conspiracy theories. Eighty-six percent sounds good when it comes to vaccination coverage, but herd immunity rate for measles, for example, requires vaccination coverage of 92 percent of the target population or above. This means that if Basham is right, and 86 percent is a pretty respectable number compared to elsewhere, then it's not just the local population who are in a whole bunch of trouble. Indeed, in Mullumbimby, which you might call the center of anti-vaccine conspiracy theorizing in Australia, less than 70 percent of five-year-olds are fully vaccinated, which is well below the herd immunity threshold.

Basham also notes that when we review videos about anti-CDC (Center for Disease Control) protests we only see about eighty people protesting, meaning that the problem of anti-vaxxers is neither considerable nor momentous. But just because only x number of people engage in a protest, that does not tell us how many people believe or are susceptible to the thesis which drives these protests. This is Stokes' actual concern: the effects of these conspiracy theories, which can be greater than the number of actual adherents. Not everyone who decides not to vaccinate their child explicitly believes in a conspiracy about vaccinations. However their decision may well have been indirectly informed by the proponents of anti-vaccine conspiracy theories. In the same way, not every politician or Supreme Court justice who is skeptical of Anthropogenic Climate Change (ACC) explicitly believes the conspiracy theory that says the notion of ACC is a pretext for socialism, but the data they use as reasoning for their position might be a product of people who do.

So, where Stokes is reluctant because of the presumed bad effects of conspiracy theorizing, Basham seems blithe about these concerns, batting them to one side. It is as if Basham is operating with a restricted definition of what counts as the proper subject for discussion of conspiracy theory—one which implicitly throws out examples which do not fit with his admirably strong particularist views—while Stokes operates with a more general definition. This has the strange consequence of Stokes—based upon his more open definition—arguing for a degree of caution, while Basham, working with a more restricted scope (notably around "politically momentous" conspiracy theories), claiming that said caution is just grounds to reintroduce some flavor of generalism to the mix.

We should resist being blithe about how we might go around assessing and investigating particular conspiracy theories. Take the kind of the examples he (and I) typically use to support the idea that fairly hefty accusations are routinely asked in our societies, from police accusing partners of being responsible for a spouse's murder to journalists accusing the government of being corrupt. These things happen, but they are also considered, as I argued in the previous section, the exceptions which prove the rule. That is, certain people or members of institutions are allowed to make such accusations in a way that the rest of us cannot. There are systems in place which license such accusations by specific members of our societies, and a blithe particularism which ignores or downplays such structures or systems is precisely the kind of thing which motives a "reluctant" particularism.

Now, it would be churlish of me to criticize Basham too heavily on this matter, because I share his aspiration (even if I do not think we are quite at the point of declaring victory). We live in an age where the appellation "conspiracy theory" no longer holds quite the opprobrium it once did. But note that is a far cry from the claim particularism is now the norm. Though some people are still worried about being construed as a conspiracy theorist, people still presage claims with "This is not a conspiracy theory, but . . ." People may be more inclined to entertain conspiracy theories as serious explanations of events, but whether this will hold true, move toward unfettered particularism, or recede into the night of a new dark age of generalism is yet to be seen. Still, like Basham, I am optimistic, just not blithely so.

4. CONCLUSION

What does the discussion between Stokes and Basham illustrate about particularism? Well, for one thing, it shows that we are, to a large extent, still talking past each other because Basham and Stokes are working from different viewpoints. For Stokes it seems that ethics decides the limits of our epistemic inquiries, while for Basham epistemology drives our ethical behavior. Stokes is concerned that particularism obliges us to engage in morally harmful social practices, while Basham thinks that wherever the evidence goes so should we.

There is a debate in both ethics and epistemology as to whether they are just one and the same. After all, both deal with "ought" claims: ethics tells us how we *ought to live* and epistemology tells us how we *ought to reason*, so surely the ethical person is obliged to reason properly, and the ideal epistemic agent should behave ethically? Both Stokes and Basham are interested in the tension between how we ought to treat conspiracy theories as propositions and what the right societal attitude toward conspiracy theory is. For Stokes ethics is primary, while for Basham it is epistemology.

As someone who has advocated for particularism in numerous papers, I do take it that epistemology is primary here, because I think an epistemology attentive to all kinds of evidence should result in ethical behavior. But Stokes' concern with conspiracy theorizing is not, I think, a concern centered on the generation and investigation of conspiracy theories. Rather, it is predicated on the actions of certain conspiracy theorists. Not everyone is going to be a good particularist, but problems in practice do not necessarily tell us that the theory itself needs fixing. It can, of course; theories which are utterly impractical, for example, might need rethinking, but in this case it is not the theory (particularism) which is impractical but rather that there is bad practice or precedent out in the world. The analogy here is with the sciences: there is a lot of bad scientific thinking, but this does not tell us that scientific methodology is flawed. It just shows us that being a scientist is hard. Being a particularist about conspiracy theories is, I think, a lot more difficult than perhaps some of us might like to think.

If there is a limit to particularism, I place it more in the grounds of economics and time. There does not seem to be enough time in the day for any one of us to investigate or assess the multitude of conspiracy theories we encounter (indeed, at the time of writing, the production of new conspiracy theories simply about the US president has increased so sharply that assessing the conspiracy theories produced in just one hour seems too arduous a task). Our engagement with particularism is limited by being an epistemic and ethical agent who must find time to eat, drink (and also be merry). But, as I will argue in chapter 15, there is a way to solve this. After all, I share Stokes' worry that, in Keeley's terms, *mature* conspiracy theories continue to persist. I, too, worry sometimes that in defending particularism (and thus endorsing the need for conspiracy theorizing) that this licenses certain behaviors or acts which can cause harms to others. But I do not think Stokes' middle ground way—a "defeasible" or "reluctant" particularism—is a live option. As Basham argues, trying to construct such a new middle ground commits us to generalism in the epistemic sense or a moral generalism which prohibits us from engaging in a particularist analysis of conspiracy theories in the first place. Given the potential threat of conspiracy, both of these two options are non-starters. The answer, then, is not to be reluctant about particularism. Rather, the solution is to embrace particularism, take conspiracy theories seriously, go out and investigate them, and then, as I argue in the conclusion to this volume, present our findings.

NOTES

1. In case people are worried, this comment is more humorous than serious.

2. Pigden disputes this in chapter 14, arguing that Stokes is wrong to generalize about conspiracy theorizing here; it is a set of practices, and thus Stokes' motivation for reluctant particularism is really centered on the activities of just some conspiracy theorists.

3. For an answer to this, see the previous chapter by Lee Basham.

4. What certain conspiracy theorists point out here is interesting: sometimes people in positions of power get away with breaking the public trust. No matter what you think of former U.K. prime minister Tony Blair and U.S. president George W. Bush's involvement in the invasion of Iraq of 2003, it seems to have had little consequence to their careers post their premierships.

5. We may well wrongly think these lapses are exceptional and not actually the norm, which is something conspiracy theorists of a certain stripe press in arguments all the time.

6. I do not want to coin the label "responsible particularism" here because particularism is a theory, and responsibility is ultimately up to the agents who practice that theory when they take conspiracy theories and investigate them.

7. Scotch whisky to our American friends.

8. Basham misses a trick here by not linking anti-generalism to the thesis so many social scientists find themselves tilting at. As I have argued elsewhere there is a notion in much of the wider conspiracy theory theory literature which relies on the characterization of conspiracy theorists as paranoid wrecks who believe all (or nearly all) the conspiracy theories they hear (2018). "Anti-generalist in tendency" is how generalists view conspiracy theorists, and anti-generalism or "conspiracism" (or "conspiracist ideation"), to give it the name said thesis often gets labeled as in the literature, is untenable simply because while there may well be some conspiracy theorists who think that way, it is by no means the norm.

9. It is also the perfect front for a conspiracy by conspiracy theory theorists to control the direction of conspiracy theory theory. I am constantly surprised that we do not feature more regularly on news sites which claim, say, that the CIA created and weaponized the term "conspiracy theory" and the like.

Section Two

DIAGNOSING CONSPIRACY
THEORY THEORISTS

Chapter 5

The Conspiracy Theory Theorists and Their Attitude to Conspiracy Theory

Introduction to Section Two

M R. X. Dentith

On June 6, 2016, eight social scientists—Gérald Bronner (Sociology, Université Paris-Diderot), Véronique Campion-Vincent (Sociology, Maison des Sciences de l'Homme), Sylvain Delouvée (Social Psychology, Université Rennes), Sebastian Dieguez (Neuro-psychology, Université de Fribourg), Karen Douglas (Social Psychology, University of Kent), Nicolas Gauvrit (Cognitive Psychology, École Pratique des Hautes Études), Anthony Lantian (Social Psychology, Université de Reims), and Pascal Wagner-Egger (Social Psychology, Université de Fribourg) published in the French newspaper *Le Monde* a piece which was critical of the French Ministry of Education and French Television efforts to produce and disseminate a video kit to teachers in order to combat talk of conspiracy theories (2016).

This may not sound like much: an opinion piece in *Le Monde* by academics critical of an educational initiative in their own country[1] is not exceptional. However, when some of the contributors to this book read said piece we found it extraordinary given that they characterized talk of conspiracy theories as a particular form of contemporary misinformation, which they labeled as "conspiracism," a problem they claimed that was on the rise and which needed to be taken seriously. They thought that the reaction by the French State to such (apparent) conspiracist tendencies among the general public had been too hasty. These social scientists thought that while the intentions of the State were laudable, this did not excuse the lack of rigor with respect to these initiatives. In turn they charged the various educational campaigns as random, expensive, and—perhaps most importantly—as taking money away from the more methodical studies of conspiracy theory that they engaged in.

The *Le Monde* piece resulted in a group of academics led by Lee Basham and myself, along with David Coady (Philosophy, University of Tasmania), Virginia Husting (Sociology, Boise State, Idaho), Martin Orr (Sociology,

74 *M R. X. Dentith*

Boise State, Idaho), Kurtis Hagen (Philosophy, retired but formerly State University of New York), and Marius Hans Raab (Psychology, University of Bamberg)—to pen a response, one which took issue with the underlying premise of the *Le Monde* piece: namely that conspiracy theories and conspiracy theorizing should be seen as *prima facie* problematic (2016). As we saw in the previous section, to philosophers (and, as we will now see, sociologists and psychologists) the thesis of particularism (evaluating particular conspiracy theories on their evidential merits) should be our *modus operandi*. The generalist conception at the heart of the *Le Monde* piece was an anathema to us. By consigning belief in conspiracy theories to a general category of problematic beliefs, they exemplified the generalist and pathologizing turn which, we argue, *unthinkingly* assumes belief in conspiracy theories to be irrational.

We responded, and in our response (a new version of which appears in the next chapter) we agreed with our social science colleagues that a reasoned response to talk of conspiracy theories in our polities is necessary. However, rather than task citizens with a vigilance crucial to the operation of a healthy democracy, these social scientists asked us to adopt a faux intellectual sophistication, one which dismisses conspiracy theories out of hand.[2]

One good reply naturally leads to another: the authors of the *Le Monde* piece (*sans* Karen Douglas) submitted to the *Social Epistemology Review and Reply Collective* a rebuttal entitled "'They' Respond: Comments on Basham et al.'s 'Social Science's Conspiracy-Theory Panic: Now They Want to Cure Everyone'"[3] (Dieguez et al. 2016). In response to our concerns, they admitted that many of the research findings coming out of social psychology on belief in conspiracy theories did indeed need further testing, even replication. However they also went on to argue that all they were advocating was for more research, and that they were just asking questions.

Yet at the heart of their reply lay a tension: they disparaged the work of philosophers, sociologists (and the occasional psychologist) who thought we should define concepts before investigating them, instead arguing that they needed empirical work *first* in order to get to the heart of *then defining* what these things called "conspiracy theories" actually are. That is, they argued that we need to know what constitutes belief in conspiracy theories before we can say what conspiracy theories are.

Now, we do not begrudge social scientists wanting to do a little social science, given that is their job. However, they also claimed the common philosophical definition of conspiracy theory—any explanatory hypothesis which cites a conspiracy as a salient cause of an event; see Dentith (2014) for more on this—was just a premature attempt to settle the issue. They wrote:

[A]sserting that a conspiracy theory is any kind of thinking or explanation that involves a conspiracy—real, possible or imaginary—and that's all there is to it, seems like a premature attempt to settle the issue, as if the topic itself was a non-topic and anyone—and that's a lot of people—who thinks there is something there of interest is simply misguided, or manipulated. (Dieguez et al. 2016, 22)

Yet our point was how can we possibly work out what constitutes belief in a thing (say, a conspiracy theory) if we are still not sure what that thing is? This is an especially perplexing problem because in their reply they end up defining what these things called "conspiracy theories" are, writing:

[W]hat the conspiracist mindset tends to produce and be attracted to, an apparently circular definition that rests on ongoing work but is firmly grounded in relevant research fields such as cognitive epidemiology, niche construction and cognitively driven cultural studies, and could be refined or refuted depending on future results. (2016, 27)

Thus, despite claiming they needed empirical work to get to a notion of what these things called "conspiracy theories" are, they were operating with a definition of conspiracy theory the entire time, one which built in the pejorative aspect so prevalent in parts of the wider academic literature.

It should be obvious by this volume alone that conspiracy theory theorists who start their work with a definition of what counts as a "conspiracy theory" do not think this renders the issue moot. Indeed, knowing what it is we are studying has led to a plethora of papers teasing out the interesting consequences of belief in such theories. In this section we both elaborate on our concerns with respect to the responses by the authors of the *Le Monde* piece, and deal with some of the interesting consequences of taking the generalist project seriously.

We approached the authors of the *Le Monde* piece and their subsequent reply to see if they wanted to reply to our concerns, and thus contribute to this volume. They declined. This puts them at a disadvantage, but not us; the chapters in this section deal broadly with issues to do with the social scientific discussion of conspiracy theories and belief in conspiracy theories. The *Le Monde* piece, and its successor, simply represent aspects of a field we critique broadly in this volume.

There is a worry that the general tenor of work coming out of the social science branch of conspiracy theory theory might be a recrudescence of the same kind of issue we saw in the treatment of religion back in the 1930s: the psychological study of religiosity ended up dissolving the phenomena (belief in religion) down to what turned out to be general psychological attitudes (or problems) common to everyone and most kinds of belief. We were worried about religion in the early twentieth century (as is witnessed by the large number of books of the time assuring people *then* that religion would soon die out, and thus no longer be a problem). Now we seem to be worried about conspiracy theories in the same way. Yet, as the last section showed, and this section demonstrates, we can take conspiracy theories seriously without attaching to them any notion that they are mad, bad, or dangerous.

For example, in the next chapter, "The Psychologists' Conspiracy Panic: They Seek to Cure Everyone," Lee Basham and I argue the danger of condemning conspiracy theorists and their conspiracy theories as *prima facie* problematic has, and has had, grave consequences, both epistemically and politically. Lee Basham follows this up in chapter 7, "Social Scientists and Pathologizing Conspiracy Theorizing," where he critiques other representative pathologizing projects concerning conspiracy theories in the social sciences.

Chapter 8 sees Ginna Husting, in "Governing with Feeling: Conspiracy Theories, Contempt, and Affective Governmentality," exploring the conspiracy panic thesis which infuses much talk of conspiracy theories.

Kurtis Hagen argues in chapter 9, "Conspiracy Theorists and Social Scientists," that a scientific study of belief in conspiracy theories which inappropriately pathologizes conspiracy theorists makes the critics of belief in conspiracy theory as guilty as their (putative) charges are.

Chapter 10 sees Martin Orr and I argue, in "Clearing Up Some Conceptual Confusions about Conspiracy Theory Theorizing," that there is a recurrent problem in the wider academic literature on conspiracy theories—as exemplified by the *Le Monde* piece and its associated reply—which is a refusal to put theory before practice. This worry is reiterated by Marius Hans Raab in chapter 11, "To Measure or Not to Measure? Psychometrics and Conspiracy Theories," which examines the various ways in which psychologists measure belief in conspiracy theories. This chapter complements Orr and mine, as Raab argues these measurement systems could enrich our philosophical discussions, but the accuracy of their results turns out to be problematic.

Chapter 12, "Anti-Rumor Campaigns and Conspiracy-Baiting as Propaganda," sees David Coady comparing rumors and conspiracy theories. He argues their respective bad reputations are the result of a kind of anti-democratic propaganda, one that we should resist.

Patrick Stokes, in chapter 13, "On Some Moral Costs of Conspiracy Theory," argues that there is a morally costly feature to conspiracy theorizing; it is a social practice which can violate important social norms around how we maintain trust in our societies. However Charles Pigden in chapter 14, "Conspiracy Theories, Deplorables and Defectibility: a Reply to Patrick Stokes," disagrees, arguing that what might motivate us to reject certain conspiracy theories is not Stokes' "reluctant particularism," but, rather, an analysis of just how defectible certain conspiracies inherent to such conspiracy theories turn out to be.

Finally, in chapter 15, "Taking Conspiracy Theories Seriously and Investigating Them," I present an argument as to how we should go about investigating conspiracy theories once we embrace particularism. By adopting the community of inquiry method, one which prizes a diversity of views on particular conspiracy theories and conspiracy theory theory, we can avoid dogmatism about conspiracy theories both generally and particularly, and thus get to the heart of the matter of taking particular conspiracy theories seriously.

NOTES

1. For the most part—Karen Douglas is resident in the U.K.

2. It is curious how the social scientists of a country whose monarchy was torn down due to the revelation that those in power conspired against the people, and thus could not be trusted, now ask us to dismiss the same kind of speculation that inspired not one but many glorious French Revolutions.

3. For some reason the authors objected to us referring to their collective work under the umbrella term "they." This may be some difference between academic French and academic English, but given that it is not clear which authors wrote which part, "they" and "them" were simply a convenience, rather than some suggestion that we think "they" were somehow involved in a conspiracy.

Chapter 6

The Psychologists' Conspiracy Panic

They Seek to Cure Everyone

Lee Basham and M R. X. Dentith

Let us never tolerate outrageous conspiracy theories.

—US president George W. Bush, first national address following 9/11

1. INTRODUCTION

A truism: governments and corporations routinely conspire to deceive people. This should be no startling revelation, at least to anyone who is historically or politically literate. Such institutions deceive the public routinely. Sometimes they need to keep secrets in the *present* in order to realize some *future* benefit; if you are negotiating trade terms with some foreign nation you will want to keep your bottom line secret from your own public, because what is publicly known at home can become publicly known abroad. On occasion they need to deceive the public in order to investigate some claim more fully; if you are concerned that the factories you use employ child labor, you might want to keep secret your investigation so that the factory owners do not have time to cover their tracks or destroy evidence. Sometimes, of course, they conspire because they are up to no good. Sometimes politicians cover up political malfeasance, such as election rigging, corrupt spending, or the fact that the stated reasons for going to war are but a tissue of lies. Businesses also cover up that they knowingly were engaging in polluting behavior, or senior business leaders were knowingly covering up the presence of sexual predators in their ranks. But if you believe the work of a significant number of social scientists, you would almost be excused for thinking that we are not supposed to talk about examples like these.

2. AN OPEN LETTER

Exhibit one is an open letter, published in *Le Monde,* entitled "Luttons Efficacement Contre Les Théories du Complot" (Bronner et al. 2016) (summarized in the previous chapter) on June 6, 2016, by a group of social scientists who—among other things—are interested in conspiracy theories and conspiracy theory theory. In their open letter they characterize a normal, even politically necessary practice—the supposition that some events might be the result of a conspiracy—with dismay. But rather than drill down into the phenomena that is conspiracy theorizing, these researchers are more concerned about how to properly develop a *science* of how to *stop* the public from considering these things we call "conspiracy theories."

Let us first speak to their motivations. The French Ministry of Education has a program of educational initiatives designed to distinguish verifiable facts from various unprovable pieces of information, some of which are associated with the plethora of conspiracy theories which have emerged in the wake of a series of terrorist incidents in France in the past (such as the Bataclan shooting) which have produced a number of conspiracy theories. Bronner et al. state:

> The political reaction to the problem of the growth of conspiracy theories is not at all disproportionate, because it is essentially a major problem. However, the urgency of this reaction suggests undue haste, one which must give way to a reasoned political response that leans on solid scientific knowledge, and takes into account all the facts available. (Bronner et al. 2016)[1]

Note the emphasis here. This is a "major problem" and the State's reaction is of "undue haste." In effect, the Ministry of Education is being chided for not being sufficiently scientific about its efforts at *quashing* conspiracy theories and conspiracy theorizing.

3. AN OPEN RESPONSE

These social scientists ask for a reasoned response. We agree that a measured, cautious response to conspiracy theories is a must, because any allegation of conspiracy (inherent to any conspiracy theory) must be assessed on the evidence. Why? Because conspiracies—should they exist—are a *potential* threat to the polity.

Consider the examples mentioned earlier, of trade negotiations or the investigation of child labor practices in your supply chain. These secretive, conspiratorial activities may well be necessary for some greater good (although, as philosophers, we are well aware that this is an ethical mine-field). But consider our other examples of political malfeasance or corporate cover-ups. Without investigation, without taking talk of conspiracy theories seriously, we do not know why, if there is a conspiracy, what the reason is for the cover-up.

"Ah," but the defender of the position espoused by Bronner et al. might say, "they are only taking about obviously *fantastical* conspiracy theories, like those which allege false flags by the French State, or theories the scientific community is covering up that the Earth is flat, and the like." To which we reply: "How do we make such a distinction unless we've already assumed those theories are false to begin with?" There is no mark of the incredible which tells you a theory is obviously false *before you investigate it*.

The authors of the *Le Monde* open letter provide a response which is neither measured nor cautious. They focus not so much on conspiracy theories themselves, how they might imperil the public, or even what evidence there is for or against them because it is as if none of those questions matter. Rather, what we *are* told by them is scientific techniques must be developed and then deployed so that people will not even consider conspiracy as an option.

These social scientists give no attention to whether anti-government or anti-corporate conspiracy theories might be well evidenced. They pay no respect to the danger real political conspiracy threatens the public with, and they make no acknowledgment that exposing conspiracies is a critical practice in a well-functioning democracy. After all, in an environment in which people take a dim view of conspiracy theories, conspiracies may multiply and prosper. Conversely, claims of conspiracy which are taken seriously, investigated by journalists, police, and the like, are much more likely to fail. But the *Le Monde* authors seem unperturbed by this. Instead, their view is what social psychologists term a "monological belief system," a particularly intense form of single-mindedness. In this case, the monological system might be summed up as "conspiracy theory is a mental and social pathology."

Why do they take offense at the French prescription? Well, because "[t]he wrong cure might only serve to spread the disease . . . we believe it necessary to recall that current attempts to remedy the problem will only be, for the moment, an improvisation" (Bronner et al. 2016).

4. A DANGEROUS PRESCRIPTION

If the authors of the *Le Monde* piece were merely talking about theories which had been already investigated and refuted this might be well and good. Instead, we see here educated and politically empowered persons advocating that perfectly, completely sensible questions about government conduct, and the various abuses of its covert powers, should be considered off-the-table. Conspiracy theorizing is apparently a problem in need of a cure; conspiracy theorists are diseased, with a curious social ailment; these researchers aim to cure us of that.

That's dangerous. The antidote to whatever problems conspiracy theories present is vigilance, not some *faux* intellectual sophistication which dismisses conspiracy theories out of hand. It is really quite simple when you think about it: conspiracy theorizing is essential to the functioning of any democracy, or indeed any ethically responsible society.

First, consider the antithesis of democracy: tyranny. History shows there is a significant probability of the development of authoritarianism in any society which is not attentive to what its politicians are doing. The development of such tyranny typically begins and matures with conspiracies within the political leadership. As such, the prevention of any potential tyrant requires the public be able to question what is happening in their polity, and that suspicions of misdeeds be treated seriously and investigated. These are necessary precautions, and they should not be restricted just because asking such questions might cause embarrassment or lead to distrust.

We acknowledge not everything which looks like a conspiracy will turn out to be, and that some of those things which turn out to be conspiratorial might not be sinister. But vigilance is the key to a functioning democracy, so asking questions about possible conspiracies cannot be considered gauche.

It is not just the emergence of extreme, overt tyranny we have to set a moral watch for. High-placed political conspiracies of lesser ambition often lie behind the political catastrophes of recent history. For example, the catastrophe of the invasion of Iraq comes to mind. There is little doubt in the public or among scholars that NATO, and many other governments, were intentionally misled and manipulated into this war, particularly by the U.S. government. This truth, well evidenced at the time of grave decision, was silenced as an "outrageous conspiracy theory" by heads of state, mainstream media, and yes, certain members of academia. Thus, a war that ultimately led to the death of hundreds of thousands, and a desperate global refugee crisis, was powerfully enabled by an anti-conspiracy theory panic, one that these scholars would seem to like to embrace and nurture as general policy.

After all, these researchers ask we take into account all of the facts available. Well, the Holocaust began as a conspiracy. Prepared in secret councils of the Nazi party, the conspiracy culminated at the Wannsee conference of 1942. The contents of this conference were hardly broadcast to the world or its intended victims. The Nazis assured the world it was "relocating" Jews, even forcing family members already in the extermination facilities to write letters to their relatives in "ghettos" (often rural camps) encouraging them to get on the trains, as life, they were forced to write, was so much better at the extermination facilities. When officials were challenged about their intentions and actions, they argued anything more sinister than relocation was an outrageous conspiracy theory. The same was said of Stalin's Show Trials—an outrageous conspiracy theory, and the denials of a North Vietnamese attack on the United States in the Gulf of Tonkin—yet another outrageous conspiracy theory which happens to be warranted on the then available evidence. And need we point toward the words and deeds of people like Nixon, Bush, or Blair, as well as all their imitators, now and tomorrow?

Or take the various claims of conspiracy about the Russian Federation and its attempts to exert influence in other political spheres. In the United States we see plausible conspiracy theories about agents of the Russian Federation seeking to influence US presidential elections, conspiracy theories taken seriously by members of the security apparatus and various intelligence committees in the US Congress. In the U.K. Russian agents have been linked to the high-profile, Bond film–esque attacks on former FSB agents; Alexander Litvinenko (poisoned with polonium-242; died 2006) and Sergei and Yulia Skripal (poisoned with Novichok in 2018). In each case Russian authorities have denied any connection with the events in question, yet the governments of the various powers where these attacks took place maintain that the Russian government is simply trying to cover up its activities.

There was nothing outrageous about any of these conspiracy theories. All are well evidenced. So, we must ask: just how many other outrages like these have slipped through the silence caused by conspiracy-denial? While some social scientists, with the best of intentions (we do not question these) may wish to combat the conspiracy theories they dislike, we all should agree that the lesson of history is conspiracy theorizing is often necessary.

It is true that every mode of explanation can be abused. The German National Socialists used the absurd conspiracy theories about Jews in Europe in order to justify the actions of their regime. Cruel elements of various Christian denominations had long done the same (as have various groups afterwards; Stalinists, the Social Credit movement, etc.). These lies were embraced, letting the murderous nightmare of the Holocaust to proceed. These fictions should have been met with facts, but when rational, evidential considerations are not allowed to be heard, reason cannot prevail. How can we assess the particulars of claims of conspiracy if we keep being told that conspiracy theories are unwarranted, "bunk," and irrational to believe? This is why we should focus, always, on the facts. We cannot resort to conspiracy "denialism." We all know where that road goes: ask the people of Iraq, the people of Syria, Vietnam, Jewish Germany, and all the rest who have suffered from militarist human history. In one way or another, that includes everyone reading this. A denial of the legitimacy of conspiracy accusations at times of great public decision would, and did, shelter these extreme state-sponsored abuses from criticism.

Only a thoughtful attention to particular conspiracy theories, on the *merits of their evidence*, can meet the threat such conspiracies present. Evidence is the key; nothing else suffices. Poorly evidenced conspiracy theories will in all likelihood be set aside or seen by an evidence attentive polis as politically irrelevant. Well-evidenced conspiracy theories must be pursued without censor; we cannot generalize about conspiracy theories. Rather, we must look at the particulars.

5. PATHOLOGIZING CONSPIRACY THEORY

The *Le Monde* authors view conspiracy theory as a medical issue, a "disease" that "spreads," a plague to be cured. But on reflection, this metaphor backfires. Consider the dominant pattern in our emerging, horizontal, digital public information systems. The absurd is typically seen as such, and surprisingly quickly, by a significant part of the public. Such "outbreaks" are typically quelled by good questions or poor answers in response to those questions. This is the very premise of democracy; collective cognition often functions to produce evidential-cognitive antibodies. For these antidotes to form, however, requires *contact and evidential interaction with* the flawed proposal. Unwarranted conspiracy theories are cycled, then dissipate and only persevere within small groups of people. Recall the quite creative, well known but near zero-evidence conspiracy theory that our world leaders are reptilian aliens, disguised by holograms so as to appear human.[2] It may linger for decades but is of no importance. These residues certainly don't serve as justification for a universal public policy of censorship and cognitive regulation, as the *Le Monde* letter suggests. But their approach of indiscriminate mass quarantine is radically dangerous to democracy, because it views *all* conspiracy allegations as mere polis-contagion. Many times conspiracy theories are, instead, a benefit, an antidote, the expression of intelligent vaccination at work, not a harmful virus. The harmful virus is the conspiracy itself. Recognizing it requires *evidential contact*.

So, if we must insist on an infectious disease metaphor, recall that many micro-organisms are either benign, or in some cases, beneficial and necessary. Most strains of *e. coli* are, contrary to common belief, beneficial, often halting pathogenic microbes. But for this to work it requires we have contact with these useful forms,[3] much as conspiracy theories ward off and undermine pathological government activities. Just as relevant is the medical metaphor that an important problem with nonselective, "broad-spectrum" antibiotics is they kill *all* strains, needed and dangerous, which often harms the patient more than the pathogen. The dangerous and the beneficially preventative go hand in hand. To know which conspiracy theories are false, perhaps harmful, and which are true, often beneficial, requires, in a discerning manner, that we dispassionately and evidentially examine both, pursue the warranted and eliminate only the poorly evidenced. Again, we must look to particulars.

Instead, we find the *Le Monde* authors fretting about producing the wrong "broad spectrum" cure, one leading to what medical literature refers to as an *iatrogenic disease*; one brought forth by the would-be healer. Their only concern about their approach is that a government-inculcated practice of blanket dismissal only invites more suspicion within the "target population." They term this effect "Boomerang":[4]

> Even worse, research in social psychology has shown that the fight against a belief can, paradoxically, serve to reinforce it by a "boomerang effect", a phenomenon widely documented in studies of rumour and misinformation. It is therefore entirely possible that the actions of ministers and associations result in an effect that is the opposite of that desired for the target audience: a polarisation of beliefs and a growth in the conspiracist mindset. (Bronner et al. 2016)

Ironically, at this point the *Le Monde* prescription almost looks desirable. Consider the widespread initial reactions to the Watergate conspiracy theory. These were certainly polarizing. Many dismissed the allegations as "beyond the pale" or "over the line." Which line? The "outrageous conspiracy theory" one. These accusations were a conspiracy theory, plain and simple, impugning the highest office of the land. Yet many others recognized the significant probability that they were nevertheless true. From this process a politically superior, unifying consensus eventually emerged: Nixon and his co-conspirators were unmasked, and the US presidency revealed to be no sacred thing.

The blanket dismissal of conspiracy theories—an ahistorical and dangerous generalist rejection—is what really portends disease. Nixon would have been above reproach, as would all presidents to come, because of the *nature* of the allegations, not because they are false. That is irrelevant to the pathologizing approach, which is absurd. However foreign to our social hopes and political pieties as conspiracy theories might initially appear, they are logically necessary for us to recognize and stop political and economic contagions and their attendant catastrophes. We are all left with the question: If the pseudo-education proposed by the *Le Monde* group and their ilk fails, even "boomerangs," what will they turn to next?

We hope our social science colleagues and the governments they seek to advise will opt for the other solution: Concede the necessity of conspiracy theorizing to an open society, in the interests of the democracy our governments were instituted to protect, not undermine. There is much to be learned here, too.

6. A SECOND TREATMENT

Exhibit two: In a follow-up piece, " 'They' Respond: Comments on Basham et al.'s 'Social Science's Conspiracy-Theory Panic: Now They Want to Cure Everyone,' " (Dieguez et al. 2016) (most) of the authors of the original *Le Monde* piece, at first glance, signal a healthy retreat from their pathologizing project. They argue that all they were doing was advocating for more research, presumably without the *Le Monde* authors' mental-hygiene agenda:

> What "they" had in mind, as must be clear by now, was to study how people, on their own or under some external influence, think and come to endorse some beliefs about such things. That, "they" think, would need some data, rather than wishful thinking, ideological clamours or armchair reasoning.[5] (Dieguez et al. 2016)

Those who question their project are not so easily dismissed as being lost in the "ideological clamours" of "armchair reasoners." Protecting functional democracy is worth making a bit of noise over. Yet we agree that historical and conceptual literacy is encouraged by a comfortable place to study human history and the forces that animate it. We encourage our colleagues, at the first opportunity, to take up a chair and give it a try. We are confident they can learn much.

Now they insist they are just asking questions. Once again, we do not begrudge them their interest in this fascinating topic, but we do question how they approach their investigation, because we worry that they do not take the phenomenon of conspiracy theory as seriously as perhaps they ought.

At the heart of their work (as shown in the open letter and its rejoinder) lies a tension. They wish to investigate the phenomena of belief in conspiracy theories, but they want to fix the empirical boundaries of that belief before defining what conspiracy theories are. Indeed, in their rejoinder they go so far as to pour scorn on the work of other conspiracy theory theorists who would prefer we define concepts first and then investigate what constitutes belief in them second.

But how can we know what constitutes belief in conspiracy theories before we can say what conspiracy theories are? Worthwhile investigation must begin with clear conception of the focus of study and, given that, what might constitute relevant evidence for or against any hypothesis concerning it. A skewed vision, one with a preordained conclusion, is never good science.

If we do not start out with a definition of what conspiracy theories are, we cannot talk about what constitutes belief in them, and we definitely cannot work out whether those beliefs are warranted or not (see chapter 10 by Orr and Dentith in this section for more discussion on this).

But, of course, saying that you need to sort out empirical matters before you get on to definitional ones (the issues we say are central to any understanding of the phenomena of conspiracy theories) is easier said than done, and it turns out that these social scientists are working with an operating definition after all. It just happens to be embedded in their views of conspiracy theorists and the "conspiracist mindset."

> [A] conspiracy theory is what the conspiracist mindset tends to produce and be attracted to, an apparently circular definition that rests on ongoing work but is firmly grounded in relevant research fields such as cognitive epidemiology, niche construction and cognitively driven cultural studies, and could be refined or refuted depending on future results. (Dieguez et al. 2016, 30)

This is a bold claim: "[a] conspiracy theory is what the conspiracist mindset tends to produce . . ." A number of points: The definition is not just "apparently" circular, it is obviously so, as soon as we ask what is referred to by "conspiracist." This will include at least the idea of "conspiracy theory," which is the very notion to be defined. Elementary logic: One cannot rely on the very term to be defined in its definition. Unsurprisingly, circular definitions are uninformative. Not just that, it is simply a rephrasing of the pejorative approach: conspiracy theory as the manifestation of the irrational and pathological, the "conspiracist mind." If the former, the definition becomes "conspiracy theories are produced by the minds of conspiracy theorists, who believe conspiracy theories." This tells us nothing, but it also doesn't discriminate, given it includes all informed, rational persons alive. If the latter, then it means, "conspiracy theories are those unwarranted, false (or 'outrageous') conspiracy theories produced by the irrational minds of conspiracy theorists." Yet this is obviously false.

We must also wonder, what exactly *is* a "mindset"? This is a term so vague that "mindset" theories are, in contrast to clearly specified scientific ones, intrinsically unfalsifiable by "future results." The use of "mindset" appears contrived to easily shift according to the needs of protecting an approach from scrutiny, thus protecting the status of the theorists—here the *a priori* view of conspiracy theories as dangerous nonsense and status of the *Le Monde* authors and their ilk who are professionally and financially wedded to this view. Whatever this is, this is not science.

On this note, "conspiracist mindset" appears intentionally *non-rational*, *non-cognitive*, perhaps even *genetic* on their non-contextual approach. Given this definition, no prior experience, reflection on history, or current events could produce a conspiracy theory without the "conspiracist mindset" already in place; observation, evidence and normal reasoning have nothing to do with conspiratorial suspicion and accusation. But social context, especially human history and the nature of our institutions of power within it, plays an immense role in the formation and credibility of conspiracy theories. This constellation of history, institutions of power, and current events within it are the main makers of conspiracy theories. The *Le Monde* authors' approach is oblivious to what should be obvious to anyone: Conspiracy theory is not the product of a vague, disembodied mindset, but they have staked their entire research project on this simplistic notion. Once again, whatever this is, this is not science.

This open-ended talk of "the conspiracist mindset" and a call for a cure suffers an uncomfortable resemblance to social panics we've encountered in the recent past. These panics cyclically trouble a society seemingly addicted to the idea of an enemy within. Now, a "conspiracist mindset" is worming its way through decent society. All these invoke the same sort of mercurial demon, consuming the gullible, endangering the innocent, and overturning the morals and reason of Western societies.

The fact of the matter is rather different. Attention to conspiracy and the generation of conspiracy theories is normal and rational in social primates like humans; because social primates conspire. We learn this as children on the basis of evidence. Sometimes people around us work against others, and do so without announcing their cooperation. This is not a "conspiracist mindset." We learn how to do it as children, and therefore learn it as one of many possible, proper explanatory templates for the behavior of others, one among the many basic explanatory templates that we select from every day, and do so, typically, on the basis of evidence. So, the fact they claim the kind of definition of conspiracy theory we commonly find in Philosophy (and Sociology) which takes, at a minimum, that such theories are explanatory hypotheses which cite conspiracies as a salient cause of some event prematurely settles the issue of belief in conspiracy theories seems at odds with their own operating definition, which builds in the pejorative so prevalent in parts of the wider academic literature.

7. CONCLUSION: GENERALISM AND PATHOLOGY OF CONSPIRACY THEORIES, REBUKED

Philosophers and sociologists have seen work like this before. Some social scientists are advocating a generalist view of how we should talk about and appraise conspiracy theories (as we saw in the discussion of generalism and particularism in the first section of this volume). They are putting the cart before the horse, telling people that they should not bother evaluating the evidence for or against any given conspiracy theory. Rather, people are to be scientifically directed, somehow, to fixate on the cry of "That's just a conspiracy theory!", flee the room, and not reflect on any facts.

The pathologizing view affixes the label "conspiracy theory" to some claim or question in order to immediately put it in the category of the pejorative (Basham 2018). As sociologists like Ginna Husting and Martin Orr argue, this strategy of labeling conspiracy theories pejoratively effectively stifles debate and leads to questions which should be asked not being asked at all (2007). Similarly, Lance deHaven-Smith and Matthew Witt argue that the pejorative labeling that we see in such pathologizing projects about conspiracy theory "risks weakening popular vigilance against abuses of power, election tampering, cover-ups, and other genuine threats to democratic governance." (2013) The pejorative use of "conspiracy theorist" by such academics can lead to conspiracy theories being dismissed *a priori*, despite the boundary between conspiracy theories and non-conspiracy theories being contested ground, a point Jaron Harambam and Stef Aupers have pressed (2014).

After all, there is a long history of warranted theories being labeled "conspiratorial" and then effectively dismissed, allowing conspirators to get away with their misdeeds. Perhaps we and the authors of the *Le Monde* letter might disagree about the prevalence of such cases (although as one of us has argued, we likely underestimate the prior cases of warranted conspiracy theories rather than overestimate them; see Dentith (2016b)).

The problem with the pathologizing project is the generalism about conspiracy theories which underpins it, leaving such theorists to draw broad conclusions about the rationality of belief in conspiracy theories *generally*. Yet generalism rests upon claiming that a subset of what are assumed *a priori* to be suspect conspiracy theories will turn out to be representative of the wider kind (an argument one of us has pressed elsewhere; see Dentith (2018)). Yet as Michael Butter and Peter Knight have argued, we cannot produce *value-neutral* research on these things called *conspiracy theories* if we start our work with *value-laden* definitions (2016).

So, whether or not we agree with just how many conspiracy theories turned out to be true, surely an evaluation of the evidence for or against particular conspiracy theories should be the end of the matter. We should not start from the position of thinking belief in conspiracy theories is unlikely, or that such theories are prima facie groundless.

After all, we were assured the National Security Agency is a law-abiding organization that would spy neither on U.S. citizens nor trusted NATO allies. To question that (and some did, with good reason) was dismissed as just a "conspiracy theory." But the NSA did all of this (and may still do so, given the lack of punishment for those involved). Examples of this kind of behavior are legion.

Indeed, the generalizing and pathologizing view so prevalent in much of the social science literature raises a very interesting question: Where did it come from? Are generalists skeptical of conspiracy theories because that is the considered result of historical reflection, or is generalism a political piety? After all, historically conspiracies were a well-known feature of politics; the French Revolution was predicated (at least in part) by the bourgeois becoming aware of just how conspiratorial (and self-serving by default) the court of the *Ancien Régime* really was. In Elizabethan England conspiracies by and against Catholics were part-and-parcel of political life. The American Revolution was inspired by a plausible conspiracy theory about the intentions of King George III.

So, given the history of conspiracy, why are some of us so loathe to admit conspiracy theorizing into the set of tools we have for assessing what goes on in politics? Is it because we do not think conspiracies occur, or because we have been told repeatedly that we should not openly believe in conspiracies? After all, conspiracies still do occur; they are not some historical relic which have no play in contemporary politics. However, it is of use to people in positions of power to tell us—the public—that we should not believe in conspiracies about them.

While we have commented on the definitional problem in the *Le Monde* declaration, consider this: if a "conspiracy theory" is whatever the conspiracy mindset produces, what if the conspiracy mindset produces a belief, say, that fruits are healthy foods? That is, the result of the conspiracy mindset, or conspiracist ideation, produces a belief driven by evidence which reaches a simple conclusion about something without reference to collusion. The upshot of our objection is that this is not an instance of "conspiracy theory" as anyone would understand it, and thus this requires us to define what a "conspiracy theory" is first. Which, in turn, forces the authors of the *Le Monde* declaration to admit to the uselessness of their operating (but largely unacknowledged) definition.

We are not proposing social scientists like those who wrote the *Le Monde* letter are willing accomplices when it comes to the idea that our political pieties against conspiracy theories benefit a chosen (and obvious) few.[6] Rather, we are curious as to whether they have ever examined the prejudice behind their generalism. For what reason should we start our analysis with the presupposition that belief in conspiracy theories is suspicious? That appears irrational. There is nothing unusual or inherently defective about conspiracy explanations. We should *always, without exception, adopt a case-by-case, evidential evaluation of all allegations of politically momentous conspiracy.* These should never be simply dismissed and silenced because they suggest we should be suspicious of elements in the influential institutions of our societies. The anti–conspiracy theory panic, and the automatic dismissal it reveals, rests at the foundation of the declaration by these social scientists. It is not only anti-rational and non-historical, it is unethical and foolish. This panic can only help replicate the many past anti-democratic, destructive, and criminal errors of our democracies.

Much contemporary media, most political leaders, and some social scientists insist that "conspiracy theory" must mean something automatically false or irrational. Yet our historians show it does not and never did. The pejorative use of "conspiracy theory" is a use of mere convenience.

The official account of 9/11 is, after all, a conspiracy theory. No matter your opinion on the matter, whether you think the attacks on New York and Washington, DC, were the result of terrorist activity on the behalf of a terrorist group, al-Qaeda, or the product of an inside job involving influential members of the US political class, whatever explanation you come up with for the tragic events of September 11th, it will be a conspiracy theory. In all cases the multiple agents behind the felling of the Twin Towers acted in secret toward some end (either an attack on US soil or the appearance of an attack by an outside power on US soil). They are all conspiracy theories. But is the official account labeled as such? Not by mainstream media, or most political leaders. But it is still a conspiracy theory all the same.

Any pejorative use of "conspiracy theory" is intellectually suspect, as is its convenient absence when governmental institutions use conspiracy theories to promote their goals. We are facing a phrase of social manipulation, one which some academics wish to portray and empower in a way so that it cannot impugn our hierarchies of power, but only defend them. The only conspiracy theories that will be permitted will be official conspiracy theories. They will not be called "conspiracy theories." But their explanatory method will be indistinguishable.

The response to this is to say that political conspiracy theorizing in Western-style democracies should not be restricted, because to do so is a grave intellectual, ethical, and prudential error. As such, the declaration by respected scholars like these is likewise a grave intellectual, ethical, and prudential error. Conspiracy theory saves lives, by the thousands, even millions, if we would let it. Its automatic dismissal leaves blood on our hands.

It is revealing that the authors of the *Le Monde* piece and their subsequent reply never mention or discuss the ideals of representational democracy. Fortunately for the public and our democracy, the more you tell the public not to think in ways open to all possibilities, including the real possibility of political and economic conspiracies, the more likely the public is to do it and more often do it; the boomerang effect is real, well recognized, and widely attested to in our personal lives. It can also be of great benefit. Call this an "open society." Some social scientists are bothered by this and seek a scientific "remedy." But we take great comfort in the open society. If research into public concerns about government need be, it should be in ways that encourage the people's politically crucial gift, the historically proven gift of watchfulness in the citizen, and its sometimes necessary, proper and correct expression, *conspiracy theory*.

Should we really be paying for a science that teaches us not to understand this?

NOTES

1. The *Le Monde* piece was written in French; these translations come from an unattributed and uncontested English source for the text which was passed around conspiracy theory theorists at the time.

2. David Icke advocates for this claim. From a certain perspective his following is impressive, yet it has stabilized in size and is miniscule in proportion to the general population. Still, imagine if the government started harassing his followers and banning their gatherings. Perhaps in response to this apparent dead end, today Icke's emphasis has switched to the dangers of mainstream medical practice and widespread, highly processed "food-like substances." He argues keeping these threats from the public requires large quantities of industry and governmental conspiracy.

3. American Academy of Microbiology: see https://www.asm.org/images/stories/documents/EColi.pdf.

4. For a recent application of the boomerang effect to conspiracy theory, see Wagner-Egger and Gygax (2017). They write: "As a general conclusion, this research showed that the social influence of newspaper headlines is far from straightforward. We found two possible boomerang effects, illustrated by changes in belief in the opposite direction from what was presented in the headline" (22).

5. It is difficult to understand the *Le Monde* piece as other than "ideological clamours" in the narrowest sense.

6. In the preamble to their denial of any intent to "cure," the *Le Monde* authors accuse their critics of aiming a "preternatural" conspiracy theory at them. This is surprising. There appears to be no attempt to conspire and deceive the public when these authors publish their plea in one of the most widely read newspapers in the world. Rather, they are completely open about their goals. Perhaps this is more frightening than any sort of conspiracy on their part. They write:

> Basham et al. (2016) fear that "they" want to curtail the free speech of conspiracist opinions, asking, after having made the point that whoever poisoned Alexander Litvinenko, his death had to be the result of some conspiracy: "Should we pay for a science that teaches us not to understand this?" (15). Indeed, it would be ironic that innocent people would end up paying, with their hard-earned money, for a scientific conspiracy meant at making sure that no one will ever even dare to think there could be any type of conspiracy in this world. In fact, that would not only be ironic, that would be

genius, a conspiracy of the "preternatural" kind if there ever was one. "They" only wish "they" had such power and influence, but thankfully, at least for the time being, that is not what "they" had in mind. (Dieguez et al. 2016, 32)

Chapter 7

Social Scientists and Pathologizing Conspiracy Theorizing

Lee Basham

The dog the stone hits yelps loudest.

—folk saying

For a week before the operation that was to raise him from his servitude and inferiority to the level of a blind citizen Nunez knew nothing of sleep . . .

—H. G. Wells, *Country of the Blind*

1. INTRODUCTION

The *Le Monde* social scientists' statement begins:

Let's fight conspiracy theories effectively. The Ministry of Education must test its pedagogical tools against conspiracy culture. The wrong cure might only serve to spread the disease. (Bronner et al. 2016, 29)

This is a paradigm instance of a political pathologizing project. Here, it is applied to conspiracy theorizing and theorists, which includes all of us. We all are aware of, and believe on the basis of good evidence, contemporary conspiracies happen, even, and even especially, at the highest levels of power, and in this knowledge and expectation, we are not pathological.

Pathologizing projects are ordinary to establishmentarian political cultures. These political cultures understand themselves through a biological metaphor; they are the body, and what is not of the body must be identified and eliminated. Hence the purpose of the establishment: to protect its way of life. The familiar methods include surveillance to detect alien thought and activities, censorship of what might spread these and control and elimination of its sources, rather like a cancer from within, or as we witness in *the Le Monde* declaration, a disease of mysterious origin. This familiar cognitive hygiene tactic makes its entrance: society has been infiltrated by this threatening "mindset" (in the past, Communists, Satanist day-care operators, and so on), the *enemy within* scenario. They are everywhere but they look like us. Cognitive epidemiologists are then called to duty. Sometimes they even line up.

The goal of pathologizing projects is to disqualify a class of citizens from public discourse, silence them, ideally, eliminate them in one manner or another: in one way or another, to disappear them from the dominant discourse of the times. It is a method of dealing with *dissident citizens*. The formula is simple: pathologize, disqualify, silence, disappear. These are historically applied to any group deemed sufficiently efficacious in society and excessively contrary to certain political and ideological tenets. Today the pathologizing approach is increasingly applied to those who question the veracity of their governments and suspect these governments are, on occasion, involved in organized, deeply anti-democratic, improper public deception. But only a thoughtful attention to conspiracy theory, on the merits of evidence, can meet the threat such conspiracies present. Evidence is the key. In the end, nothing else suffices.

Let us be clear: These authors' motives are not in question: only their assumptions and goals.[1] They appear to actually believe in a sort of society-wide epidemic. In the United States, the U.K., and France, this small group of social scientists has been used by governments to play a key role in the first stage of this pathologizing project. Now they ask to directly assist the government to fund their development of sophisticated psychological techniques to successfully *prevent* the public from conspiracy theorizing, or as they put it, "just asking some questions." The disappear phase. To this end, they offer their services.

As one philosopher prominent in the field proposes, the *Le Monde* piece is merely an appeal for more funding, marketed as a cognitive hygiene crusade. This is a kindly, if minimizing, apologetic. And they might devise some clever disqualifying-silencing techniques as a result, too. The question that faces our democratic polis is more pressing: Why should we wish them to? And pay them for it?

They never address this in their original statement or subsequent response (Dieguez et al. 2016). It is a given. Most philosophers in the field and a significant number of social scientists and cultural theorists, as well as the public at large, are rightfully skeptical of such a project by any government. They have increasingly, and with good reason, come to recognize that conspiracy theorizing is a thoughtful, normal, and democratically necessary social activity. There is no mention of these critical facts in the *Le Monde* statement, but a rather disturbing omission of them. Conspiracy theorizing is treated simply as a personal and social disease. Fortunately, the *Le Monde* authors initially seem to concede a pathologizing stance is politically dangerous, as they take umbrage at the very idea they would be involved in such a thing. By itself, this seems to represent a total retraction, a very welcome one. They will no longer participate in these manipulations of public thought. Unfortunately, this hope—at this time—vanishes as we read on.

2. A RESPONSE TO A LETTER OF CONCERN

M R. X. Dentith and I replied to the *Le Monde* statement in "Social Science's Conspiracy-Theory Panic: Now They Want to Cure Everyone" (2016). Our reply was reviewed and improved by other philosophers active in the field, as well as social scientists studying the same. All pointed to the obvious political perils of a psychologically sophisticated government "combating" conspiracy theories challenging the government, the questionable pathologizing assumption at the heart of the *Le Monde* piece and within much (but not all) social science on conspiracy theorizing. Now our colleagues feel the need to explain themselves.

The authors of the *Le Monde* statement responded, claiming:

> Basham et al. (2016), fear that "they want to cure everyone" of conspiracy theories. Here, "they"[2] respond and try to put this concern to rest. The commentary "they" published in French newspaper *Le Monde*, with which Basham et al. take issue, cautioned against governmental initiatives to counter conspiracy theories among youths. (Dieguez et al. 2016, 20)

The *Le Monde* statement objected to government initiatives to counter conspiracy theorizing that are *ineffective*, and suggested social psychology could improve upon these, fighting the disease effectively. Our letter of concern cautioned against *government initiatives*, psychologically sophisticated or not, to counter conspiracy theorizing. The *Le Monde* authors continue,

> "They," in fact, are "just asking" some questions, which Basham et al. surely agree is always a good thing. Perhaps, by clarifying such and related issues, some pertaining to the conceptual and others to the empirical domains, one could get a better sense of how to address conspiracy theories, and even ascertain whether there is a problem at all. (2016, 21)

When they already view conspiracy theory as a disease, it is unlikely they are curious to discover if conspiracy theorizing is a disease or not, and so whether it is a problem or not. That ship has sailed. For them it is a pressing problem, and they have moved onto the how to cure stage of the project. Accordingly, when the purposes of questions are highly suspect, we might wonder if asking such questions is always a good thing: the economic lethality of hydrogen cyanide, for instance. Questions, when in the service of bad motives, easily lend themselves to far worse answers and results. Immediately thereafter we are told, "Doing things right would benefit everybody: the authorities, social scientists, the kids targeted by the programs, and yes, society at large, including taxpayers" (2016, 21).

What is intended by "doing things right"? And while we are "targeting kids"? And why target children in such a charged political context if not to direct their thoughts and behavior as adults? In the *Le Monde* statement what "doing things right" means is explicit. It remains so in their response to critics: preventing the public from indulging the disease of conspiracy theorizing. The authors then present us with their prize discovery: There is mass social disease, the "conspiracist mindset." From this something, that comes from seemingly nowhere, conspiracy theory suspicions and beliefs are to be best explained. Of course, this strange theory is rather like arguing all Muslims are Osama bin Ladens in the waiting: beware the "Islamic mindset."

This pattern of "giving with one hand and taking back with the other" becomes familiar as we read through the response and indeed, study the entire literature. This logically contradictory oscillation appears defining of the pathologizing project in its relation to critics in our larger, demo-cratic society. While historically literate people agree our governments have long resorted to conspiracy, we must pathologize those who note this and suggest it is still occurring. When critics point to the problematic nature of the pathologizing assumption guiding their research, the authors briefly deny they are pathologizing anyone, then resorting to questionable studies, proceed to explain why conspiracy theorists are pathological. This invi-tation to double-think, a self-contradictory oscillation between explicitly pathologizing and silencing citizens who explore conspiracy explanations while denying as researchers they are doing this, but instead are "just asking questions," appears to be the blueprint for their entire response.[3]

3. THE PATHOLOGICAL MINDSET DEFINITION OF "CONSPIRACY THEORY"

The *Le Monde* authors' unusual definition of "conspiracy theory" lays bare the internal logic of the pathologizing project:

[A] "conspiracy theory" is what the conspiracist mindset tends to produce and be attracted to, an apparently circular definition that rests on ongoing work but is firmly grounded in relevant research fields such as cognitive epidemiology [disease], niche construction and cognitively driven cultural studies, and could be refined or refuted depending on future results. (Dieguez et al. 2016, 30)[4]

This is a typical pathologizing "enemy within our society" hypothesis. The difficulties appear numerous, so it is hard to know where best to begin. First, "firmly grounded" appears to simply mean, "firmly repeated"; the mindset theory has only been assumed, used as a template for interpretive distortions and never demonstrated to exist within our populace.

It is also an empirical nonstarter: Most normal, rational people accept conspiracy theories for rational reasons, including contemporary ones like the US/U.K. Weapons of Mass Destruction (WMD) hoax. In the WMD hoax, evidence indicates a lion's share of what people did before mainstream media was forced to concede that we were being lied to (and that the media was the deception's megaphone) was they worked it out on their own.[5] Further, if we view it as an actual definition, there's nothing "apparently" circular about it; it is straightforwardly so, a logical nonstarter: Conspiracy theories are those theories created and believed by conspiracy theorists, victims of the "conspiracist mindset," and victims of the conspiracy mindset are those irrational people who believe in conspiracy theories.

It also appears to be a case of confirmation bias, a self-fulfilling presupposition: If we insist on the "conspiracist mindset" story before reflecting on our fellow citizens, designing questionnaires and interpreting responses only accordingly, we will only become more and more convinced of mass-pathology and the progress of our pathologizing project. If additional critique is needed, it lies again in the fact that all of us believe well-evidenced conspiracy theories, including the authors of the *Le Monde* statement. So either very few of us suffer a "conspiracist mindset," or there is nothing whatsoever pathological about it. Either very few people are subject to a "conspiracist mindset," or almost every rational person is. Either way the "mindset" theory is reduced to one of trivial interest.

No surprise, in hundreds of interviews with rational people who explore and sometimes accept conspiracy explanations counter to mainstream media, the pattern observed is the same: evidence for a conspiracy theory, suspicion others may be true, and an entirely appropriate openness to considering others. Sound familiar? It should. That's virtually all of us.

4. THE SOCIAL MORALITY ISSUE

Some have recently argued that, whatever the evidential status of conspiracy theorizing, it is a morally suspect activity.[6] It attacks the shifting claims our hierarchy of knowledge prescribes to all members of our society, ultimately undermining its background self-narrative of representational democracy and manifest scientific and moral objectivity. I have no objection to evidential objectivity, nor even moral objectivity. The abuse of both stances is clear in the *Le Monde* statement's generalist rejection of conspiracy theory. Nothing these generalists write appears to contravene this. Instead, it is entirely predicated on it.

5. GOING PATHOLOGICAL: THE SOCIAL SCIENCE LITERATURE

What is the caliber of the pathologizing ("conspiracist mindset") literature? Much data reported is interesting if expected.[7] But then we come to the *interpretation* of results stage ("discussion"). Here things frequently fall apart. A full survey isn't possible for reasons of space, but those of us not participating in the project are often struck by the implausible interpretations it indulges.[8] For an extreme instance, the *Le Monde* authors rhetorically ask "why should it be the case that people merely interested in uncovering the lies of would-be tyrants by carefully gathering, evaluating and presenting the best evidence, would also turn out . . . [to] simultaneously endorse flatly contradictory conspiracy theories?" (Dieguez et al. 2016, 25). The *Le Monde* authors' reference is to Michael Wood, Karen Douglas, and R. M. Sutton, "Dead and Alive: Beliefs in Contradictory Conspiracy Theories" (2012) (hereafter, "Dead and Alive").[9] The *Le Monde* authors' rhetorical question is a textbook case of the disqualify-silencing strategy. A more de-rationalizing, dehumanizing accusation against people who entertain and explore conspiratorial explanations is hard to imagine: Conspiracy theorists routinely, simultaneously believe obviously contradictory conspiracy theories? Rather surprising. But do they?

Fortunately, they do not. The accusation is an empirical non-starter. Instead these citizens are keenly aware of the contradictions between alternative explanations and work hard to evidentially resolve these impasses, much like any good detective or forensic scientist would. Even a cursory glance over the writings of conspiracy theorists many of us may find disturbing and offensive, like those within the "Inside Job" 9/11 community, amply demonstrate this logical meticulousness. The contrasting recklessness of the authors' accusation is a bit stunning, but not entirely, if we recall again the power of the "monological" (one explanation fits all) pathologizing belief system the authors have been limited to. Obviously something has gone wrong with this alleged demonstration. But what?

The Wood et al. paper remains a flagship of the pathologizing approach to conspiracy theorists by social psychology. I hasten to add I consider Wood and Douglas friends and gifted scientists.[10] But while producing this paper they were operating within a culture defined by the pathologizing goals and assumptions we are questioning. It would be surprising if we expected them to deviate from these. They did not. Let's look at a quick summary of their methods and their interpretation of results.

In the Osama bin Laden scenario participants were asked to rate on a scale of 1 ("definitely not true") to 6 ("definitely true"), with a "somewhat" gradient 2, 3, 4, and 5 in between, the following:

1. Osama bin Laden was killed in the American raid [in Pakistan]. Rate 1–6.
2. Osama bin Laden is still alive. Rate 1–6.
3. When the raid took place, Osama bin Laden was already dead. Rate 1–6.
4. The actions of the Obama administration indicate that they are hiding some important or damaging piece of information about the raid.[11] Rate 1–6.

Pencil in hand, suppose we rate (1) as "5" and circle it accordingly; we suspect the reports are fairly likely to be true. Next we rate (2) as "4"; we harbor some suspicions about the veracity of government reports. We are not entirely certain about these, especially in such a politically charged context. For instance, the body was reported to be disposed of at an undisclosed location but bin Laden's capture, interrogation, and even perhaps a trial seem like valuable options. Next, recalling numerous government and mainstream media reports that bin Laden was killed in Afghanistan, but his body could not be retrieved from the blasted caves of Tora Bora, we are also willing to entertain (3), so we circle "4" again. Coherent with the above, when we reach (4), we are content to circle "4" once more. We put our pencil down.

This, we are told, is the profile of a lunatic.

Notice we never report a settled belief. Wood et al.'s interpretive mistake is so surprising because it is so clear. Simply, the researchers conflate participants' reports of *strong suspicions* with *settled beliefs*. This is an easy way to contrive irrationality in anyone about almost anything. Imagine you have misplaced your key ring. You suspect you left it in the front door lock. You also suspect you left it in the kitchen. Given your previous behavior, you rate as quite probable, "agree" that it is in the front door and equally as probable, "agree" the keys are in the kitchen.[12] This is an entirely rational cognitive practice. But according to the interpretation of Wood et al., you *believe* your keys are located, at the very same moment, in both your front door and in your kitchen.

For those with lost-key beliefs, believing one has left the keys in the front door is apparently no obstacle to believing the keys are simultaneously in the kitchen. Clearly, those with lost-key beliefs are irrational. Also, it would seem, are scientists who, given current evidence, view likely but contrary explanations as equally probable. For instance, when scientists noted the cancer-driven decline of the Tasmanian Devil, they recognized that a bio-logical pathogen or an artificially introduced carcinogen would equally well explain the animals' plight. Given the evidence, both were quite probable. At that juncture only additional investigation could distinguish which hypoth-esis was more likely, in this case a viral pathogen.[13] Ignoring the diversity and contrasting logical properties, the propositional attitude is the "sleight of hand" here, however unintentional. This is strange for psychologists; but not when a pathology-hunt defines their research culture.

Wood et al. shelter their "Dead and Alive" conclusion from participants' predictable protests, participants who could be any of us. They provide no opportunity for them to disambiguate what they mean by drawing circles "on a scale of 1–6." That would no doubt undermine the *suspicion* is *settled belief* maneuver. They certainly don't ask them, "Do you believe Osama bin Laden is *simultaneously* both *dead and alive*?" That would up-end the whole study, requiring heroic efforts to indict the participants of massive self-deception: They wouldn't find many participants acknowledging they believe Osama bin Laden walks the earth while moldering in a watery grave, nor witness many participants gasp in astonishment when they discover the extremity of their mindset disorder. The thesis is a non-starter, unless, per-haps, when uttered in the halls of the pathologizing project. No clarification is allowed. Instead Wood et al. go behind the participants' backs, reinterpreting the data in the most de-rationalizing way they can.[14] While this is understand-able in some research, here it is all too convenient. So, the *Le Monde* authors' claim that Wood et al. have scientifically established conspiracy theorists simultaneously believe flatly contradictory theories fails to inspire confidence in their standards of science.

Among a number of examples in the pathologizing literature, another seemingly transparent instance of forced and fallacious interpretation of data can be found in Robert Brotherton and Christopher C. French, "Belief in Conspiracy Theories and Susceptibility to the Conjunction Fallacy" where, as the title suggests, "conspiracy theorists" are alleged to be more susceptible to the conjunction fallacy than the rest of us (2014). But the participants are not committing the conjunction fallacy. The probability of two conjuncts cannot be greater than the probability of *either* conjunct. The participants are reasoning to the *best explanation* for the facts presented. Consider one of Brotherton and French's examples:

> Josh is now on the verge of perfecting a device which will increase the fuel efficiency of any car by 500%. The response options were (i) the CEOs of several major petrol companies hold a meeting in which they discuss the implications of Josh's invention; (ii) Josh is found dead in his home before patenting the invention; and (iii) the CEOs of several major petrol companies hold a meeting in which they discuss the implications of Josh's invention, and Josh is found dead in his home before patenting the invention. (2014, 241)

The authors claim participants who rate (iii) as more likely than (i) or (ii) are irrational. But there is nothing irrational, let alone paranoid, in this cognitive practice; (iii) has greater explanatory power and unifies in a rational manner seemingly disconnected phenomena. These are primary goals of both scientific and ordinary reasoning. The "and" in (iii) is naturally and rationally interpreted as causation, not as mere conjunction, as in "the car crashed *and* caught on fire." Since explanatory power and unification are positively correlated with rational acceptability and the truth, so until additional information and considerations are forthcoming, we should rate (iii) as more probable in this scenario than (i) or (ii), rationally interpreting the "and" as causation, just as any competent police investigator would. The pathologizing project blinds Brotherton and French to the obvious epistemic considerations, ones that also loom large in the empirical sciences. A verdict of "participants are rational" would, after all, have to follow. The authors brush this sort of devastating objection aside with a brief footnote, saying this issue is complex. But really, it's not. Such troubling examples are endemic to the pathologizing literature, starting as it does with the universal, and apparently false, "conspiracist mindset" hypothesis.

These are two ordinary, not outlier, examples of the pathologizing project. Instead of science, a standard of forced and fallacious interpretations of results, as required by the pathologizing project, appears to be the guiding light of this literature, followed with almost unwavering allegiance across dozens of papers. This problem has been noted for several years.[15] Need it continue to develop?

6. CONCLUSION: BEING FAIR TO CONSPIRACY THEORIZING AND OUR FUTURE

The "conspiracist mindset" hypothesis is an effigy of conspiracy theorists, demonstrably distorting current research, supporting a project perfectly suited to disqualify, silence, and socially disappear dissident citizens. But an anthropology of people who entertain conspiracy explanations—again, all of us—reveals a very different tale. We almost universally proceed from a rationally suggested hypothesis, evidence for or against, typically deploying sound inference, and reach rational conclusions: rejection, suspicion, acceptance, or agnosticism. Sound familiar? It should. In the massive contemporary media flux, conspiracy allegations need evidence to gain the slightest notice, and in this competition, conflicts within or between accounts need to be resolved if this attention is to be sustained.

In our original letter of concern we wrote:

> [The authors] believe people shouldn't bother evaluating the evidence for or against, even though an evaluation of the evidence for or against really should be the end of the story. Rather, people are to be scientifically directed, somehow, to fixate on the cry of "That's a conspiracy theory!," flee the room, and not reflect on any facts. (Basham and Dentith 2016, 13)

For the *Le Monde* authors, little seems to have changed. Indeed, their pathologizing stance seems not to have become more nuanced, but more aggressive.

History shows enemy-within "mindset" theories, applied to large swaths of society in charged political contexts, are almost certainly false. Yet they are politically useful reductions of thoughtful persons to "mindset pathogens": victims and carriers of a mental plague. It is unseemly and dangerous in the long run for governments to contrive—worse, "scientifically" contrive—to censor and disable their critics because government officials classify them as "conspiracy theorists." Such a label is correctly applied to anyone who claims a group within the government is being intentionally deceptive about certain programs, actions, or plans that it should not be.

There is also much cause for hope. We can be fair to conspiracy theorizing. This begins by approaching conspiracy theorists as rational persons, not inflicting designs and forced interpretations contrived to make them appear insane or variously deranged and dangerous. It rejects the broader "outlier" obsession of social psychology, and its application to conspiracy theorists. Of course, those who explore conspiracy explanations are not outliers unless we all are "outliers"; but then it follows none of us are. In the final paragraph, the authors propose a peace treaty. They will study only the *non-rational* components of conspiracy theorizing, and please leave us alone (Dieguez et al. 2016, 34).

Dare to dream. Why should these researchers restrict themselves to such a narrow vision in a bid for social control? When hundreds of thousands were killed and continue to be killed in Iraq? A counter proposal: unbiased, good science. Seek out the rational elements, be careful not to be blinded by a pre-opted, establishmentarian pathologizing project, and see what we really can discover by pursuing *all* the cognitively relevant questions.[16] Jack Bratich insightfully summarizes conspiracy panics: "Conspiracy panics operate only via a series of contradictory analyses, self-delusional claims, even its own paranoid projections. They often operate in similar ways to the objects they problematize . . . seeking a figure for incrimination" (Bratich 2008, 166). Draped, as all conspiracy panics are, in establishmentarian politics and dubious analysis, this certainly appears to apply to our colleagues in the *Le Monde* statement and their subsequent defense of it. But the day is bright and the canvas wide. Conspiracy theorizing is not a disease. Social scientists increasingly recognize the "conspiracist mindset" story and its political pathologizing and silencing project are suspect, both as politics *and* science.

In the background, we are faced with a political collision, one both foreshadowed and feared by J. S. Mill's monograph, *On Liberty* (Mill 2008). Mill's attempt at reconciliation of truth and consequences fails—in the min-imum, with his distinction between direct and indirect harm. We need not detain ourselves with this. There is a deeper problem: The correlation between utilitarianism and the deontology of rights-based democracies is not nearly as strong as Mill hoped for and argued for, not in the short term of community conduct, nor, arguably, within entire life-spans of civilizations. It repeatedly breaks down at critical junctures.[17] Truth or consequences don't always play nice. But consequentialist betrayals of democracy accumulate rapidly, and democracy dissipates accordingly and in that proportion. We face one of these betrayals now. We know this from the conduct of even our personal lives. Even if we embrace short-term consequences as the governing standard, any attempt at compromise between the two, in a democratic setting, on the time scale current democracies operate on is a mistake.

There may be a good argument for a distant intersection of truth and consequences. But manipulating the belief-abilities of the public by govern-mental powers, especially those of the young, is not where this intersection will ever occur. It is contrary to it. We might conclude the information hier-archies as they currently exist are in need of significant displacement by new, social epistemic structures, particularly horizontal information exchange and democratic response. This is happening before our eyes, and the *Le Monde* declaration is a conservative reaction to it. This evolution must be tempered with responsible epistemic standards that develop within, like a child learning to walk. There is evidence the child is learning to walk. The development of a more epistemically responsible and capable population is a vast and organic development. It should not be attempted, let alone inflicted in a foolish and ahistorical fashion, by a few social psychologists and essentially conserva-tive, opportunistic legislatures. We should not pathologize those who side with warrant and accountability over short-term stability and political continuity. If we side with truth and warrant, we will view the project of the *Le Monde* pathologizers and those like them with extreme concern. Admittedly, when historical amnesia beckons, their approach is dangerously seductive and to that measure, dangerous to our future. The public's access to evidence and the ability to individually and then collectively reason, not top-down manipulation, either clumsy or well contrived, is the key to long-term success of our human democracies.

NOTES

1. The *Le Monde* authors report they suffer popular hatred: "The whole issue [in] numerous online discussions and the type of hate mail 'they' regularly receive from 'historically or politically literate' defenders of the truth, sometimes also called 'conspiracy theorists': 'But what about the *real* conspiracies?'" Why anyone would think this "hate mail" is unclear. Perhaps there may be other examples more clearly hateful. I hope not. But a sense of popular rejection may go some way to explaining the spirited tone of their response, and reinforce their commitment to pursuing the pathologizing project.

2. Dieguez et al.'s peculiar scare-quote motif, "they," appears throughout the *Le Monde* authors' response. As Kurtis Hagen playfully quips, "Would it have been better if we had called them 'it?'"

3. It appears to be the public face of this latest of "cognitive hygiene" projects. The constant shuffle between disinterested science and social-political policy is revealing. The authors also refer to "cognitive epidemiology," another medicalization and venue for public policy. Envision the future "Ministry of Cognitive Epidemiology and Health," and all else follows.

4. This definition would render, for instance, croissants "conspiracy theories" too, at least when conspiracy theorists make them or seek to eat them.

5. Later in the *Le Monde* authors' response they inform us social psychology has established these same billion-plus people are simultaneously certain Mr. Hussein secreted away vast stockpiles of WMD, an ideation on their part that speaks for itself.

6. See, for example, Patrick Stokes' chapter in this volume.

7. Weak correlations to rational attitudes like suspicion of authorities, a sense of powerlessness, distrust of public information, a willingness to commit similar behavior if in power, and so on. All are rational responses to the evidence-driven acceptance, or suspicion that, any given ambitious (not minor) political conspiracy theory is true.

8. M R. X. Dentith, Peter Knight, Ginna Husting, Martin Orr, Kurtis Hagen, David Coady, Jack Bratich, and Charles Pigden, among a number of others.

9. In this paper, "endorsement" literally means "settled belief."

10. It's nice to discover how much you have in common at lunch and a night on the town.

11. Notice that (4) has profound implications for any ordinary person about the evaluation of 1, 2 and 3; these are reduced to speculations by it.

12. Perhaps a 5 or 6 on the authors' 1 (strongly disagree) to 6 or 7 (strongly agree) point scale.

13. At times Wood et al. retreat from explicit talk of "belief" to the ambiguous term "endorse," which can be interpreted as either "belief" or "suspicion," among other things. In "Dead and Alive" there is no occurrence of "suspicion" or similar language in the description of respondents, but ironically it does occur in their initial characterization of concerns over the handling of the bin Laden assassination, "Conspiracy theories alleging that bin Laden had not actually been killed in the raid immediately started to propagate throughout the Internet and traditional media, mostly. Proponents claimed that their *suspicions* were aroused by several actions of the Obama administration, including a refusal to release pictures of bin Laden's body and the decision to bury him at sea shortly after the raid (emphasis added)." Yet subsequently, "those who distrust the official story of Diana's death do not tend to settle on a single conspiracist account as the only acceptable explanation." So yes, they "have suspicions" concerning multiple mutually excluding explanations. But no logical contradictions can be derived from that.

14. This is an instance of the broader "why don't you just ask them?" problem plaguing this literature: People are treated as non-rational, malfunctioning automatons from start to finish.

15. In talks in the United States, Nordic countries, Germany, and Eastern Europe, these criticisms and others of much of this literature have been met with surprising agreement by social psychologists. Perhaps this is what Marius Hans Raab, in signing our letter of concern, "est allé faire dans cette galére?"

16. Such unbiased rationality-testing research designs are now in the works with the help of accomplished social psychologists in the United States, Germany, and Sweden.

17. The problem of toxic truths, for instance. See Basham (2018, 2011).

Chapter 8

Governing with Feeling

Conspiracy Theories, Contempt, and Affective Governmentality

Ginna Husting

When people ask me about my work, I often explain that I study media and conspiracy theories. The ensuing conversation unfolds in a strikingly uniform way. Last week, for example, during an appointment a podiatrist asked me about my academic specialty. I brought up conspiracy theories, and he immediately launched into a conversation about JFK. Had I seen the 1992 JAMA articles reviewing the medical data on the assassination? (I hadn't.) He mentioned a conspiracy theory running through the medical profession. "Which just goes to show," he said, "that even really intelligent, educated people believe in these things!" He then tested me on my knowledge of conspiracy theories. He said he hears them almost every day; most of his clients are "the real middle American public" (he later clarified "the working class," much of his clientele). and he is stunned by the things they tell him. He even said he's actually baited patients a couple of times—just to see if he can construct a theory too extreme for his most "paranoid" clients. He's never yet succeeded, he said. We spent an extra ten post-biopsy minutes of his packed schedule talking about conspiracy theorists; his nurse fluttered behind him, unable to interrupt but anxious about the passing time.

One of the oddest and most predictable parts of this conversation is that I wasn't able to get him to understand what it is I study: "conspiracy theory theories" (Dentith 2014), or people's ideas, anxieties, and obsessions about conspiracy theorists, and the term's discursive punch as it throws those so labeled into the category of wingnuts (Husting and Orr 2007; Aistrope 2016). When I told my podiatrist that I'm interested in the rhetorical force and cultural politics of the phrase, he simply returned to his list of prominent theories. "Have you heard of the Bilderburger? Strauss-Kahn? . . . What do you think of Roseanne Barr? Alex Jones?"

My doctor's visit provides an apt entry point into my concern about conspiracy theories: even "smart, educated people" find it hard to "go meta" (in Simon's 1994 term) and think about, *inter alia*, the cultural uses of the phrase, particularly the anxiety-filled popular discourses on the dangers of conspiracy theorists in our midst. Investment in the problem is so deep that interlocutors can rarely bracket it to consider how a label like "conspiracy theorist" is itself part of a culture of fear. In fact, use of the label is part of a cultural politics sculpting the limits of what we can reasonably say, think, feel, and know. To bracket the phrase and examine the cultural political work it does is not to suggest that Elvis lives, aliens shot JFK, or Obama had no US birth certificate; it is, however, to suggest that each knowledge claim must be taken on its own terms and evaluated without binding it to a sloppy category of "kooky" conspiracy theories. Media studies scholar Jack Bratich is right to point out that the fuzziness of the phrase "conspiracy theorist," its openness as a category, "closely approximates that of the 'terrorist' (the whatever enemy)" (2008, 12).

In this paper, then, I trouble some key analytical moves in the burgeoning field of conspiracy studies and explore alternative approaches that link it to two strands of current social theorizing—governmentality and the politics of affect. First, I "go meta" to ask how the production of knowledge about knowledge itself becomes a form of politics. Here I follow Bratich's work on conspiracy theories as part of neoliberal governmentality, understanding public anxiety over conspiracy theories to be one instance of a set of "series of prevention strategies for dissent" (2008, 12) in neoliberal political economies. Second, I show how a fuller analysis of conspiracy theory discourse requires developing our theorization of the cultural politics of contempt, or the notion of affective governmentality (Ahmed 2004b; Illouz 2007; Ferguson 2010). I argue that current struggles over the use of the phrase "conspiracy theory" work in and through a politics of contempt. Finally, I ground the analysis in Hannah Arendt's theorization of political action. Here I argue that the emotionality of US conspiracy panic discourse (Bratich 2008) effectively polices the boundaries of what is sayable, knowable, thinkable, and perhaps "feelable," by cordoning it off from the unsayable/unknowable/ unthinkable—from the patently ridiculous, pathological, and emotionally suspect. Such abject kinds of knowing place the knower out of bounds of reasonable politics, and for Arendt, violate the conditions on which political action must rest.

1. THE TROUBLE WITH CONSPIRACY STUDIES: ASKING ONE SET OF QUESTIONS, FORECLOSING ANOTHER

Since the work of Lippman and Hofstadter (1965), a cross-disciplinary literature on conspiracy theorizing has emerged, ranging from political science and neuropsychology to cultural and literary studies. Much conspiracy scholarship focuses on conspiracy theory as a pathology of individuals, polities, and social systems (Husting and Orr 2007; Dentith 2014; Bjerg and Presskorn-Thygesen 2016). In this section I examine how the proliferation of anxious stories over the dangers of conspiracy theories does certain kinds of political work. It calls into being a particular kind of other: the conspiracy theorist, who believes in "Roswell" *and* the Kennedy conspiracies, but who, all the same, is often difficult to identify, since the theory itself looks reasonable on its surface. Ultimately, this pathologizing discourse, like other moral panics, works to reaffirm for an anxious public the value of political norms of openness, trust in democracy, and faith in the transparency of government and corporate politics. This boundary maintenance and social unification may be critically important in an age of staggeringly large-scale organizations and inequities of access to power and resources. But in popular and scientific writing they do more than simply maintain boundaries. In searching clinically (or logically) for the inner truth of the individual who manifests conspiracist ideology, we behold a Foucauldian technology of the conspiratorial self or "game of truth" par excellence (Foucault 1988).

These generalist arguments (Buenting and Taylor 2010; also see the chapters in Section One of this volume) urge us to dismiss, pathologize, and impugn conspiracy theories and theorists in general, rather than asking after the particulars of any given case of conspiracy accusation. Dentith (Dentith 2017b, 2) points out that "often the generalist claims that . . . a conspiracy theory is not *merely* a theory about a conspiracy but, instead, a theory about a conspiracy which has certain features which dictate its implausibility or ir-rationality as a belief." Much academic and popular conspiracy theory discourse attempts to diagnose traits like character and intelligence, intent on identifying hidden, usually individualized causes of constructing, believing in, and circulating conspiracy theories.

Such dietrological work (Bratich 2008) constitutes the dominant form of analysis among academics, journalists, and political bloggers. It asks why conspiracy theories propagate in a particular place, period, or society. Answers range from the increasing deluge of digital information and the easy spread of rumor on the Internet to paranoid styles, cultural primitivism, status anxiety, and alienation (Aistrope 2016). A whole swathe of this literature points to dispositional characteristics of certain groups which are associated with "conspiracy thinking"—in US conspiracy discourse, these consist of people in the Middle East, citizens of nondemocratic, non-Western nations, and disenfranchised whites and communities of color in the United States. Some of this literature is racist and nationalist: for example, positing the tribal mind of the Arab other as one unable to grasp how democracy works.

Much of this literature, when not overtly racist, is a patronizing form of "these people aren't crazy, just ignorant and backward given their history of oppression" (Goertzel 1994; Simmons and Parsons 2005). Some is not. Witness, for example, Kelman's study of the reasonableness of African American stories framing the failure of the levee in New Orleans as intentional on the part of the Army Corps of Engineers (2009). His analysis demonstrates a history of intentional forms of sabotage from white government and corporate actors in taking, polluting, and weakening residential areas inhabited primarily by African Americans in Louisiana. Under such conditions, stories about the levee and flooding become not "crazy" but legitimate attempts to understand a confusing and difficult phenomenon.

Done well, the dietrological approach to conspiracy theorization reveals some of the more troubling aspects of globalized political economies and its inequalities. But because it tends to psychologize the subjects of its analysis, it misses the political work done by the labels themselves. Ironically, these same conspiracy theorists are often described in the literature as dangerously persuasive; they "appear" logical and coherent, which makes them dangerous to the rest of us. We might be taken in by their seductive skepticism and magical thinking (Pipes 1997; Arnold 2008; Bale 2007). This narrative of danger is continually rearticulated in left, right, and center popular political discourse, and displays fear and moral indignation toward its target.

2. CONSPIRACY THEORY, GOVERNMENTALITY

Conspiracy discourse is a moralized discourse exemplary of neoliberal governmentality. Central to Foucault's work on modernity are the practices and techniques by which subjects are produced and governed. By government Foucault does not necessarily refer to the state; instead, governmentality's referent hearkens back to older usages of "govern"—as in guiding or governing one's behavior, governing one's self or one's child or a household (Foucault 2010, 48). Unmoored from the state, governmentality is the "conduct of conduct," or a form of "government from a distance," in which knowledges, rationalities, procedures, beliefs, and "best" practices (from statistical analysis of a population to techniques for positive thinking) govern a population by creating subjects who govern themselves.

Said differently, neoliberalism has particular practices, working definitions, and values that define rationality in particular ways, and link it to the practice of democracy and the activities of citizen-subjects; "rationalities of rule are specific ways of thinking about how to govern at particular times and places. [They] are discursive; they propose strategies, suggest reforms, identify problems, recommend solutions and constitute a series of suppositions, instructions and assumptions which are encapsulated in discourses and knowledges that guide, advise and inform our ways of being in the world" (Campbell 2010, 36). Governmentalized selves in a neoliberal society guide, advise, inform, and constantly surveil themselves and each other on everything from optimal weight and bodily fitness to the amount of negative thoughts and emotions we allow ourselves to have (Illouz 2007); we are "responsibilized" as we produce and follow expert advice to optimize well-being and health of body, mind, and polis.

To understand any political culture, then, we want to look at how it defines truth versus falsehood, and reasonable versus unreasonable thought. We must look at how certain discourses, organizations, experts, and programs construct "fields of possibility" for what counts as fact, truth, reason, reasonable political thought, action, and speech. What particular notions/practices govern the reasonable limits of freedom in any particular moment? Foucault asks us to recognize the following *as effects of neoliberal governmentality*: citizens; the freedom they exercise in acting, questioning, thinking about politics; the moral limits of rational inquiry into the honesty of political and journalistic authorities, also into the fairness and transparency of political and economic power. One of the signal violations of a conspiracy theorist is that s/he does not govern her reason well, something which requires the classification, monitoring, and analysis of conspiracy theories.

Approached this way, conspiracy theory discourse serves to construct, circulate, and enact a "well-tempered" citizen in liberal politics who is vigilant but not obsessive about the state and its power. Much popular discourse on conspiracy theorizing attempts to gauge its distance from sane, reasonable discourse. A classic example here comes from Democratic Underground, a prominent liberal online site rife with long, heated threads on conspiracy theorizing. Characteristic of these are finely detailed arguments and definitions, as illuminated in this response to a poster trying to calm a dispute:

[The other disputant] provided one definition (or explanation) of "conspiracy theory"—of course, it isn't the only possible one. It is true both of conspiracy theories . . . and many conjectures that turn out to be true, that they are constructed from bits and pieces of evidence. That doesn't mean that CT is indistinguishable from conjecture in general. (2011)

Witness here the responsibilized citizen's calculation and cautious measurement of the distance between reasonable skepticism and paranoia (and it is
strikingly similar to much pathologizing academic work on CTs). On this site,
conspiracy discourse has become so common that members now routinely
joke-worry about posts and comments being moved to the "conspiracy dungeon." The dungeon is slang for removal of posts that violate a key rule on the
website—no conspiracy theorizing. The dungeon was developed after a raft
of conspiratorial conjecture over the 2004 Indian Ocean Tsunami:

> Do not quote or link to "conspiracy theory" websites, except in our September
> 11 forum, which is the only forum on Democratic Underground where we
> permit members to debate highly speculative conspiracy theories. A reasonable
> person should be able to identify a conspiracy theory website without much
> difficulty (2006).

Conspiracy discourses like the ones quoted above both specify that conspiracy theories are "kooky" (in the words of Democratic Underground's
administrators), easy to identify in their fringeness, and persuasive and
dangerous.

Conspiracy panics are governmentalized to the extent that they embody
discourses (news, blogs, conversations, congressional hearings, political
advertisements) and practices (e.g., the US State Department's 2005–2007
webpage on "How to Identify Misinformation," posted during the Bush
Administration) that sculpt the range of possibility for the well-tempered
citizen. A whole host of popular political knowledges about pluralism and
democracy do boundary maintenance by rehearsing the dangers of paranoiac
thinking styles and calling for good self-regulation or control of suspicion, to
take care that it does not go "too far."

An example which by now is old and cold, and therefore easier to study, is
the case of Cynthia McKinney, an American politician, one year after 9/11.
In Congress and on Pacifica News, McKinney said: "We know there were
numerous warnings of the events to come on September 11. . . . What did the
Administration know, and when did it know it about the events of September
11? Who else knew and why did they not warn the innocent people of
New York who were needlessly murdered?" (Cardindale 2008).

She became a conspiracy theorist célèbre in US mainstream news almost
immediately. Stories insistently highlighted quotes calling her disgusting,
loony, and dangerous. For example, the *Washington Post* asked: "Did she
say these things while standing on a grassy knoll in Roswell, New Mexico?"
(Eilperin 2002) A fellow democratic politician, Zell Miller, repeatedly called
her "loony," describing her as "dangerous and irresponsible."

These descriptors, widely repeated in the news, point to the meanings circulating through the condensed symbol "conspiracy theorist" (McKinney 2002). McKinney's case is one to examine with care; she made no assertions, but she did ask suggestive questions. Presidential spokesman Scott McClellan attacked McKinney, saying "The American people know the facts, and they dismiss such ludicrous, baseless views. The fact that she questions the president's legitimacy shows a partisan mind-set beyond all reason" (Eilperin 2002, A6).

Yet while McKinney made a particular claim (that there were warnings in advance about the attack), and asked questions about timing and profit, she did not claim that the Bush Administration let it happen (although it can easily be read as within the implied scope of her question). Yet in 2006 the mainstream press confirmed that, in fact, the Bush Administration had forewarnings of the imminent possibility of al-Qaeda attack (Draper 2006). The CIA had reported these both to Secretary of Defense Donald Rumsfeld and to Secretary of State Condoleezza Rice, but was ignored (Draper 2006). In 2002, making such claims and asking for independent inquiry was evidence of political distemper; McKinney became paranoid, beyond reason, and "dangerous."

Because these are still such loaded topics, note that this example in no way promotes McKinney's or any other "LIHOP" or "MIHOP" question ("Let It Happen on Purpose" and "Made It Happen on Purpose"—two popular theories about the Bush Administration's complicity in 9/11). It highlights instead that conspiracy panic is about the production and marking of "danger," which Foucault posited not as something outside a liberal political economy, but something essential to the ongoing production of it; "liberalism nurtures danger, it subjects danger to an economic calculus . . . it must never fix security, since the striving of securing and the danger of insecurity are complementary aspects of liberal governmentality" (Lemke 2009). Instead of an absolute abjuration of that which is dangerous, then, governmentalized political culture has a sphere of reasonability, circumscribed by the boundaries of the well-tempered citizen. The McKinney coverage reveals some of the boundaries constructed when we hear the phrase "conspiracy theory" or "theorist" invoked. The term works to separate those who think "rationally," reasonable citizens/thinkers, from paranoid, irrational, or delusional ones; and in fact this is the stated goal of those concerned with conspiracy discourse—that conspiracy theories muddy the liberal public sphere with "dangerous" theories.

Gary Webb's case provides another striking example. In 1996 Webb, a journalist for the *San Jose Mercury News*, published a three-part story on the link between the CIA, Nicaraguan Contras, and cocaine transportation into California. Webb's exposé, highly documented with primary sources, showed that CIA-backed Nicaraguan Contra fighters repeatedly used CIA planes to transport cocaine into the United States. The series was repeatedly vilified in the US news as the story of a mentally unstable conspiracy theorist. Webb had done vast painstaking research to substantiate his claims of drug-running (profits funneled to Nicaraguan Contras) and the CIA's awareness of it (Webb 1998). Additionally, he posed questions about links that might exist; he did not have the data to support them and made that clear. Webb was flayed in the press, subsequently fired, and issued anonymous death threats because of both his founded claims and claims falsely attributed to him.

In one of its thirty-two condemnatory stories on Webb, the *New York Times* reported gossip that the board of the Northern California chapter of the Society of Professional Journalists met and discussed stripping Gary Webb of his 1996 Journalist of the Year award: "Dark Alliance . . . continues to echo among journalists nine months after the series was published . . . the series overstated its provocative findings and omitted important details." The *Times* quoted a journalist saying, "I think it's clear that a lot of people came out feeling dispirited and troubled. . . . You could hear a lot of people saying, 'I know if I did something like Gary did, I'd be out the door.'"

PBS's *Frontline* reported the story again several years later with a piece entitled "Cocaine, Conspiracy Theories and the CIA in Central America" (Golden 1996). This story reiterated false claims:

> Amongst Webb's fundamental problems was his implication that the CIA lit the crack cocaine fuse. It was conspiracy theory: a neat presentation of reality that simply didn't jibe with real life. Webb later agreed in an interview that there is no hard evidence that the CIA as an institution or any of its agent-employees carried out or profited from drug trafficking (Delaval 2003).

But the CIA itself had confirmed that drug-running was happening with CIA planes, and with the knowledge of some members of the CIA (Schou 2006). His evidence was meticulous, and vindicated later (Schou 2006; Fenster 2008), but he was attacked precisely for not having evidence (see Golden 1996) and for creating conspiracy stories about drug-running. The conspiracy panic around Webb worked not by evaluating, or disproving his evidence, but by derision.

The reception of Webb's exposé illuminates the problem of stepping outside the bounds of "reasonable" skepticism of governmental and corporate agents. Questioning too much, as Gary Webb did in "Dark Alliance," met with widespread public defamatory response, most of it centering on the supposed illogic of arguments and the paranoia or psychosis of the arguer.

Even academics can fall into the trap of making strange claims while trying to cordon off conspiracism from "reasonable" thought. Vincent, for example, in a provocative essay on conspiracy theory writes:

> [T]he strength of paranoiac thought lies in its perfect coherence: it does not leave any space for error, failure or ambiguity. Conspiracy theories . . . are attempts to find a narrative for the contradictions and transformations that are animating the world . . . to make them more intelligible . . . to reduce the tension arising out of the pressure exerted by reality. (2006, 45)

This is as true of what usually counts as science or "non-paranoiac thought." Decades of media research document journalistic failure (forget non-professionals) to allow for ambiguity, failure, or error (Altheide 2002; Zelizer and Allen 2004; Tolley 2015; Drok and Hermans 2016; Gutsche 2017 fail to scrape the surface of this literature). But the next step in developing a theory of conspiracy panics and their political work is to recognize that conspiracy discourse functions not just on a cognitive register, but an affective one as well. It is to this problem that we now turn.

3. HANNAH ARENDT, CONTEMPT, AND ITS CORROSIVE EFFECTS

The charge "conspiracy theorist" is in fact a form of what symbolic interactionists call "identity spoilage"—talk or action that sullies and tarnishes the self as well as the specific content of the self's action (Goffman 1963). In public discourse, as McKinney's case shows, conspiracy theorists are often framed as untrustable and thereby dangerous, both because of their illogic and, ironically, because of their excess of emotion—in other words, contempt, one of the most caustic emotions (Melnick and March Nevis 2010), becomes a vehicle for positioning certain illiberal subjects as too emotional. Underlying much conspiracy panic is a fear of emotional excess overwhelming reason and creating socio-pathological disorder and paranoia; to engage in conspiracy theorizing is to step out of the sphere of reason and logic, and enter the terrain of the emotional and the psychotic. But conspiracy panic discourse is itself a form of emotional and political engagement driven by contempt and laced with anger and fear. The affect running through conspiracy panic performs discursive work, degrading and dismissing both claims and claimants. It polices or manages the boundaries of reasonable political doubt, delineating a relatively uncorrupted democratic sphere in an age of increasing economic inequality and massive concentration of political and cultural power in the hands of corporate, governmental, and increasingly nongovernmental organizations (Sassen 2006). In this section I trace the emotion running through conspiracy theory discourse, linking it to Hannah Arendt's work on natality and plurality to show the damage done by public contempt.

A trend in the new work on affect and emotion is to think about the relation of both to place, culture, and political life; but only just now is governmentality being linked to emotion (Ohnuma 2008; Campbell 2010; Vrasti 2011; Sauer and Penz 2017). While work on emotions has begun to focus on specific kinds of emotions (Ahmed 2004a; Ferguson 2010), little work specifically examines contempt, and none of it links contempt with governmentality or considers contempt's effects on democratic culture. Disgust has received far more attention (Nussbaum 2010; Miller 1997; Ashworth 2017). Both Miller and Nussbaum focus on the destructiveness of disgust, noting that both disgust and contempt are bound up with the maintenance of social hierarchy in a culture. But while Miller proscribes disgust in the public sphere, he recuperates contempt as vital to the persistence of democracy in the face of rigid social hierarchies. In this he agrees with Bell (2005) and Mason (2003), who also attempt to normatively ground contempt as a justified, warranted, and useful emotion that can be used to resist oppression in interpersonal relationships. These scholars roughly agree on the nature of contempt; for all of them, contempt is an intertwining of affective and cognitive elements, roughly synonymous with derision, scorn, and judgment of another's worthlessness.

These scholars share the belief that contempt is both a fully social and an extreme emotion that regulates the boundaries between acceptable and reprehensible, unforgivable actions. Contempt demeans not just one or several qualities about another, but constitutes a judgment *tout court* in which the other, as a whole and in every particular, is a failure (Miller 1997; Mason 2003). Contempt is constructed in and through relations and interaction; we have contempt for humans, and perhaps other animals, but it is an emotion reserved for the animate world. It is precisely only useful when it is witnessed interpersonally—we do not hold a rock in contempt, because a rock, or other rocks, cannot recognize their devaluation.

In this way, and especially in popular and political culture, contempt is a performative emotion—the expressing of it in public effects the movement of another to a status that is both beneath the contemner's and unworthy of attention or recognition as fully human. Contempt, focused on selves rather than acts, creates an irreparable distance between the contemned and the contemner (Bell 2005); it cuts off the contemned from community. When we perform contempt in public, we *emotionally* push people from the realm of belonging, toleration, and worthiness of interaction. They fall from the state of being recognized by us—of being worthy even of attention or consideration.

To earn contempt is to be marked as un-reasonable, as unworthy of rational interaction.

In that way to hold another in contempt is to hold his/her humanness in abeyance, to radically decouple him/her from what Hannah Arendt would call our life in common. Arendt is a good theorist for the emotional politics of conspiracy theory; her conceptualization of agonistic political action is not inhospitable to Foucauldian inflections (Honig 1995; Zelizer and Allen 2004; Braun 2007; Blencowe 2010). Political action and speech for Arendt are bound up with the performance or ongoing creation of the self and the world we have in common; political action is bound to performance and thereby to emotion. How does contempt work in such a politics?

To answer this question we must recognize how Arendt theorizes political action. She defines political speech and action as that which makes us most fully human. We continuously recreate ourselves through the act of speaking and acting in concert (cooperatively or competitively) with others. Much of identity is constative—given to us through our work and labor, with few parameters for variation, play, or experimentation (Honig 1995). But as political selves we can continually become what we are not yet—we are less bound to the requirements of work, which determine and focus the "what" of us, our activity, thoughts, and behavior. A democratic political space is an agonistic one, where we can come together to argue, fight, agree, act, and speak in common with one another. Under those conditions we do not know what we will say or do, or what others will say or do—there is a spontaneity to political action. Through political action (which includes speech) we create and perform new selves through interaction with others. The sphere of concerted action in public is performative—it is a theatre for the improvised selves which we call into being even as we take action and speak with others.

Two qualities of life in public make this possible: natality and plurality. They are *sine qua non* for Arendtian agonistic democracy. Life in public happens through plurality, in which we are seen and heard by others in a context where we can, through action and speech, affect material and symbolic conditions (Arendt 1998, 57). Life in public arises whenever people engage each other through the agonistic confrontation of identities, opinions, and differences. Indeed, for Arendt the only way we can think for ourselves is through encounters with others, which transform opinion into thought. Thinking requires a form of "interior" plurality, in which we use the dialogic process of thinking from more than one perspective (our own) to examine our beliefs and actions. Being seen and heard by others is requisite both to construction of the world in common and to the self interwoven with it. But natality shows us most clearly the damage done when conspiracy discourse catapults selves from the ongoing process of world-making in common. Natality, carrying as it does the resonances of birth and newness, is our capacity to continually re-construct and renegotiate our world in concert with others who are in political contest with us. Through my ability to talk or act in new ways I create who I am; I participate in what can only be a collective, if profoundly conflictual, process of crafting the world. To permanently exclude others from this process is to enact a form of violence that in turn forecloses the spaces of democracy. It erodes the condition of plurality, or the inclusion of maximal differences in play in world-making.

We can now spell out the political functions of the label "conspiracy theorist/theorizing" in relation to plurality and natality. Contempt runs through it, and contempt is a radical excision of the so-labeled from the community of interlocutors who, even as they profoundly disagree with one another, must interact, recognize, and speak across difference. Contempt separates the contemned from the ability to be seen and heard; it end-runs around any utterance or action another might make. Once the label "conspiracy theory" sticks to someone, it impugns their intellectual and moral competence and relieves hearers of the need to consider the validity of her or his claims (Ashworth's 2017 analysis of disgust in relation to Uganda's anti-homosexuality laws shows parallel processes). It robs the contemned of the capacity to re-negotiate our world in concert with others.

"Democratic Underground" is particularly interesting in this regard since conspiracy theorizing is a frequent topic both among posters and among commenters. The nature and detailed reasoning and argumentation in these discussions illuminates an anxiety over the nature of truth and how it can be distinguished from conspiracy theory. In one thread (Democratic Underground 2008), for example, a commenter writes: "When I want to evaluate a theory, 'conspiracy' or otherwise, I look for the emotionalism employed in its service."

Thread titles often reflect the contempt, anger, and defensiveness: "The Troof Is Out There" (T_i_B 2007), "Fun with Tinfoil" (Guaranteed 2004), "Paranoid Shift or By Their Fruits You Shall Know Them" (Champion 2004), "Soylent Green is Made Out of People!!!" (Bonobo 2009) and "Why You Conspiracy Theorist, You" (NNN0LHI 2007). Ironically, perhaps, some of these, like "Paranoid Shift" or "Why You" were in fact created by posters who embrace the label "conspiracy theorist." Vitriol twines through the interactions on many of these posts. In an argument over 9/11 and the Pentagon's damage, one commenter indicates "I don't know what happened." In response, another commenter says: "And they were able to jigger up the crime scene in only a few minutes and so well that it fooled hundreds of investigators from other agencies?" and another enjoins: "RIGHT. You are being sophomorically stupid. And juvenile." The affect running through conspiracy theory discourse suggests anything but a well-tempered set of citizens; it is an ill-tempered exchange, with animated emoticons smirking, derisively dancing, and vomiting in responses to others' comments.

This is by no means limited to the Left: since conspiracy theorizing is supposed to come from the fringe, Right and Centrist analyses also posit the problem as extremists at the crazy edges of the political spectrum (Bratich calls this "fusion paranoia" among those concerned with conspiracy theories). A case in point comes from Bill Keller, former New York Times CEO, who built a reputation for attacking Julian Assange and Wikileaks. Keller's *New York Times Magazine* piece on Assange (2011a) seethed with contempt; he attacked Assange as a "conspiracy theorist," and the epithet is nested in a chain of signifiers through which affect circulates (Ahmed 2004a). Assange is "childish," "coy about his secret stash," "manipulative and volatile," "disheveled, like a bag lady," "unwashed," and "arrogant." Descriptors become vivified through contempt, which binds them together, and links them to Assange's selfhood, rather than to discrete acts. Contempt transfers across circuits, from one kind of quality and personhood to another.

Through such usage "conspiracy theorist" becomes a condensed assemblage of characteristics, through which contemptuous affect both circulates and intensifies the discourse. Keller taps a whole range of non-accidental meanings or "sticky associations" (Ahmed 2004a)—sticky in that they bind characteristics to one another in a chain of negative signification. Childishness is to homeless scrounger as unclean body is to paranoiac and pompous narcissist is to Wikileaks. The chain of associations is glued together by contempt, which jumps from one association or quality to the others.

Conspiracy panics, then, are full of emotionality, and we can do more than simply say that emotions like contempt are tools by which politics get done. Conspiracy theory discourse both mobilizes and is mobilized by a cultural politics of affect; it proliferates across micro-discourses on- and offline, in official and unofficial spaces, governing what we say and how we feel about what we say.

Some of the best evidence for this is the rise of the disclaimer "I'm not a conspiracy theorist but . . ." which has become a regular feature in popular political culture (Husting and Orr 2007). As with most disclaimers, this one functions to distance the utterer from a category that can spoil not just the intended claim, but the personhood of the claimant as well. In Mary Douglas's terms, such categories are dirty, or ritually polluted. Disclaimers like "I'm not a conspiracy theorist, but . . ." inoculate us from that which can spoil our speech/actions and personhood. Once conferred, the stigma permanently removes us from the possibility of political speech and action, and forms of human becoming/self-production. Fear of the accusation leads most of us to govern our own thoughts and speech to ensure we are not so labeled.

When we cannot avoid it, the result is shame; Keller (2011b) quotes Mark Fenster, a generalist scholar of conspiracy theory, saying; "I admit I was a little drawn to the D. S. K. [Dominique Strauss-Kahn] plot at first," Fenster told me. "Then I heard Nina Totenberg explain the case on NPR, and I was ashamed of myself." Fenster exhibits what most of us experience: shame at the possibility of fitting into the category.

The affective politics of conspiracy discourse is such that many of us—good governmentalized subjects—continually manage, reflect on, and monitor ourselves to ensure that we do not come to fit the label. Bratich (2008, 140) highlights precisely the encouragement of this governmentalized strategy by the State Department in its online site "How to Identify Misinformation": "it is important to note the state's preferred orientation of detection techniques: of the people by the people. Peer-to-peer suspicion . . ." quickly identifies the dangerous theorist among us, but it also turns us into self-managers as we evaluate how far our thoughts are from conspiracy theorizing, and as we try to avoid being shamefully stuck with the condensed assemblage of the label. Conspiracy panics fuse not just "reason and politics in a way that promotes the technology of citizen subjectification" but emotion as well. Both affect *and* "reason must become part of the ethos of the self, a work of the self on the self . . . [panics] are not just about making people reasonable, but making reason [and, we add, contempt] a people's enterprise" (Bratich 2008, 46).

This emotionalized form of governmentality fits with recent work on the emotional construction of neoliberal economic selfhood and behavior. As Vrasti and Illouz elucidate, neoliberal political economy is the outcome of the long twentieth-century reconfiguration of subjects and lifeworlds by which emotional life is reconstructed through "the metaphors and rationality of economics" (Illouz 2007, quoted in; Vrasti 2011). While conspiracy theory discourse does not directly work on the "entrepreneurial self," we can expect that popular political culture would be recrafted slowly over the same period and through the same technologies, practices, and values that govern that self and its culture. These technologies replace solidarity-based political action based with individualized, tightly managed skepticism that largely evaluates and corrects potential spinoffs into "crackpot" theories.

4. CONCLUSION

This chapter has shown how conspiracy panics bring into being, sustain, and continually renew neoliberal politics through contestation across a prolifer-ating series of micro-contexts. Contests over conspiracy theories concern the well-tempered reasonability and proper skepticism needed for citizens to govern themselves. Such contests are part of a host of similar capillary forms of knowledge production about healthy and unhealthy styles of thought and critique. Together they are part of the practices and discourses that govern neoliberal political economies. The circulation of knowledge, argument, and emotion provides the boundaries needed to define an integrated population (an "us"). It also creates potential outsiders and resistance to the well-tempered nature of the managed citizen. It creates the boundary contests needed for the continuing process of responsibilized regulation of the self and the public. We regulate ourselves by regulating, judging, and contemning others, and keeping our own thoughts and styles of reason and emotion clear. Endless disputes over reason, falsehood, and conspiracy theory become the networked sites of ongoing performance of a regime of truth and the maintenance of a neoliberal "consensus state" and global politics.

Chapter 9

Conspiracy Theorists and Social Scientists[1]

Kurtis Hagen

1. INTRODUCTION

Conspiracy theorists labor under considerable abuse from ostensibly reliable sources in the media, government, and academy. Often judged collectively, conspiracy theorists are commonly dismissed as irrational and deluded ignoramuses. While it is true that *some* conspiracy theorists appear only weakly tethered to reality, and logical and factual mistakes can easily be found in their work, not all conspiracy theorists are equal in these respects. And so grouping all conspiracy theorists together and judging them as if they formed a homogeneous class is both unfair to the better-grounded conspiracy theorists and is seriously misleading. Judgments about Alex Jones (a provocative host of a conspiracy-oriented radio show) may not apply to Peter Dale Scott (a scholar whose books are published with the University of California Press), even though they both find the official narrative of the September 11 attacks, as well as the JFK assassination, to be dubious. Further, and more to the point of this chapter, while it is not surprising to find errors and sloppiness of reasoning in the work of some conspiracy theorists, we should expect more from mainstream and "authoritative" sources, such as the academics who study conspiracy theorists. So, it would be particularly troubling to find that some social scientists—often social psychologists—have engaged in sloppy reasoning in what appears to be a self-serving agenda to "scientifically" reinforce the stigmatization of conspiracy theorists. But that is precisely what we find.

Our saga begins with a joint statement published in *Le Monde* by a group of social scientists calling for more research on conspiracy theorists in order to "fight" the "disease" of conspiracy theorizing more effectively. In response, a number of scholars, including myself, signed an open letter criticizing this agenda (Basham and Dentith 2016).[2] In response to us, the authors of the *Le Monde* statement (minus Karen Douglas) published a sprawling rebuttal entitled, "'They' Respond" (Dieguez et al. 2016), published in the *Social Epistemology Review and Reply Collective* (which is summarized in the introduction to this section). Several of us, in our own ways, responded in the same venue. Here I extend my initial response.

2. UNCRITICAL CITATION OF SERIOUSLY FLAWED STUDIES

The *Le Monde* authors claim merely to want more "rigorous empirical research" on conspiracy theorists (Dieguez et al. 2016, 25). Some of this supposedly "rigorous empirical research" on conspiracy theorists does, it turns out, just happen to have unflattering conclusions about conspiracy theorists. However, at least some of these conclusions are based on flagrant errors in reasoning[3]—errors that the *Le Monde* authors uncritically overlook, citing these studies as if they are unproblematic and authoritative, and thereby implying that there is some kind of noteworthy problem in the reasoning of conspiracy theorists.

For example, citing Wood, Douglas, and Sutton (2012) and Swami et al. (2011), respectively, the *Le Monde* authors state that conspiracy theorists "simultaneously endorse flatly contradictory conspiracy theories [and] readily accept experimentally made-up conspiracy theories" (Dieguez et al. 2016, 25). That makes it sound like there is some pretty sloppy reasoning going on. And there is. But it turns out that it is the social scientists doing the research that are guilty of it, as are those who uncritically cite this research and exaggerate its findings. Specifically, the claim that conspiracy theorists "simultaneously endorse flatly contradictory conspiracy theories" is not supported by the evidence and is presumably false, and the claim that they "readily accept experimentally made-up conspiracy theories" is a misleading exaggeration. In the former case, the authors of the study conflated *belief* with various ways of *giving some degree of credence*. For example, the respondents judged various conspiracy theories to be relatively more "plausible, convincing, worth considering, and coherent" than did others (Wood, Douglas, and Sutton 2012, 771). Notice that, while "endorsing flatly contradictory conspiracy theories" sounds irrational, there is nothing irrational about giving two contradictory theories more credence in the relevant respects than someone else does. Indeed, being alive to conflicting theories is not just unobjectionable; it is often an epistemic virtue, emblematic of a good detective or scientist.[4] In addition, the subjects were, in a significant sense, *justified* in giving more credence to these views than did their conventionalist counterparts, as I will explain below.

As for the claim that conspiracy theorists *"readily accept* experimentally made-up conspiracy theories" (emphasis added), this is an exaggeration of the finding. The subjects rated "the extent to which they agreed" with statements regarding a fictitious conspiracy theory. The authors of the study find that "[B]elieving in real-world conspiracy theories appears to make it more likely that an individual will also be more accepting of fictitious conspiracy theories" (Swami et al. 2011, 460). Notice first that to be "more likely" to accept a theory than some others (who are more skeptical about conspiracy theories in general) is not the same as to "readily accept" the theory (that's the exaggeration). Notice too that "[B]elieving in real-world conspiracy theories" *ought to have the observed effect.* And thus, the study does not tell us anything interesting about the reasoning of conspiracy theorists. For all we can tell from these studies, conspiracy theorists are simply reasoning the way reasonable people should.[5]

The phenomena stems, in all likelihood, from the participants giving some weight to prior probability considerations—just as one should. Judging the prior probability of a hypothesis is simply a matter of estimating the likelihood of the hypothesis *before considering any direct evidence about the particular case.* In the case of the fictional conspiracy theory, the participants know nothing about the proposed theory (because it is fictional—but they don't know *that*). So, in making a judgment of how likely the proposed conspiracy theory is, they have nothing to go on except prior probability considerations. The most obvious and salient prior probability consideration in a case like this is the prevalence of relevantly similar phenomena. Obviously, people who tend to believe that other conspiracy theories are true will tend to (and indeed *ought* to) believe that a newly proposed conspiracy theory is "more likely" than people who tend not to believe other conspiracy theories.

And this is also why, compared to conventionalists, conspiracy theorists are *justified* in giving more credence to conspiracy theories that happen to be mutually inconsistent. The mutual inconsistency, as I have already mentioned, is a non-issue, since the participants in the study did not indicate that they simultaneously *believe* inconsistent theories. But given their other beliefs, namely, that various other conspiracy theories are true, they are justified in assigning a higher prior probability to various other analogous theories, compared to conventionalists. And thus they are justified, in a significant sense, in giving more credence to those theories, all else being equal. One might be tempted to say they are not *ultimately* justified, because their other beliefs about conspiracy theories are false. But that move would prejudge the most significant issue in question and reveal precisely the bias that I worry is undermining the attempt at science we are discussing.

Now, the reasoning process just described relates to what the *Le Monde* authors proclaim to be "the most robust finding in the rather recent field of social-psychological conspiracy theory research." Namely, "[P]eople who believe in one conspiracy theory tend to believe in other, unrelated, conspiracy theories" (Dieguez et al. 2016, 24). They cite ten studies, Wood, Douglas, and Sutton (2012) and Swami et al. (2011) among them, along with Goertzel (1994).[6] From this documented tendency, which is entirely epistemically unproblematic (as just explained), the *Le Monde* authors posit an inauspicious-sounding "conspiracist mindset." Now note, first of all, that "conspiracist" is even more clearly derogatory than "conspiracy theorist." The word "conspiracist" implies belief in conspiracy theories *where no such belief is warranted*. So a central question has been begged, per usual. And, the rhetorical slant of much of the social scientific work suggests, "Of course, being more inclined to believe in one conspiracy theory just because one believes in another is surely irrational." *But it isn't.* It is no more or less rational than not believing in one conspiracy theory because one does not believe in another. Both are products of perfectly normal and reasonable inference making, as explained above.

So, the *Le Monde* authors, like at least some of the social scientists they cite, take a perfectly innocuous type of inference, which is not at all peculiar to conspiracy theorists, and, with the help of exaggeration and uncritical appeal to flawed studies, frame it as though it represents some sort of abnormal cognitive error that applies uniquely to conspiracy theorists. They thereby appeal to faulty science to unfairly malign an already marginalized group.[7]

3. OVER-GENERALIZING PARTICULARISM

The first part of this book highlighted the distinction between particularism and generalism. But if the *Le Monde* authors are right, this distinction makes no sense. If their arguments are successful, "particularists" such as myself will have to hang our heads in shame and admit that our whole project is incoherent. But how strong are their arguments? Read on, and judge for yourself.

Let's begin by reviewing the definition of the distinction in question, as it was first proposed by Joel Buenting and Jason Taylor:

According to the *generalist view*, the rationality of conspiracy theories can be assessed without considering particular conspiracy theories. On this view, conspiratorial thinking *qua* conspiracy thinking is itself irrational. The *particularist view* about conspiratorial thinking denies that the rationality of conspiracy theories can be assessed without considering particular conspiracy theories. (2010, 568–69)

That seems like a perfectly reasonable distinction. But the *Le Monde* authors claim that, "[O]n closer inspection, this partition turns out to be meaningless, self-serving and self-refuting." Ouch, that's a real zinger. How do they show this? They have several strategies. First they accuse us self-proclaimed "particularists" of inconsistency. Specifically, they try to show that we are equally generalist. They explain, "Basham et al. (2016) essentially claim that conspiracy theorizing is generally warranted because there are conspiracies: that is a generalist view."

Ah . . . well . . . yes . . . one could say that this is a "generalist view" *in some sense* of that phrase. It is, after all, a *generalization*, though we never intended to imply that we reject all generalizations of all kinds. That would be crazy. The important thing to note is that the idea that "conspiracy theorizing is generally warranted" is *not* a generalist view in *the specific sense in question here*. If we had asserted or implied that, "conspiracy *theories* are generally warranted" then they would have us. We would have been caught *assessing* conspiracy theories in general rather than evaluating particular conspiracy theories each on their own merits. But we did not do that, for we do not hold that position (if I may presume to speak for the group). Although the two claims *sound* very similar, they *mean* two very different things. To say that conspiracy theorizing is warranted is just to say that there is nothing inherently wrong with theorizing about conspiracies, and since conspiracies sometimes occur, it is reasonable to consider them. This tells us nothing about the warrant of any particular conspiracy theory, which has to be investigated on its own merits. Indeed, conspiracy theorizing is warranted in general *because* particularism (in the specific sense in question) is true.

Now, the *Le Monde* authors should have understood this, for they accurately understood that, in their words, "[Particularism] refers to an approach to conspiracy theories based on the examination of each specific claim of conspiracy and its respective argumentative and evidential merits (or shortcomings)" (Dieguez et al. 2016, 23 n4). And so, according to this view, we cannot rule out a conspiracy theory because of the mere fact that it is a conspiracy theory. That is, generalism is false. So, in order to evaluate a conspiracy theory, we need to "theorize" (if you will) about it, determining what is the most plausible version of it and exploring how well the evidence seems, on the whole, to support it. To point out the fact that this can be characterized as "a generalist view" in the larger sense of involving one sort of generalization or another is a silly non sequitur. It certainly does not make the distinction between generalist and particularists *as it applies to the evaluation of conspiracy theories* "meaningless, self-serving and self-refuting."

However, that was just their first swing. They follow with the assertion that "conspiracy theorists are generalists, in that they tend to endorse several and varied conspiracy theories." But this is another non sequitur. Whether or not conspiracy theorists tend to be generalists themselves would not be germane, *even if* that meant they tend to be generalists in the *relevant* sense. The debate is about what perspective a person *should* take regarding conspiracy theories, not what conspiracy theorists themselves happen to think. In other words, particularism would still be true even if all conspiracy theorists happened to be generalists in the relevant sense. And further, once again, the *Le Monde* authors are *not* referring to generalism *in the relevant sense*. For endorsing several and varied conspiracy theories does not make one a generalist in the relevant sense. What is important is whether conspiracy theorists consider the particulars of these "several and varied" conspiracy theories, which any acquaintance with the arguments put forward by conspiracy theorists suggests that they typically do.

The *Le Monde* authors do say one thing that is right on this issue. They point out that generalism might not only lead to the inappropriately flippant rejection of conspiracy theories, but a generalist orientation *in favor* of conspiracy theories might equally "lead to their uncritical acceptance." True indeed. However, that just shows that generalism is epistemically problematic regardless of its directional orientation. If their point has any relevance to the merits of particularism at all, it gives one further reason to endorse it. It certainly does nothing to advance the claim that the distinction between generalism and particularism is "meaningless, self-serving and self-refuting."

But the *Le Monde* authors are still not done. They also claim that they themselves are, in some sense, particularists. If they are particularists in the *relevant* sense, as they seem to suggest rather tentatively, that would be good news. They *ought* to be. But if they are merely particularists in some other sense, as their more concrete examples suggest, that wouldn't be germane even if their status as particularists in the relevant sense had some bearing on the issue—which it doesn't. The claim that they happen to be particularists themselves is simply not germane. Even if it is true in the relevant sense, it does nothing to support their bold claim regarding the conceptual incoherence of particularism; if anything, it undermines it.

Now, this distinction between particularists and generalists was first articulated *for a reason*. The distinction was designed to make it easy to point to two contrasting perspectives actually taken by philosophers engaged in the debate over conspiracy theories.[8] There are those who think that the whole class of ideas counting as "conspiracy theories" can be regarded as unwarranted based on quasi–a priori reasoning (these are the generalists), and those who think that one must treat each conspiracy theory on its own particular merits (the particularists). It is a clear and useful distinction that makes it easy to refer to two actual and distinctive camps. If making the distinction clear also makes generalists feel a little silly and inclines them to forsake generalism, either by claiming to have been some kind of a particularist all along, or by reframing the distinction as a spectrum along which they can take some middle position (perhaps by pretending that we particularists don't already occupy that position),[9] then the distinction is not just conceptually coherent but is doing some real work. It seems to me, then, that the *Le Monde* authors' assertion that the distinction is meaningless is both poorly supported and wrong.

4. THE MISREPRESENTATION OF THEIR OWN AGENDA

Let's now consider the original agenda of the *Le Monde* authors. What were they up to? The very title of the *Le Monde* statement makes it clear, "Let's fight conspiracy theories effectively." They worry that the "wrong cure might only serve to spread the disease" (see Basham and Dentith (2016, 17)). The "disease," of course, is conspiracy theorizing,[10] which they conflate with "conspiracism," expressing their desire to help "fight against this particular form of contemporary misinformation known as 'conspiracism'" (17). In putting it this way, they reveal their bias: the generalist presupposition that conspiracy theories are a form of misinformation. They believe that "the growth of conspiracy theories" is "a major problem" (17). And so, they aim to provide research that will help "remedy the problem" of "adherence to conspiracy theories" (18). This research is necessary, they reason, because "Conspiracism is indeed a problem that must be taken seriously" (17)—again conflating conspiracy theories with conspiracism.

It was this objective with which we took issue. But now, in response to our criticism, they have recast their position. Although they had originally characterized the intentions of governmental initiatives to undermine conspiracy theories as "laudable" (17), they have reframed their original *Le Monde* letter in the following ways:

> [Our commentary] cautioned against governmental initiatives to counter conspiracy theories among youths and advocated for more research on the topic. (Dieguez et al. 2016, 20)

> [We] took issue with French governmental and local initiatives designed to tackle the apparent proliferation of conspiracy theories among youths. (2016, 20–21)

Both of these statements are technically true, but quite misleading. These ways of putting it make it sound as though they are *against* governmental initiatives to counter conspiracy theories. Reinforcing this impression, they go so far as to suggest that they are, in part, trying to "ascertain whether there is a problem [with conspiracy theories] at all" (21), and that they want to "help everybody become *better* conspiracy theorists" (20). But that is not at all the impression one gets from the *Le Monde* statement, as indicated above.

In reality, the original *Le Monde* statement was *not* cautioning against governmental initiatives to counter conspiracy theories. Rather, they expressed full support for that *objective*. They were merely cautioning against doing it without first funding more research (to be done by themselves), so that, armed with this research, the government could counter conspiracy theories *more effectively*. Here is how they pitch it:

> [The current] more or less random campaigns [to combat belief in conspiracy theories] are *expensive*, and *this investment is automatically taken from more methodical studies of the phenomenon.* It is therefore urgent that we launch widespread research programmes aimed at evaluating present educational initiatives rather than continuing to promote them (Basham and Dentith 2016, 18, emphasis added).

As an aside, it seems a tad hypocritical of the *Le Monde* authors to charge us with a "self-serving" interpretation (Dieguez et al. 2016, 22, 23n4) while they are calling for more funding for research in which they would like to engage. But for critics of conspiracy theories, double standards are the norm.

In our response we took issue with their objective, namely, to aim scientific research (much of which turns out to be seriously flawed) toward pathologizing and fighting a perfectly legitimate, and indeed important, cognitive activity. But now I am taking issue with something different. I'm taking issue with the way they, in their response to us, have misleadingly characterized their own previously expressed purpose.

Though they attempted to recast their intentions, they have not fully retreated from activism. They say that they "thought . . . that something should be done" (21). About what? Why, about "ideological polarization . . . hate-speech and misinformation" (21). But who said anything about those things? It seems that a number of questions have suddenly been begged. Then, almost admitting what their original position had been all along, they worry that "early and hasty endeavours had the potential to misfire or simply be ineffective" (21). Endeavors to do what? Now they seem to be suggesting that they are for efforts to reduce hate speech and misinformation. But their original statement was about being ineffective in undermining conspiracy theories. Rather than straightforwardly defend *that* position, they equivocate between conspiracy theories and "ideological polarization . . . hate-speech and misinformation."

Regarding conspiracy theories, they now present themselves as perfectly neutral, writing:

> So, what were "they" up to? Quite simply, "they" advocated for more research. "They" figured that, before "fighting" against, or "curing", conspiracy theories, it would be good to know exactly what one is talking about. Are conspiracy theories bad? Are they good? Are they *always* bad, are they *always* good? . . . "They," in fact, are "just asking" some questions. (Dieguez et al. 2016, 21)

Once again, this is a clearly misleading representation of what they were up to. They now ask in a neutral voice, "Are conspiracy theories bad?" Yet they had already answered this when they described belief in conspiracy theories as a disease and conflated it with "contemporary misinformation known as 'conspiracism'" (Basham and Dentith 2016, 17). Have they suddenly turned over a new leaf? If so, why not be honest about what they had originally said, and admit a change of heart?

Later in their response, under the heading, "A Cure?" they once again reframe their purpose in neutral terms. They write, "What 'they' had in mind, as must be clear by now, was to study how people, on their own or under some external influence, *think* and come to endorse some *beliefs* about such things" (Dieguez et al. 2016, 32). They maintain that they just want to use objective science to answer questions such as whether a new "remedy is not needed after all, as the disease might be transitory, or even not a disease at all" (33). They continue, "Scientific research turns out to be the best currently available tool to answer such questions, and that's where the analogy lies with programs devised to counter conspiracy theories." It's a curious position, if we are to take it seriously. They support "programs devised to *counter* conspiracy theories," wanting to try to make such programs *more effective*, because, they seem to suggest, "Who knows? We might end up finding that there was no problem to begin with!" But how likely is it that biased researchers, funded by grants directed for a purpose that aligns with that bias, are going to produce findings that run directly counter to that purpose and so support the conclusion that no more such funding is warranted? No conspiracy theory is needed to recognize this as a flawed, if not intellectually dishonest, approach.

5. THE MISREPRESENTATION OF OUR CRITIQUE

Naturally, since they misrepresented their original position, they needed to misrepresent our critique of it as well. And so they did. They did not focus directly on the substance of our actual critique, namely, that seeking to use what passes for science to assist the state in undermining belief in conspiracy theories (without concern to whether or not there is justification for those theories) is a bad idea. Instead, they attributed to us a number of positions that we never asserted. Then they produced a wide variety of points in response to these positions, some of which are unobjectionable, others quite problematic, but none directly germane to our central complaint.

For example, they suggest that our objection to their project involved the idea that "everything there is to know on the matter is in fact already known, and that any further attempt to investigate the topic would be a 'grave intellectual, ethical and prudential error,' or worse, a genocidal crime against the masses, destroying lives 'by the thousands, even millions'" (21). Wow! Did we write anything as crazy as that? Or, more likely, is this a rather egregious misrepresentation of our critique? Let's find out. While it is true that much of the social science research on conspiracy theorists is deeply flawed (as discussed above), we did not even mention this in our objection to their proposal. We certainly did not claim that "any further attempt to investigate the topic" would be necessarily problematic. After all, we ourselves, in our own ways, investigate the topic. No. *That* was not the problem we were pointing out. Neither did we suggest, needless to say, that *merely investigating the topic* would destroy lives by the thousands or millions. So, what exactly *did* we write? We wrote this:

> Political conspiracy theorizing in Western-style democracies should not be restricted, because to do so is a grave intellectual, ethical, and prudential error. As such, the declaration by respected scholars like these is likewise a grave intellectual, ethical and prudential error. (Basham and Dentith 2016, 15)

So, quite plainly, we were not saying that any investigation would be inappropriate. We were saying that there should not be an effort to restrict (it would have been better to have said "undermine") political conspiracy theories. *That* is what would be the "intellectual, ethical, and prudential error." And, remember, that is precisely the goal that the *Le Monde* authors were originally supporting, though they are now, in their response, not straightforwardly admitting.

We continued, writing:

> Conspiracy theory saves lives, by the thousands, even millions, if we would let it. Its automatic dismissal leaves blood on our hands. (16)

What were we talking about? Certainly *not* that merely investing the topic would result in untold carnage. Perhaps our explanation bears repeating:

High-placed political conspiracies of lesser ambition often lie behind the political catastrophes of recent history. Very recent. For example, the catastrophe of the invasion of Iraq comes to mind. There is little doubt in the public or [among] scholars that NATO, and many other governments, were intentionally misled and manipulated into this war, particularly by the U.S. government. This truth, well-evidenced at the time of grave decision, was silenced as an "outrageous conspiracy theory" by heads of state, mainstream media and yes, certain members of academia. Thus, a war that ultimately led to the death of hundreds of thousands, and a desperate global refugee crisis, was powerfully enabled by an anti-conspiracy theory panic. One that these scholars would seem to like to embrace and nurture as general policy. (14)

We gave other examples as well. So, quite plainly, we were saying that it is engaging in an effort to disable a mechanism for thwarting potentially disastrous conspiracies that "leaves blood on our hands," not merely investigating the topic. Further, let me be emphatically clear about this: the *Le Monde* authors were *not* originally advocating investigating the topic in a fair and neutral way. They have a clear bias: they assume that conspiracy theories are a disease that needs to be cured. And they have an explicit agenda: to "fight conspiracy theories effectively."

Now, I am not opposed to activism, and there is nothing inherently wrong with having an agenda. Indeed, I have an agenda in writing this. I am making a case for what I believe to be true, and defending what I think is important. But here is the crucial difference: I am not pretending to be a neutral scientist, objectively collecting the data and letting it speak for itself. These scholars, on the other hand, do claim to be in precisely that business. Perhaps that is why they have a hard time admitting their agenda. And so, having been called out for their agenda, they are now trying to claim that all they wanted to do was to dispassionately and scientifically investigate the topic. They are "just asking questions" (Dieguez et al. 2016, 28; cf. 20, 21) and gathering data, they claim. But they are not convincing. As shown above, that position is refuted by their own words in their original statement.

They also claim that we "call . . . for more conspiracy theories and less 'conspiracy theory panic'" (20). Here they are half right. It seems fair to say that we are against "conspiracy theory panic," but it is silly to say we want "more conspiracy theories." For my part, I would say that I want fairness toward conspiracy theories (a desire also expressed by Basham (2017)). I do not want to see the state allied with biased social scientists for the purpose of producing research designed to help the state undermine legitimate conspiracy theorizing. But that is not the same as calling "for more conspiracy theories," as if we think that the more conspiracy theories in circulation the better, regardless of their merits. No. We were calling out those who would employ science to try to undermine a legitimate and important activity.

In addition, they also suggest that we accused them of being part of a conspiracy (Dieguez et al. 2016, 30). But we did *not* maintain that they were *secretly* up to something morally dubious. Their morally dubious agenda was *openly* articulated in a public forum. However, given their bizarre response, it now seems that they are retrospectively trying to pretend that they were up to something different from what they clearly and repeatedly stated originally. But I, speaking just for myself, do not maintain that they *plotted* any of this. No, in this case, I favor a cock-up theory.[11]

6. PATHOLOGIZING CONSPIRACY THEORISTS

Another central concern that we raised was their pathologizing of conspiracy theorizing, suggesting that conspiracy theories are a "disease" (Basham and Dentith 2016, 17). Basham (2018) addresses this issue more broadly. I've chosen here to focus narrowly on reasoning errors in their attempt to vindicate themselves by suggesting that we are equally guilty of the same offense. They accused us of inconsistency since we oppose the *general* pathologizing of conspiracy theories and yet some of us had, on their reading, pathologized certain *particular* conspiracy theories. Hmmm. Actually, even if they had read us correctly (which in at least one case they have not), there is nothing inconsistent about that.

Since I was one of those accused of this supposed inconsistency, and since they have indeed misread me, I'll use their critique of my work to set both matters straight. Specifically, they accuse me of "delegitimiz[ing]" Roswell conspiracy believers (Dieguez et al. 2016, 26). Neither did I intend to do that nor would it have been in any way significant if I had. Here is what I wrote:

> [Sunstein and Vermeule's] deliberate intent to be dismissive becomes unambiguously apparent. Immediately after the mention of Operation Northwoods they write: "In 1947, space aliens did, in fact, land in Roswell, New Mexico, and the government covered it all up. (Well, maybe not)." This trivializes a whole list of significant conspiracies that they could not but admit were real, though the list could have been much longer. (2011, 13)

I was objecting to an obvious appeal to ridicule and inappropriate trivialization of agreed upon facts by throwing in a widely disbelieved example, accompanied with a snarky comment. As for my own position on the issue of alien visitations in general, and the Roswell incident in particular, I have no firm opinion, as I have not studied these issues in any depth (interesting though they are).

The point of the claim that I delegitimized Roswell conspiracy believers is that I had thereby, presumably, engaged in the pathologizing of a *particular* group of conspiracy theorists, as others in our group are likewise accused. This is a problem, they think, because we were critical of their attempt to pathologize conspiracy theories *in general*.

There are multiple layers of problems with their analysis. To begin with, as I have just explained, I had not even claimed that Roswell conspiracy believers were wrong, or that their belief is poorly evidenced. I did not take a position on that, and I have none. But even if I had, it would not follow that I pathologized them. Asserting that someone's position is wrong, or is not well evidenced, does not suggest that the person is defective. But that *is* what the *Le Monde* scholars seek to do. They aim to describe a presumed-to-be-defective conspiracist "mindset" (Basham and Dentith 2016, 18; Dieguez et al. 2016, 20, 23–25, 29–30, 34). And they advertise that their studies will help make efforts to undermine conspiracy theories more effective. Their project is a delegitimizing one. Ours is not. And further, even if I had pathologized *a particular group* of conspiracy theorists, that would not mean I had acted hypocritically in criticizing the *Le Monde* scholars for pathologizing conspiracy theorists *in general*. (After all, while it is wrong to generically pathologize atheists, Republicans, or Norwegians, that does not mean there are no individuals in those groups who may legitimately be regarded as, in some sense, pathological.) At minimum, pathologizing conspiracy theorists in general is an instance of *inappropriate* pathologizing, since believing in conspiracy theories is not necessarily, or even typically, pathological—even *if* there are particular instances that are (about which I have taken no position). In sum, their argument goes wrong at every turn. No wonder they value "data" and disparage reason—contrasting data, data collection, experimental designs, and empirical research with "armchair" reasoning and various derogatory versions of the same (Dieguez et al. 2016, 22, 25, and 32).

7. CONCLUSION

In their statement the *Le Monde* authors worried that without further scientific study government programs aimed at undermining conspiracy theories might backfire. Indeed, they might have; such programs are fundamentally ill conceived. What is clear is that the *Le Monde* authors' defense of their scientific project in support of this objective has itself backfired. It undermines confidence in their ability to conduct fair and reasonable studies of conspiracy theorists, or of any subject for that matter. And thus their response calls into question the wisdom of their original proposal, even if its objective had been defensible, which even they seem unwilling now to maintain. Mere incantations of the holy words *science* and *data* will not turn invalid arguments into valid ones.

This chapter should be troubling, not because it exposes the bad reasoning of a handful of social scientists, but because it raises a more general worry: How pervasive is this kind of thing? Is the research on conspiracy theorists, in particular, significantly biased, perhaps to the point of being seriously misleading? Is the scientific research on other topics likewise biased? While it is well beyond the scope of this essay to offer answers to these questions, I would like to highlight one particular issue that will be impacted by the answer: the plausibility of conspiracy theories. The less fair and reliable supposed "epistemic authorities" turn out to be, the weaker the argument against conspiracy theories based on their opposition to the views of such (supposed) epistemic authorities. From this I derive two conclusions: (1) So long as these questions have no clear and comforting answer, one should be careful about dismissing conspiracy theories based on the pronouncements of scientists or other (supposed) epistemic authorities. At least, due diligence involving critical review of their findings, rather than uncritical acceptance of them, is in order. (2) Scientists and other would-be epistemic authorities ought to be exceptionally careful to hold their biases in check, lest they unwittingly undermine their own disciplines. Everyone benefits when science is genuinely trustworthy. The costs of unreliable science are high. One cost is that false conspiracy theories cannot easily be dismissed by appealing to the judgment of those who *ought* to be epistemic authorities.[12]

NOTES

1. A shorter version of this paper, addressing only the last three points, was first published under the title, "What Are They Really Up To? Activist Social Scientists Backpedal on Conspiracy Theory Agenda." See Hagen (2017).

2. Regarding the original critique of the *Le Monde* statement (namely, Basham and Dentith 2016), it should be noted that while eight scholars, including myself, endorsed the critique, only two of us, Basham and Dentith, actually did the writing. Just to be perfectly clear, while I am proud to be associated with the critique, and refer to it as "our" response, I did not substantially contribute to it, other than offering some comments on a couple drafts. So, it seems to me perfectly sensible for it to be published as, and referenced as, "Basham and Dentith 2016," giving credit where it is due.

3. These flaws are discussed in more detail in other articles. For example, a special issue of *Argumenta*, which focuses on the ethics and epistemology of conspiracy theories, includes articles by M R. X. Dentith ("The Problem of Conspiracism" (2018)), Lee Basham ("Joining the Conspiracy" (2018)), and myself ("Conspiracy

Theories and Monological Belief Systems" (2018a)). In addition, "Conspiracy Theory Phobia," by Lee Basham and Juha Räikkä, is forthcoming in *Conspiracy Theories and the People Who Believe Them* (Oxford University Press), edited by Joseph Uscinski and Joseph Parent. Basham and Räikkä make essentially the same case as I have regarding Wood, Douglas, and Sutton (2012).

While the critiques of these studies were not yet published at the time of the *Le Monde* authors' response, and thus they can be excused for being unaware of these particular explanations of the problems with the studies in question, they are not excused from failing to notice the flaws themselves, as they were fairly obvious.

4. I thank Brian Keeley for pointing this out to me.

5. Elaborating on this point, I (2018a) provide an extensive critique of both Wood, Douglas, and Sutton (2012) and Swami et al. (2011). I (Hagen 2018b) take issue with Swami et al. (2011) (and others) on a related issue, a prejudicial conflation of "conspiracy theories," "conspiracist ideation," and "the paranoid style."

6. Citing Goertzel they write, "regardless of the facts available in the outside world, the *mind* of some people attracts and is attracted by conspiracist cognitions, which come to form a monological belief system involving conspiracies" (Dieguez et al. 2016, 22). Ted Goertzel (1994) first articulated the notion that conspiracy theorists operate within a "monological belief system." This topic is critically analyzed in Hagen (2018a).

7. This is, admittedly, a strange case of marginalization, since almost everyone is a conspiracy theorist. But it can hardly be denied that the epithet "conspiracy theorist" is often used for the purpose of marginalization and discreditation.

8. The *Le Monde* authors imply that we are "build[ing] artificial rivalries and point[ing] to imaginary enemies" (Dieguez et al. 2016, 23 n4). But the rivalry is real. Consider the title of David Coady's book, *Conspiracy Theories: The Philosophical Debate* (2006c). The "debate" is essentially between the particularists, represented by Coady and Charles Pigden, and the generalists, represented by Karl Popper, Steve Clarke, and (seemingly) Brian L. Keeley, with Lee Basham being hard to nail down at that point. (Basham is now clearly in the particularist camp, of course.) In addition to Keeley (1999) and Clarke (2002), Buenting and Taylor cite Pete Mandik, as representing the generalist camp (Buenting and Taylor 2010, 568n3). Neil Levy (2007) could also be added as offering a position that is generalist in spirit. And the distinction is not merely applicable to scholars who publish on this issue. Snooty generalist dismissal of conspiracy theories is commonplace, especially by media personalities and government officials, as well as in the academy.

Keeley's position requires some clarification. He did *explore the viability* of generalism. His "initial motivation," he writes, "was to present an analysis of conspiracy theories in the spirit of Hume's analysis of miracles" (Keeley 1999, 126), which is clearly a generalist project. As Keeley notes, "For Hume, miracles are *by definition* explanations that we are never warranted in believing" (126). However, Keeley ultimately finds this kind of analysis of conspiracy theories not to be viable. He concludes, "There is no criterion or set of criteria that provide a priori grounds for distinguishing warranted conspiracies from UCTs [unwarranted conspiracy theories]" (118). So, Keeley is not, in the end, a generalist in the sense criticized here. Still, his emphasis on (purported) problems with what he regards as *unwarranted* conspiracy theories reflects an interest in determining whether generalism can work for some *subsets* of conspiracy theories.

9. I am alluding here to an article by Stokes (2016), an expanded version of which is included as chapter 2 of this volume. I find Stokes's discussion of "defeasible generalism" and "reluctant particularism" to be useful, in part because it encourages us to think of the distinction between generalism and particularism as two ends of a spectrum, inviting the articulation of a middle ground. But I'm not sure that the ground pointed to by Stokes is not already taken. I believe that those of us in the "particularist" camp already agree that there is some degree to which general observations can give us guidance in judging particular cases. That is just to say that prior probability considerations are *relevant*, which I don't think we ever denied. Indeed, I think particularists explicitly insist on this. We simply deny that such considerations *by themselves* could lead to *the blanket dismissal of all conspiracy theories*, which is the generalist move.

10. "Conspiracy theorizing" here means theorizing about something typically regarded as a "conspiracy theory" (e.g., the JFK assassination, 9/11). Whether or not such a theory is warranted must be judged on the relevant evidence; that is the point of particularism. And it must be acknowledged that such theories are often vigorously, and in some cases cogently, defended. In contrast, "conspiracism" implies being unwarranted, "a form of misinformation." Conflating the two ideas is a way of begging a central question.

11. "Cock-up" is a British expression equivalent to the American expression "screw-up." Conspiracy theories have often been contrasted with "cock-up theories," in which unplanned blundering, rather than secretly coordinated activity, is pointed to as an explanation for some phenomenon.

12. I would like to thank M R. X. Dentith and Lee Basham for their helpful comments on earlier drafts of this chapter.

Chapter 10

Clearing Up Some Conceptual Confusions about Conspiracy Theory Theorizing

Martin Orr and M R. X. Dentith

1. INTRODUCTION

Scholars have developed two main approaches to the understanding of conspiracy theories. One position takes as its central research question the determination of the psycho-social profile of those who believe in conspiracy theories. For these scholars, whom we can call "generalists," studying conspiracy theory is important because such knowledge may enable us to prevent those inclined to believe in conspiracy theories from believing in conspiracy theories. Underlying this is the belief that conspiracism—belief in conspiracy theories—is a threat to democracy. The other approach, to which we subscribe, seeks to interrogate the concept of the "conspiracy theory" itself. The failure to do so on the part of generalists leads to conceptual confusion, and research programs such as these, based on a common-sense conceptualization of "conspiracy theory," risk producing flawed conclusions. For us, studying conspiracy theory is important because the blanket dismissal of any claim that a conspiracy is afoot will tend to blind people to the very real conspiracies that even those in the other camp acknowledge do occur. Our concern is that, in democracies that are imperfect at best, ignorance of an actual conspiracy can be at least as dangerous as the belief in a false conspiracy theory. A recent debate, in which we participated, serves to describe these two positions, and offers us an opportunity to respond by clarifying our stand.

In June 2016, a group of social scientists published an opinion piece in *Le Monde* applauding the efforts of the French government to combat the spread of "conspiracism,"[1] but lamenting that, in the government's haste, experts in the study of conspiracy theories, like the authors themselves, had not been consulted. In response, Lee Basham and M R. X. Dentith penned a reply, cosigned by David Coady, Kurtis Hagen, Ginna Husting, Martin Orr, and

Marius Hans Raab. In that, we took the authors of the *Le Monde* piece to task for advocating a cure for conspiracy theorizing (Basham and Dentith 2016). An extension and elaboration of that reply constituted the previous chapter.

Most of the authors of the original piece—Gérald Bronner, Véronique Campion-Vincent, Sylvain Delouvée, Sebastian Dieguez, Nicolas Gauvrit, Anthony Lantian, and Pascal Wagner-Egger—subsequently responded, claiming:

> What "they"[2] [the authors of the *Le Monde* piece] had in mind, as must be clear by now, was to study how people, on their own or under some external influence, *think* and come to endorse some *beliefs* about such things. That, "they" think, would need some *data*, rather than wishful thinking, ideological clamours or armchair reasoning. (2016, 32)

Because their response to Basham and Dentith left us with more questions than answers, misrepresenting our work and position along the way, we (the authors of this chapter) wrote a response. This chapter sets out to develop the points presented in that essay. Here we will engage with three systemic issues. The first is that they misrepresent the work of the scholars to whom they are responding. This seems to be an attempt to defend their position by suggesting that we agree with their characterization of the "conspiracy theory" as inherently irrational and false. Second, we point to the naive empiricism of their research project. Believing that careful consideration of one's conceptual framework can be set aside until things have been counted, they not only fail to do that essential work, but ignore the scholarship that has wrangled with these fundamental issues. Third, we believe they are engaging in a sort of special pleading; rather than engaging with this conceptual work, or contributing to it, they want more time to allow their data-gathering to resolve the conceptual issues. But as they acknowledge, in defining the "conspiracy theory" as an epistemologically unsound belief held by a "conspiracy theorist" (someone suffering from pathological "mindset" that needs to be cured), they end up embracing this circularity; they start with a working definition which presupposes the kind of evidence that will be needed to develop the definition they seek to confirm.

2. MISREPRESENTATION *EN MASSE*

A curious feature of their response is to try and make out that the authors and co-signatories of the response to the *Le Monde* piece are inconsistent, or even hypocritical. We address this first, as this is a curious move. The objective of this approach seems to be to dismiss our arguments because it turns out that, much to our surprise, we really agree with them about what a conspiracy theory is. Despite our objections to their position in Basham and Dentith's reply specifically, and despite that the corpus of the authors and co-signatories is clear in objecting to this generalist approach, they claim we conceptualize "conspiracy theory" just as they do—the irrational belief of a pathological mind, damaging to our otherwise vibrant democracies. We take issue with that for two reasons.

In general, this seems a strange approach, since inconsistencies between the publications of the co-signatories are easy to explain. First, any group of interdisciplinary scholars, no matter how closely aligned their research projects turn out to be, are bound to have points of disagreement—it is by exploring and prodding our disagreements that we advance this collective enterprise. Pointing out (relatively minor) points of contention is no substitute for looking at the merit of each of our publications individually. Second, some of the earlier work of the co-signatories (some of it over ten years old) may no longer reflect perfectly their current thinking. You would think that people refining their views would be considered an academic virtue, but it seems we are expected to hold fast to outdated views, or toe certain disciplinarian lines.

More troubling is that, in the attempt to demonstrate that our work is inconsistent and (at least occasionally) in line with their position, they achieve their goal only by misrepresenting our work. The number of these errors in their piece are too numerous to detail, so let us just point out four examples.

The first is that they misrepresent one of our own works by claiming "Dentith seems very worried by those he calls 'conspiracists'" (Dieguez et al. 2016, 26). They back up this construal by selectively quoting Dentith in such a way that seems to show a generalist skepticism towards conspiracy theories, but fail to note that Dentith is using the terminology of Quassim Cassam (2016) (whose article Dentith was critiquing) in order to show up the errors in Cassam's arguments. Dentith's point is that if Cassam is right in his construal of conspiracist ideation, then, conversely, the same faults are going to be true of the non-conspiracists as well.

Indeed, Dieguez et al. seem to have missed in their haste to find an apparent inconsistency in Dentith's work section 7 ("Stipulating Conspiracism") of the article they are critiquing, where Dentith states quite clearly:

> It might be also be the case that once we investigate Conspiracism, it turns out to be a fairly useless thesis, especially if it turns out there are not many (if any) conspiracists. However, if we are going to treat the thesis of Conspiracism seriously—and investigate it—we need to keep in mind that conspiracists are simply one kind of conspiracy theorist. The putative existence of such conspiracists does not tell us that belief in conspiracy theories *generally* is problematic. The question should be "When, if ever, is a conspiracy theorist

a conspiracist?" rather than presupposing that conspiracy theorists suffer from conspiracist ideation. (2018a, 341)

"When, if ever" are hardly the words of someone who is vexed or troubled by the existence of conspiracists. Rather, Dentith is signaling his agreement with the work of Charles Pigden, who has persuasively argued that if we are historically or politically literate, then we all end up being conspiracy theorists of some stripe (Pigden 2007). If anything, Dentith is worried that conspiracism is often portrayed in social scientific work as the only way to characterize belief in conspiracy theories, a stance which effectively assumes the answer to the question "Can belief in conspiracy theories ever be rational?"[3]

A second example of this misrepresentation is in reference to another of our works, a piece co-written by Ginna Husting and Martin Orr. It gets a similar treatment. Rather than attempting to "delegitimize the claims of alien believers" (Dieguez et al. 2016, 26), Husting and Orr write:

> While it is *tempting* to argue that Hofstadter is simply pointing to certain claims and claimants who *seem* truly misguided—for example, those who argue that aliens walk among us—*this conclusion neglects a fundamentally important process*. (2007, 140) [emphasis added]

Similar arguments can be found in the work of Lance deHaven-Smith and Matthew Witt (2013) and Jaron Harambam and Stef Aupers (2014). Michael Butter and Peter Knight argue that we cannot produce *value-neutral* research on belief in *conspiracy theories* if we are working with *value-laden* definitions (2016). Husting and Orr's meaning is clear, and the use of the example is to make a point about our inability to establish a priori the truth of a belief or claim (whether a theory or not) simply by affixing the label "conspiracy theory" to it.

A third example, also from Husting and Orr, is Dieguez et al.'s claim that people who believe that the death of Elvis Presley was faked are "extreme," suggesting, in the end, that we are in agreement that conspiracy theorists are, as a group, beyond the pale (2016, 26). Even a cursory reading makes clear that we are objecting to the use of this example, and only this example, to reject all "conspiracy theories" as a class of knowledge-claim. When we argue that "some claims characterized as conspiracy theories are false" (Husting and Orr 2007, 131), the qualifier "characterized as" is rather important to our meaning. We believe the intent in this piece seems plain enough, and our position should be obvious: the point is that not all claims characterized as conspiracy theories are false.

Fourth and most critically, while we can debate the willfulness or sloppiness of these misrepresentations, what is even worse is that they misrepresent the central argument of the piece they are directly replying to. By dropping essential qualifiers from the co-signatories' argument they commit us to views we never expressed. They claim that our position:

[C]an thus be framed as the following two-fold hypothesis: *because real conspiracies have happened and still happen, conspiracy theories are not only warranted but necessary; the only reason this is not obvious to everyone is that "conspiracy theories" have been made to reflect badly on those who assert them by the very people they purport to unmask, and their enablers.* (Dieguez et al. 2016, 21)

Yet that is not what we said in the original cosigned piece. Indeed, we are not committed to any *general* claim that "conspiracy theories are not only warranted but necessary." Rather, at best, we are committed to the following two claims that:

1. We should not dismiss theories as unwarranted *merely* because they are labeled as "conspiracy theories," and
2. We should not downplay the necessity of *conspiracy theorizing*. There should be no proscription against theorizing about conspiracies, especially in a democracy, even if it turns out that some of those conspiracy theories will be pernicious, even damaging.[4]

It is this latter point that our critics seem to have glossed over in their haste to respond. We think conspiracy theorizing is necessary in a healthy democracy even if some conspiracy theories turn out to be damaging. This is not the same as thinking each and every conspiracy theory is a public good, let alone that every conspiracy theory is warranted.

So, at best, we agree that conspiracy theories are necessary, in that open democracies should tolerate (if not promote) investigating claims of conspiracy (the investigation of which will be predicated on the expression of conspiracy theories), but nowhere do we claim that conspiracy theories are *in all cases* warranted.

Now, it seems that what our colleagues meant to say is we think conspiracy *theorizing* is warranted, given that they go on to claim:

Basham *et al.* (2016) essentially claim that conspiracy theorizing is generally warranted because there are conspiracies: that is a generalist view. (Dieguez et al. 2016, 23)

Do we think conspiracy theorizing is *generally* warranted? We certainly think it is warranted on a case-by-case basis, and that we should not dissuade people from theorizing about conspiracies generally. This distinction is

important, because the original piece in *Le Monde* argues that conspiracy theorizing *generally* is an ill that needs a cure. Our response is to say that a stipulation against such theorizing is in itself an ill, one which will likely allow
conspiracies to thrive and prosper, because to question whether there are
conspiracies occurring here-and-now will simply be considered a symptom
of conspiracism.

Perhaps, then, we might extend an olive branch and say, yes, we think
that—on some level—conspiracy theorizing is generally warranted. But this
does not commit us to any generalism about conspiracy theories; there is a
huge difference between talk of conspiracy theories and conspiracy theorizing. Thinking we should not dissuade people from theorizing about conspiracies is a long way from saying that we think conspiracy theories are *in
all cases* both warranted and necessary. Perhaps our permissiveness about
conspiracy theorizing makes the existence of conspiracy theories in our polities necessary, but it does not commit us to any claim that said theories are
necessarily warranted.

Taken individually, these errors are troubling. Taken together, these errors
indicate that our interlocutors have, to paraphrase words of Sherlock Holmes,
"seen, but not observed" (Conan Doyle 1891). It is errors like these which
make us think they wrote their response in haste: quick to anger; faster to
reply. Rather than searching the corpus of seven scholars for evidence of
apparently inconsistent views, they might look at what we have written *in
context*. A few isolated or partial quotes might make us look inconsistent, or
even foolish, but we trust our readers to be more careful.

3. A NAIVE EMPIRICISM

Misrepresenting our work is one thing, but a bigger worry is the thread that
runs throughout their reply: they are scientists, and our "armchair theorizing"
should be divorced from their method.

The tenor of their reply reminds us of Bill Murray's line from *Ghostbusters*.
"Back off man, I'm a scientist!" (Reitman 1984). Leaving to one side doc-
trinal disputes about the role of the social sciences in the grand schema of
the sciences, the lack of engagement by these social scientists in pursuing the
conceptual analysis of conspiracy theories by philosophers, sociologists, and
the like is a marker of science done badly.

They, seemingly, would find it a distraction to consider the kind of theoretical concerns we are interested in. Rather, as scientists they see their job as
going out to collect data, and then, perhaps, to theorize about said data later.
While they are timid when it comes to conceptualizing the problem, there is
no such restraint when it comes to advocating for responses to it.

The issue here is that our social scientists are taking the specter of conspiracism and conspiracists seriously, without either doing the conceptual work to first identify what counts as conspiracist ideation *before going off to find people who might suffer from it*, or acknowledging that much of this work has already been done. The work of other scholars is noticed only to misrepresent it, and to deride it *in toto* as the product of "a spiraling and self-congratulating clique of insulated theorizers" (Dieguez et al. 2016, 21). That they avoid the difficult preliminary work of clarifying concepts and their relationships appears to be our fault. However, we have made every effort to make our work public, and we do not see ourselves as members of an exclusive club. There is no secret handshake, and we encourage others to contribute to the debate. (And that the work that needs to be done can often be most comfortably performed in an armchair is beside the point).

Indeed, their whole project depends on taking the "conspiracist mindset," both cause and consequence of "conspiracy theories," as established empirical fact. Now, maybe the whole enterprise is scientific per se, but, if so, its conceptualization is taken as read, and operationalization has become operationalism. Having a ruler in hand, whatever it is we are measuring will be determined by the very act of holding a ruler up against it. This is science done badly, because it presumes the very thing it seeks to measure. What we hope to bring to this debate is a conceptual rigor, in that we think we should start with conceptual definitions prior to testing these definitions against what we take to be the evidence. This, they too, seem to want. Throughout their response our colleagues ask for more time to work out definitions, or answer fundamental questions. But even a cursory look at the literature in philosophy, sociology, or anthropology shows that many of these questions are—if not outright answered—carefully considered (as we will show in the final section). The work has been done. But rather than engage with that work, they opt for special pleading: we need more time to work out the answers for ourselves!

This disciplinarian silo-ing is disappointing, particularly in an age of interdisciplinary work and ease of access to research. Perhaps in the 1970s and 1980s being ignorant of work outside your particular field was explicable (even if it was not necessarily understandable) but here-and-now ignoring the work of other scholars on any topic comes across as deliberate, rather than accidental. It smacks of the kind of thinking which says "This is our field of interest, and you should stay away."

4. A CASE OF SPECIAL PLEADING

This brings us to our final set of worries, the fact that the reply piece penned by our colleagues ultimately rests upon special pleading.

Understandably, our social scientist colleagues present their project in the best possible light, suggesting only that they continue to conduct research in order to know what we are talking about. They write:

> So, what were "they" up to? Quite simply, "they" advocated for more research. "They" figured that, before "fighting" against, or "curing," conspiracy theories, it would be good to know exactly what one is talking about. (Dieguez et al. 2016, 21)

The problem is this: they do not consider the work from the middle of the century which shows that their naive empiricism is untenable. As W. V. Quine argued persuasively, evidence does not determine the truth of theories, because there are a potentially infinite number of theories consistent with a limited set of data points. Rather, our pre-existing theories (whether held explicitly or implicitly) end up being part of what determines what gets counted as evidence for said theories (Quine 1951). But perhaps requiring social scientists to be *au fait* with mid-twentieth-century metaphysics is unfair. However, as social scientists, they are more likely to be familiar with the work of C. Wright Mills, who might suggest that "only within the curiously self-imposed limitations of their arbitrary epistemology have they stated their questions and answers. . . . [They] are possessed by . . . methodological inhibition" (Mills 1959).

You cannot gather evidence without already assuming something about the phenomena you are studying, so the claim they are simply advocating for more research before they settle upon the definitional issue gets things back-to-front. Knowing "exactly what one is talking about" should be a precondition of sound operationalization. If one is to measure something, it is important to spell out what you are trying to measure. This is especially important if you are trying to quantify phenomena that may by nature be better understood as qualities than as quantities.

The idea we can research a topic without knowing the terms of the topic seems rather backwards. If we do not define what counts as a "conspiracy theory," how do we begin to measure when someone believes in such a theory, let alone whether that belief is rational or irrational? It is clear "they" think they know what a conspiracy theory is, because they research belief in them. So why the reluctance to settle on a definition? Is it because settling on a definition would lead to problems in making their work seemingly fit together as the product of a coherent research program?

This is an especially galling problem, because they specifically ask:

> Are conspiracy theories bad? Are they good? Are they always bad, are they
> always good? Who endorses them, who produces them, and why? Are there
> different types of conspiracy theories, conspiracy theorists, and conspiracy con-
> sumers? (Dieguez et al. 2016, 21)

These questions have already been addressed in research published by
scholars such as ourselves. Indeed, for a fulsome accounting of the problems
of defining what counts as a conspiracy theory, and how our chosen
definitions often presuppose answers to the research questions we are asking,
they could do worse than look at the first three chapters of Dentith's book,
The Philosophy of Conspiracy Theories. (2014)

Indeed, for researchers in search of a definition, they seem to have an awful
lot to say about the definition they claim to have not yet settled upon. For
example, they claim:

> [A]sserting that a conspiracy theory is any kind of thinking or explanation that
> involves a conspiracy—real, possible or imaginary—and that's all there is to it,
> seems like a premature attempt to settle the issue, as if the topic itself was a non-
> topic and anyone—and that's a lot of people—who thinks there is something
> there of interest is simply misguided, or manipulated. (Dieguez et al. 2016, 22)

That is to say, not only are they at least *aware* that scholars have presented
definitions of what counts as a "conspiracy theory," but they have found said
definitions *wanting*. That—at the very least—means they are operating with
some definition of the subject-at-hand.[5] (And we would be the last to suggest
that conspiracy theories are not of interest.)

So, what is their definition?

> For the time being, thus, a "conspiracy theory" is what the conspiracist mindset
> tends to produce and be attracted to, an apparently circular definition that rests
> on ongoing work but is firmly grounded in relevant research fields such as cog-
> nitive epidemiology, niche construction and cognitively driven cultural studies,
> and could be refined or refuted depending on future results. (Dieguez et al.
> 2016, 30)

Where do we start? They define conspiracy theories as irrational to believe
despite earlier in their piece admitting some conspiracy theories have turned
out to be warranted. Either they think those warranted theories somehow
only became rational to believe over time (at which point we can say they
are ignorant of the history of certain prominent examples) or they are being
inconsistent with their terminology. Both issues have long been addressed

in the wider academic literature (see Dentith (2014) for a summary of those discussions).

It follows from their definition, then, that a conspiracy theorist is simply a believer in some irrational theory about a conspiracy. That is, they portray conspiracy theorists as being *merely* conspiracists. It is telling that they defend their scientific endeavor by pointing only toward weird and wacky conspiracy theories. They ask why alien shape-shifting reptile theories persist, and, yes, that is a good question. Yet they do not talk about the alleged conspiracy theories which turned out to be warranted nonetheless, like the Moscow Show Trials, the Gulf of Tonkin Incident, or Watergate. They ask us to explain why unwarranted conspiracy theories persist. We could ask them to explain how they would have reacted to John Dewey's claim the Moscow Trials were rigged back in the 1930s, or to the claim that US intelligence agencies were sweeping up intercontinental communications (subsequently documented by Edward Snowden). It is as if these examples of people theorizing about actual conspiracies (yet being accused at the time of being irrational conspiracy theorists) are not of interest to them. Could it be because the theoretical basis for their scientific endeavor is entirely predicated on the idea that conspiracy theorists are not only gullible or subject to confirmation bias, but pathologically so—to the point that scientifically-informed state intervention is desirable?

What makes this all the worse is they *acknowledge* they start with a circular definition (or at least a definition that is "apparently circular"—although how this circularity is only apparent or illusory isn't addressed). They are quite clear in what they believe: a conspiracy theory is the sort of thing that attracts a deficient type of person, one plagued by a conspiracy mindset (which is assumed to be a problem from the get-go, rather than, say, the more widespread problems of confirmation bias, or premature closure of inquiry). Even more damning is that they seem completely unconcerned that research based on a circular definition is problematic. Even the most sophisticated research designs will produce indefensible conclusions if based upon shifting and illogical definitions. Yes, people who believe things that are not true is potentially a problem, so why not start there? That they proceed from a circular definition of the core concept, and then expect empirical research to fix fundamental conceptual problems, is just bad research design.

5. THE CRUX OF THE MATTER

We stand, then, by our earlier claim that these social scientists seem to be committed to shutting down talk of conspiracy theories (see the previous chapter; see also Basham and Dentith 2016). After all, why would they not?

While they repeatedly acknowledge that there are "good" (i.e., warranted) conspiracy theories, these have no place in their research. They believe them to be, in all cases, the flawed beliefs of defective people.

Before you decide something needs fixing, you need to come up with something other than a circular definition that rests on the existence of something that is demonstrated only by the research conducted premised upon your circular definition.

This, then, is the heart of our disagreement. We (both the authors of this article, and the undersigned of the piece the social scientists replied to) have done the conceptual work the social scientists claim they want to uncover in their empirical work. Now, they could embrace that, and consider the work of their academic peers seriously, using it to look at the cases where beliefs in conspiracy go awry (and also at those wonderful examples where it turned out the conspiracy theory was not just true, but well-evidenced and warranted to believe from the outset). This might require them to rethink some of their assumptions, but the thing about unexamined assumptions is that they can lead to research programs which end up being quite unscientific. While they claim that their research might even demonstrate that conspiracy theorizing is not even a disease at all, reaching that conclusion seems unlikely at best. Their diagnosis is baked into their premises.

They believe that conspiracy theories are important to study due to the "apparent proliferation of conspiracy theories among youths, a trend many deem worrying in the wake of several terrorist attacks on French soil, and in a context of ethnic and religious tensions, increased ideological polarization and ready online access to hate-speech and misinformation" (Dieguez et al. 2016, 30). Given their objective, reducing the pernicious (yet wholly undocumented) effects of conspiracism as such, it seems that they've already reached the "conclusion" that we are dealing with a serious social pathology.

Above all, in dealing with social pathology, what you do not do is assume the beneficence of those concerned about "the kids targeted by the programs" (Dieguez et al. 2016, 30). That governments might discourage children from thinking critically about their governments (and the corporations they often serve), despite the very real history of the criminal abuse of power, seems to concern them only because they had not been consulted. True, children should be taught critical thinking. They should be shown the evidence and taught how to assess the arguments that vaccines do not cause autism, that the Earth is round, and that Elvis probably is in fact dead (at least by now). They should also be taught that people, most dangerously people in positions of power, sometimes conspire. After all, if we want subsequent generations to be historically or politically literate, then we need to show them the evidence that past and current generations have had a tendency to engage in conspiracies. Telling people that it would be silly to suggest that the France, the United States, and the United Kingdom have not conspired against much of the rest of the world is unlikely to be persuasive.

Apparently, though, "armchair philosophizing" (or, better put, careful conceptualization of research problems) might interfere with their research and advocacy. This tendency to ignore the work of philosophers, sociologists, anthropologists, and the like shows a stunning lack of insight into the role such theorists have had on the development of the scientific method over the twentieth century. Yes, those with a conspiracist mindset might conceivably sully a democracy (were there a good example to test against). Conversely, if we treat all conspiracy theorizing as pathological (as *merely* conspiracist in nature), then we run the risk of ignoring very real conspiracies in our polities. That is, are we more concerned with false positives or false negatives?

The conceptual work being ignored by social scientists such as Dieguez et al. is the underpinning of good, rigorous science. We do not exist in opposition to their work. Rather, we clarify the theoretical definitions upon which quality research is grounded. Scientists who work without definitions (or try to hand-wave away their need for them) ultimately produce results which can be easily questioned. If we start our work without defining what a "conspiracy theory" is, how can we possibly measure what counts as belief in one? And if we do not know what a conspiracy theory is, how can we ultimately identify who the conspiracy theorists are? Perhaps getting to grips with the theoretical work would just get in the way of their "science," but if they are not willing to engage with the conceptual analysis of these things called "conspiracy theories," then they—we argue—open their research to questions they are ill-equipped to handle.

NOTES

1. We use "conspiracism" here to refer to belief in conspiracy theories. The term itself is typically a pejorative, and refers to a general unwarranted belief in conspiracy theories. One of us has taken this pejorative to task; see Dentith 2018a.

2. A curious artifact of Dieguez et al.'s reply is their reference to themselves as "they" throughout; they seem to have mistaken the authors of the original co-signed piece's references to them as "they" as if they were being presented as members of a sinister cabal (as opposed to it simply being the convention in English to refer to members of a group as "they" or "them").

3. See also Dentith (2017b).

4. As for the second clause; we do not know what they are trying to say, and have to assume that as the authors are French, it is a bad translation of some otherwise pithy point.

5. We leave to the side that, once again, our social scientist friends have failed to capture or present this work accurately. These definitions they claim make the topic

a non-starter are, in fact, aimed at looking at the broad class of theories covered by such a general definition, such that we can get to the heart of the question of how we judge and appraise such theories.

Chapter 11

To Measure or Not to Measure?

Psychometrics and Conspiracy Theories

Marius Hans Raab

Abstractly, it would seem illogical to try to measure the worth of a religion's fruits in merely human terms of value. How CAN you measure their worth without considering whether the God really exists who is supposed to inspire them?

—William James, *The Varieties of Religious Experience* (1902)

Psychology is measuring. When Wilhelm Wundt established the first institute for experimental psychology in 1879, he founded modern psychology as an independent academic discipline. The first experiment: Measuring the time passing between an acoustic signal and a participant pressing a button. The research question: Does conscious thinking take time?

Psychological experimentation introduces the problem of measuring psychological states and variables. Getting the time between a bell ringing and a button press with millisecond precision and accuracy was already possible in 1897. Yet we often are interested in emotions, in personality, and in the processes and results of cognitive labor. Can we translate those latent concepts into numbers? Can we measure the worth of a religion's fruits in mere human terms of value without considering whether God really exists, as William James asked in 1902? Applied to our topic we can ask: Can we measure the belief in conspiracy theories without knowing exactly what a conspiracy theory (CT) is supposed to be?

Luckily, the answer is *yes*. However, it is an "in principle yes, but . . ." Understanding the power and the pitfalls of contemporary conspiracy theory research makes some understanding necessary as to how psychologists measure. This chapter is set out to give a very brief overview of theoretical principles of testing. It will then describe examples of different data collection methods, as well as methods that have not yet been widely used

155

in conspiracy theory research. The chapter will conclude with considerations about the current psychological focus of conspiracy theory research, and why looking at the interactions of believers with the structure and content of theories would contribute to a deeper understanding of the phenomenon.

1. THEORETICAL FOUNDATIONS OF PSYCHOLOGICAL TESTING

Wilhelm Wundt's psychological lab is just one example of the roots of modern psychology. Alfred Binet and Théodore Simon published the Binet-Simon-Test in 1905. Intelligence was for the first time the subject of a standardized measure. Hugo Münsterberg, at the beginning of the twentieth century, developed instruments to assess job performance, and founded what we today know as organizational psychology.

Concepts like *intelligence* and *job performance* are complex. To handle them in a meaningful way, they have to be defined and mapped to a finite set of statements. The more specific the statements, the better. This operationalization is more straightforward when specific behavior is involved. To explore environmental awareness, the question "I take the bike instead of the car on ___ days per week, if possible" does have an apparent behavioral connection to an environmental impact. The motives behind this decision (maybe environmental awareness; saving money; or appearing progressive), however, are not captured by this question.

Concerning beliefs, such behavioral grounding is not always possible. There is an epistemic paradox. For example, to measure conspiracy belief, we might ask if a person believes that Lee Harvey Oswald shot JFK. That this question is even valid for measuring conspiracy belief is, however, first and foremost a hypothesis (Gadenne 1984). We can match this question with similar questions, and with other conspiracy scales, but without some objective criteria for what constitutes conspiracy belief in the first place, the tautological character of such questions will remain (Galliker 2016). It is advisable to ground such questions in theory; but as soon as these questions are used to evaluate theories, we are trapped in circular reasoning. At the end of the day, we rely on consistency and face validity for non-observable psychological features—and on academic discourse to clarify and improve our operationalization.

A set of questions that bears a high face validity, which is clear in language, refined through discussion with experts, and grounded in theory, is a good starting point for belief and attitude research. However, when confronted with such questions, some things have to happen in a participant's mind before he or she will be able to mark the answer in the questionnaire. Let us consider the first item from the Conspiracy Mentality Questionnaire (GMQ) (Bruder, Haffke, Neave, Nouripanah, and Imhoff 2013):

I think that many very important things happen in the world which the public is never informed about.
certainly not ___   0 1 2 3 4 5 6 7 8 9 10 ___   certainly

Components of the response process in the participant's mind are (see also Tourangeau, Rips, and Rasinski, 2000 for detailed discussion and a comparison of relevant literature):

- **Comprehension**: A participant has to identify what the question is about—here, important things happening without the public being told—and what is meant by that: Who is "the public," and what is meant by "important things"?
- **Retrieval**: "[E]xisting evaluations, vague impressions, general values, and relevant feelings and beliefs" (Tourangeauet al. 2000, 194) are drawn from memory. In this response model, attitudes are not seen as some fixed evaluation resting in a cognitive file drawer. Rather, they are generated or updated when needed. Context effects, cognitive heuristics (see Tversky and Kahneman, 1974) and recent encounters will influence what "comes to mind." *Important things* here are not straightforwardly retrieved from memory, because they must be something hidden, *which the public is never informed about.*
- **Judgment**: The evaluation of the material retrieved is subject to distortions, too. Memories can be dismissed as too specific, too general, too recent or too distant. Context (instructions, other questions) will influence what is considered relevant.
- **Response**: The judgment is then mapped to the question's scale. The scale's anchor points and granularity influence this final step.

Not all of these steps are necessarily conscious (or even present for every answer). The retrieval and judgment of relevant memories, for example, will be a fast and automatic process when the participant is familiar with the questionnaire's topic, and has relevant experience. Yet, even then, responding is a multi-step process—and thus, susceptible to distortion.

Test theory has become an important branch of psychology (for an introduction, see Embretson and Reise, 2000) with refined models. The supposed additivity (inherent to the General Linear Model, GLM, that underlies many common inductive statistics like Pearson's correlation, t-test, and Analysis of Variance/ANOVA) is one of the most criticized assumptions. In the majority of personal psychological tests—intelligence, personality, attitudes, clinical psychology—all the answer scores are summed up. When a test is supposed to measure different facets (i.e., factors) of a phenomenon, the summing up is done for each scale. Among the most famous multi-factorial psychological approaches is the five-factor model of personality (Costa and McCrae 1992), also known as the *Big Five*. A person's personality is understood here in terms of *openness to experience, conscientiousness, extraversion, agreeableness*, and *neuroticism* (neuroticism translates more or less for *emotional instability*).

Two sample items for big five neuroticism are: "I get upset easily" and "I worry about things" (five-point Likert scale, from *strongly disagree* to *strongly agree*). Already there are several answer combinations that would result in the same overall score. One person might get upset easily, without ever worrying. Another one might ruminate constantly, while being calm as a rock. Do both persons have the same *amount* of neuroticism? After all, is it justified to treat neuroticism as something purely *quantitative*? The same goes for conspiracy belief: When two individuals differ in a conspiracy belief score, then what is the psychological nature of said difference? The prima facie assumption that the difference is a quantitative one is hard to test, and especially hard to falsify, "and, so, in the absence of additional, relevant evidence; [there is] not a sound basis for the conclusion that the numerical data procured via the contrived devices is a measure of anything" (Michell 1999, 22).

The epistemic questions inherent to any psychological measurement—of which only some were mentioned here—is definitely something many researchers are aware of. We can safely assume they do not take such concerns lightly, and take precautions when validating their instruments.

Yet, when those measures, instruments, scales, and inventories are applied to conspiracy-related research questions, those epistemic uncertainties are usually not made explicit. The scale is taken as given. The results are then related to measures (personality, values, attitudes, . . . whatever psychology has to offer) that should be treated with caution, too, even if they are regarded as "standard instruments." We should, then, pause for a moment when reading the latest conspiracy-related study, given that the epistemic feet of contemporary, empirical psychological research are part iron and part clay.

2. GETTING DATA ON CONSPIRACY
THEORIES: CURRENT APPROACHES

Ted Goertzel's "Belief in Conspiracy Theories" (1994) is one of the most influential academic publications on conspiracy theories. It is remarkable for several reasons:

- It identifies (some) conspiracy theories as examples of *monological systems*; that is, belief systems that "speak only to themselves, ignoring their context in all but the shallowest respects" (740). Up to this day researchers continue to seek to understand what constitutes such a monological belief system (e.g., Swami et al., 2011; Wood, Douglas, and Sutton, 2012).
- It is an empirical paper, drawing conclusions from a telephone survey with 348 New Jersey residents. Participants were asked about their approval of ten common conspiracy theories (e.g., the assassinations of JFK and Martin Luther King Jr., and the spread of AIDS).
- It identifies anomia and interpersonal trust as factors influencing conspiracy belief. These concepts have been explored further in the following years (e.g., Abalakina-Paap, Stephan, Craig, and Gregory, 1999; Leman and Cinnirella, 2013; Miller, Saunders, and Farhart, 2015).
- It calls for more sophisticated empirical approaches, namely "time series data to determine how change in belief about one conspiracy affects change in belief in another [. . .], content analyses of published literature or [. . .] depth interviews" (741).

However, that last point—the necessity for more refined empirical approaches—has not been seen in subsequent years. Temporal dynamics—the condition that believers and narrations might change over time—have not been focused on so far as this would require longitudinal studies and tenacity on the part of the researchers. Depth interviews—a structured approach where the person interviewed has the freedom to explore feelings, thoughts, standpoints, and to shape the conversation's direction—have similarly not been part of the agenda in the years subsequent. Psychological research has, instead, confined itself to surveys and questionnaires, where assessments of common conspiracy topics (like JFK and HIV) have been routinely employed.

3. QUESTIONNAIRE APPROACHES
TO CONSPIRACY BELIEFS

With all the different definitions (see, for example, Brotherton and French, 2014; Coady, 2006; Popper, 1958) measurement of what constitutes conspiracy belief is all but straightforward. There is a hypothetical construct that we might call "conspiracy belief" or "conspiracist ideation": We assume that, in people's heads, cognitive, emotional and motivational processes are intertwined in such a way that they relate to narratives we call "conspiracy theories" in a non-random way. This assumption is necessarily an axiomatic one, as we cannot verify or refute something that is hypothetical in the first place. If we accept this premise, we might then ask: How do people differ? Can they have more or less of this feature? By asking the right questions, we might discover such individual differences.

The first widely acknowledged attempt at compiling a canonical set of questions aiming at conspiracy belief was the *Belief in Conspiracy Theories Inventory* (BCTI) (Swami, Chamorro-Premuzic, and Furnham 2010), a compilation of fourteen items describing common conspiracy theories. For example, participants have to state if they agree with the notion that JFK was not killed by Lee Harvey Oswald, but instead fell victim to an organized conspiracy. In the same publication, a seventeen-item 9/11 conspiracy belief scale was compiled and evaluated. Around the same time, an unpublished collection of thirty-eight items by Bruder and Manstead, the *Conspiracy Theory Questionnaire* (CTQ), was also being used in research (e.g., by Darwin, Neave, and Holmes 2011).

Two years later, two novel scales entered the stage of psychological conspiracy theory research. The *Conspiracy Mentality Questionnaire* (CMQ) (Bruder et al. 2013) is a scale comprised of five items. It is derived from the CTQ, focusing on the five items out of the thirty-eight that do not ask about specific instances of supposed conspiracies, but, rather, relate to a general mindset. For example, one item states: "I think that there are secret organizations that greatly influence political decisions." The authors also provide a German and a Turkish translation.

At the same time, the *Generic Conspiracists Belief* Scale (GCB) (Brotherton, French, and Pickering 2013) was published. In the process of constructing the scale, the authors had compiled seventy-five items aiming at generic conspiracy belief. In those questions, actors like "powerful organizations" and "the government" were connected to concealed activities and cover-ups. Employing a factor analysis, the authors settled on five facets of conspiracy belief: *governmental malfeasance, extra-terrestrial cover-up, malevolent global conspiracies, personal wellbeing,* and *control of information.* In the final scale, each factor is represented by three items.

Each of the aforementioned scales went through a thorough empirical process. The BCTI was validated with a sample of 257 participants (with demographic characteristics being representative of the British population) by relating the BCTI score to the 9/11 score, to personality traits, and to political cynicism (Swami et al. 2010). In a study with 7,766 volunteers from five different countries, the CMQ data was said to be "consistent with the assumption that conspiracy mentality—at its core—constitutes a one-dimensional construct" (Bruder et al. 2013, 10). For the GCB, the authors concluded that a "five-factor model was a better fit for the data than a unidimensional model" (Brotherton et al. 2013, 8), with a sample of 500 participants recruited online.

So, then, there are two distinct approaches: Going for specific conspiracy beliefs using the BCTI—or aiming at generic conspiracist ideations with the CMQ or the GCBS (raising the question as to whether conspiracist ideation is a one-dimensional or a multi-faceted construct). To add to this confusion, a recent re-examination of different measures found "poor factorial and convergent validity" for the CMQ that "may reflect underlying problems with the construct validity of this measure" (Swami et al. 2017, 22). Correlations with other measures were also rather low, and the one-dimension assumption could not be validated. The five-factor assumption for the GCB scale did not hold either, with "confusion about its latent structure and whether it taps a single or multiple dimensions of conspiracist ideation (Swami et al. 2017, 23).

A recent addition to the zoo of conspiracy belief scales is a one-item measure by Lantian, Muller, Nurra, and Douglas (2016), where the whole concept of conspiracy belief is reduced to the question "I think that the official version of the events given by the authorities very often hides the truth" (1 = completely false to 9 = completely true). In contrast, Wood (2017) proposes a scale, the *Flexible inventory of conspiracy suspicions* (FICS), for a detailed exploration of a single belief. The FICS consists of seventeen (long-form) or five (short-form) statements of conspiracy suspicions, where the conspiracy theory in question has to be filled by the researcher.

For all these scales, there is, to a certain extent, convergent validity; that is, there are intercorrelations between the measures when applied to the same sample (for example, see Swami et al., 2017).

For any survey, participants are necessary. Psychological research over the past few decades has often relied on convenience sampling; that is, young white people, mostly women, with a high education, and who happen to study psychology. The requirement to participate in studies was, and is still, commonplace in most psychology undergraduate programs to receive mandatory course credit (a practice increasingly coming under fire, see for example Shore (2016) and Samrai (2017). In recent years, Amazon's Mechanical Turk (MTurk) has also gained popularity. Work—like the filling-out of surveys—can be outsourced on demand at low cost (for example, Craft, Ashley, and Maksl, 2017, paid fifty cents for a completed survey), allowing for large sample sizes (recent examples of studies using MTurk are: Castanho Silva, Vegetti, and Littvay, 2017; Craft et al., 2017; Lantian, Muller, Nurra, and Douglas, 2017; Joanne M. Miller, Saunders, and Farhart, 2015; Swire, Berinsky, Lewandowsky, and Ecker, 2017). Analyses of MTurk's sample representativeness and data quality have been positive (Buhrmester, Talaifar, and Gosling 2018; Buhrmester, Kwang, and Gosling 2011), but some authors have pointed out that MTurk participants might be younger and more liberal than the general population. Also, habitual responses, shown by more routine

MTurk workers, might present concerns about the validity of their responses (Berinsky, Huber, and Lenz 2012).

As we have seen, research on conspiracy belief and conspiracist ideation does not suffer from a lack of measurement scales. Thanks to platforms like MTurk, it also does not suffer from a lack of study participants. Yet, one pitfall here is the danger of *reification*. We have to keep in mind that conspiracy belief is a hypothetical construct, and all these questionnaires ask for self-assessments—and those are prone to error. Comprehension, retrieval, judgment, and finally mapping of the judgment onto a given scale (Tourangeauet al. 2000) all introduce ambiguity. The assumption that test results for attitude questions are a measurement on an interval scale is controversial. A strict statistical interpretation would suggest that we should refrain from procedures like bivariate/Pearson correlation and fall back to more robust statistics like Spearman's rho. Standard procedure, however, is to treat all data as interval scaled—even for single attitude items (like in Lantian et al., 2016).

The bottom line: We get a score for each participant that is related to how he or she thinks about conspiracy theories; we do not get the belief itself. The discussion over the dimensionality of conspiracy belief further indicates that there is some level of ambiguity—and that different scales cover slightly different aspects of what we might call "belief in conspiracy theories." Also, the luxury of easily accessible samples via MTurk might allow for sample sizes with $N \gg 1000$; but that does not automatically translate to a greater validity of the results.

4. CONTENT ANALYSIS: BLOGS, FACEBOOK, AND THE NEWS

A different line of research has focused on digital records. Instead of asking people about their conspiracy beliefs (which requires reaching out to people to answer our questions in the first place), we are now looking at the traces: the trails and footprints people leave in digital environments.

The article "Private Traits and Attributes Are Predictable from Digital Records of Human Behaviour" by Kosinski, Stillwell, and Graepel (2013) is remarkable on several levels. While many knew (or, at least, suspected) for years that activities in the digital world might be used to profile people, most of them were shocked how easily accessible data—here, Facebook "Likes"—can be used for quite accurate predictions about a single person. For this study, the "Likes" of 58,466 people who had volunteered to participate were matched with psychometric scores and survey data. Ethnicity, religion, gender, political sway—all these attributes could be guessed with a prediction accuracy of greater than 80 percent. The authors were also able to predict intelligence and personality traits like openness and emotional stability. Rather harmless preferences might also allow for some far-reaching conclusions: Liking "Hello Kitty," for instance, was associated with a less agreeable and emotionally stable personality, with the users "more likely to have Democratic political views and to be of African-American origin, predominantly Christian" (Kosinski et al. 2013, 5805). "[T]he predictability of individual attributes from digital records of behaviour may have considerable implications, because it can easily be applied to large numbers of people without obtaining their individual consent and without them noticing" (Kosinskiet al. 2013, 5805). All the (conspiracy) theories about Cambridge Analytica and the supposed targeting of swing voters in the Brexit debate and the 2016 US elections are rooted in the technology that was successfully implemented in this paper. Fear of surveillance, fear of being manipulated, fear of being transparent for the algorithms of multi-billion companies—Kosinski et al. (2013) have demonstrated that these fears are more than just unwarranted paranoia. At the same time, they have demonstrated that we can learn quite a lot about people by looking at their behavior on the Internet.

The online discussion of 9/11 in comment sections has been investigated by Wood and Douglas (2013). They searched for news articles in the wake of the tenth anniversary of the 9/11 attacks. Human coders determined which conspiracy theories were mentioned, how hostile the comment was, and if expressions of mistrust and powerlessness were present. In a re-evaluation of the data gathered here, Wood and Douglas (2015) regard the content analysis of comment sections a "sound" and "instructive insight into the conspiracist mindset" (6) that might be especially useful for "populations that would be averse to filling out questionnaires" (6).

Lewandowsky, Oberauer, and Gignac (2013) used blogs to post links to an online survey about climate change denial and other conspiracy theories including the rejection of science. They found a strong correlation (r = .80) between the rejection of climate science and the advocacy of an unregulated, free market.

The authors did not stop here. They closely monitored the blogosphere's response (Lewandowsky, Cook, Oberauer, and Marriott, 2013) where posters hypothesized that, for example, the initial survey was scammed, or that data was suppressed. This second paper, "Recursive Fury: Conspiracist Ideation in the Blogosphere in Response to Research on Conspiracist Ideation," sparked discussions in the publisher's comment section about ethics and consent. While the publisher did not find issue with the "academic and ethical aspects" (Frontiers in Psychology Editorial Office 2014), the paper was eventually retracted (Zucca and Fenter 2014).

The phenomenon of *echo chambers* (beliefs being amplified or reinforced through repetition within a closed system) was investigated by Quattrociocchi, Scala, and Sunstein (2016). The authors found that debunking—that is, the exposing of false or exaggerated claims—does not reach the intended audience: "[O]ut of 9,790,906 polarized conspiracy users, just 117,736 interacted with debunking posts" (13), that is about 1.3 percent.

Three million comments made by thirty thousand users—in Bessi (2016)—and the posts of over four hundred Facebook groups (science and conspiracy related) for a period of five years, have been subjected to automated analysis, and features like punctuation, usage of emoticons, vulgarity, and word length are supposed to reveal the character traits of the posters (Mairesse, Walker, Mehl, and Moore 2007). Bessi concludes that "the prevalent personality model is the same in both echo chambers" (9), with a tendency to be suspicious and antagonistic that was even stronger for the science fraction.

Nied, Stewart, Spiro, and Starbird (2017) have similarly undertaken an exploratory analysis of the propagation of conspiracy-related information on Twitter, and they found that alternative explanations were shared by people spanning many different political mainstream views (and that about one quarter of all tweets containing alternative narratives were made by bots).

Network analysis is not confined to Facebook and Twitter. Any data source that includes conspiratorial content and allows for cross-references might be harvested, as demonstrated by Zinoviev (2017) for the Amazon recommendation engine ("Customers who bought this item also bought . . .").

Instead of asking people, these researchers were looking at traces left in blogs, in comment sections, and on social media. This saves us any consideration about which scale to pick; and we do not have to recruit participants. The conspiracy stories are there, accessible via web-scraping programs, or directly via application-program interfaces (APIs) that are provided by social media sites for scientific purposes.

From an epistemic point of view, the waters are a bit muddy for such content-based approaches. With questionnaires, the focus of research is clearly on people. A story, be it a short tweet or a long blog post, is a deliberate and motivated action carried out by an individual. Personality, topic, language skills, and intended target audience are influencing factors; acute conditions like time pressure and mood will also play a role. We get valuable insights on a group level, on the propagation of information, and on hot topics and the surrounding discussion climate. But we should not assume that those people who are very active in online discussions are the most representative of their kind, and that the stories they propagate are the most relevant for a given discourse.

It would be foolish not to use the treasure of data floating around the Internet. Especially for communities that are hard to reach in real life, online communication is valuable data (see Holtz, Kronberger, and Wagner, 2012, also for a discussion of methodological issues). For conspiracy theories, message boards and social media can be considered a natural habitat. A recipe to avoid arbitrariness—given enough data, there will always be some correlations—however, would be to be strict in formulating clear and testable hypotheses before the analysis.

5. BEYOND QUESTIONNAIRES— OTHER RESEARCH METHODS

Questionnaires, as well as content analyses, are valuable but of limited means. We do not know if, and to what extent, beliefs measured with a questionnaire will guide a person's everyday actions. Which stories will he or she adopt and propagate? Will there be consequences with respect to important life decisions? Even studies addressing behavioral aspects mostly operate with hypothetical behavior. Jolley and Douglas (2014), for instance, in a study on vaccination intentions, asked participants "to *imagine* a scenario in which they were the parent of an infant (Sophie, aged 8 months)" (3, emphasis added).

Content analysis, on the other hand, operates with conspiracy *theories* directly and all their shades and varieties in content, structure, and habitat. Yet even here, we're missing the people behind the stories. Their beliefs, attitudes, hopes, and fears are hidden behind pseudonyms.

One major challenge in CT research will be to bring together people's beliefs, people's actions, and the stories people adopt and share. Depth interviews, as suggested by Goertzel (1994), have not been a standard method in conspiracy research so far. A notable exception is Franks, Bangerter, Bauer, Hall, and Noort (2017). They saw that the content and structure of conspiracy theories are a blind spot in much psychological research: "[I]t remains unclear how individuals use elements of a conspiratorial worldview in sensemaking. [. . .] [F]urther insight would be gained into the symbolic foundations of a conspiratorial worldview. For example, epistemically, does a person believe all of the CTs they believe in the same way [. . .]? And ontologically, do the CTs all draw on the same everyday commonsense ontology [. . .]?" (3)

Franks et al. (2017) describe how hard and laborious it can be to find participants for interviews. People in online forums, for example, did not respond to requests for interviews. When the authors tried to talk to people outside a Bilderberg Group meeting, they were even physically assaulted. After gaining the trust of some gatekeepers, eighteen people finally decided to participate. The semi-structured interviews which followed focused on personal background, David Icke, religion, and social contacts; analysis and interpretation was abductive and focused on the following themes: reality, ontology, self-view, group affiliation, political action, and their view on the future. The authors conclude that "the sense of community, the pantheon of leaders, the personal conversion journey, the link to political action, and the optimistic future—are at odds with the typical image of monological conspiracy theory believers as paranoid, cynical, anomic, irrational individuals (Douglas et al., 2016). Instead, the conspiracy theory worldview may be the underpinning of a nascent social movement, prefigurative political mobilization, or, at the very least, an inchoate, but distributed community of engaged citizens, albeit with alternative beliefs."

Another approach to connect people and their stories was suggested in Raab, Auer, Ortlieb, and Carbon (2013); and Raab, Ortlieb, Auer, Guthmann, and Carbon (2013). For their method of *narrative construction*, short statements about a given topic were compiled from real world sources. They used information from the official 9/11 commission report and statements from blog posts and comments implying that the US government was completely taken by surprise (SURPRISE), had known about the 9/11 terror attacks beforehand without taking countermeasures (Let it happen on purpose; LiHoP) or even had orchestrated the attacks itself (Make it happen on Purpose; MiHoP; a distinction made by Daniele Ganser, 2006). The statements were printed on cards, and participants had to construct the 9/11 course of events they deemed most plausible.

Obviously, it is crucial to balance the information, so that SURPRISE/ LiHoP/MiHoP are present for different narrative categories (like motive, perpetrator, or role of the media). The method allows participants to actually engage in a cognitive story-telling mode, that is, to actively evaluate and connect information. At the same time, the restriction to a limited number of statements/cards allows for a better comparison of stories between subjects (compared to unrestricted source material). The emphasis here is on cognitive and behavioral aspects of storytelling; but it can be combined with any other questionnaire to connect beliefs, attitudes and stories.

On a continuum from *fast and easy* to *extremely cumbersome*, there's one psychological method that marks the upper bound of resource-intensive, structured, not appliance-driven research: the Heidelberg Structure-formation Technique or *Heidelberger Struktur-Lege-Technik, SLT* (Scheele and Groeben, 1988; Scheele and Groeben 1986). It is a multi-stage approach where depth interviews are just the first step. For every individual in the sample, the topic in question is explored by discussing pre-defined aspects and categories. For example, researching subjective work-related identity theories of LGBT people, Frohn (2013) asked six people about identity, discrimination, resilience, and competences related to personal LGBT experience at the workplace. Key statements are written on cards. In a second step, the person is

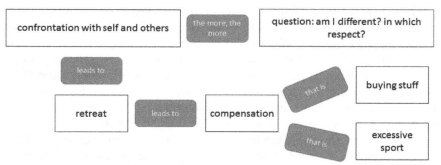

Figure 11.1:   Part of a subjective theory for workplace-related LGBT experience, freely adopted from Frohn (2013).

asked to connect these statements using a set of operators (like: *leads to, only when, the more . . . the more*). In the end, rather complex *subjective theories* are laid out, visualizing the important aspects and their connections for the given topic (see Figure 11.1).

This second step emphasizes a person's cognitive-reflexive capabilities. It is idiographic, that is, a case-oriented description of individual experience.

In a third step, several subjective theories can be condensed with respect to relevant topics. For example, all theories can be scanned for statements indicating political activism; the structure reveals what predates this activism, and what the individual consequences are. If, however, this resource-intensive approach will really give us insights surpassing our current know-ledge remains to be demonstrated (Semle and Raab, in prep.).

6. TOWARD A HOLISTIC APPROACH

Right now there are two major research strands. One focuses on people by taking samples from the general population (often via MTurk), and employs questionnaires. Conspiracy belief is seen here as quantifiable, and as a continuum without qualitative leaps. Beliefs and attitudes are measured with questionnaire items aiming at either (a) approval of conspiratorial suppositions regarding specific past events, or (b) generic attitudes toward government, companies, science, and society. Depending on the measure-ment device, conspiracy belief is either (a) a monological, one-dimensional concept or (b) a multi-dimensional system of discernible facets. The resulting questionnaire scores are related (more often than not: simply correlated) to other psychological concepts that are measured with questionnaires too.

The other strand focuses on stories—conspiracy theories and circumstances—that can be found in various corners of the Internet. Some studies went the cumbersome way—analyzing and categorizing posts manually—which is time- and resource-intensive. In the past few years, however, data mining techniques have gained traction. They can process a text corpus with literally millions of posts. Their algorithms, however, are bound to miss finer details (like irony), and cannot resolve social and discourse deixis. Furthermore, the infamous bot armies might sully the corpus.

Other approaches, like interviews or the method of narrative construction, remain niche. More exotic methods, like the Heidelberg structure-formation technique, have yet to demonstrate if they allow for deeper insights.

This leaves conspiracy theory research in a kind of split-brain state: On the one hand, we examine *believers*—but not the narratives they believe. On the other hand, we examine *conspiracy theories*—but not the people who believe in them. Obviously, this is problematic—all the more so, as both research strands rely on each other when defining their concepts, resulting in a "circular definition; a conspiracy theory is the sort of thing that attracts a deficient type of person, one plagued by a conspiracy mindset" (Dentith and Orr 2017, 15). As long as those research strands do not heed the dynamic interaction of theorists *and* theories at the same time, the tautology will not be broken. Our concepts will remain blurred. Much of current debate and confusion stems from this split-brain state, and after many years of empirical research, the diagnosis by Dentith and Orr (2017, 15) is more relevant than ever: "After all, if we do not define what a 'conspiracy theory' is, how can we possibly measure belief in one? And if we do not know what a conspiracy theory is, how can we identify who the conspiracy theorists are?"

Shall we measure conspiracy belief? Absolutely! The relation with anomia (or trust; or alienation; depending on the instruments used in the study), for example, was found by Goertzel (1994), and has been established in many empirical studies in the following years. When participation in rational discourse is a matter of trust, we might conclude that debunking and shaming will not foster rational discourse but, rather, have the opposite effect. And trust goes both ways: by showing faith in their abilities as cognitive-rational agents we might start to hear what conspiracy believers have to say. Without quantitative studies, the role of trust (and the co-variates moderating this influence) would be much less clear.

This should not blind us to the fact that dynamic aspects of conspiracy belief, their multi-faceted interaction with personality *and* culture *and* narratives over time, remain a desideratum. Do conspiracy theories erode trust over time? Or do they re-establish a sense of agency? Most likely, both assumptions are true—but depending on the theory *and* the theorist, a conspiratorial narrative can be detrimental or beneficial. A theory's content is a good indicator if it is promoting freedom and transparency. But even the most enlightened and positive narrative might become a dangerous tool at the hands of a fanatic.

This ambiguity is far from understood. We need: theoretical work about the nature of conspiracy narratives; longitudinal studies; a combination of qualitative and quantitative methods; and more creativity in applying those methods. "We must go on into the unknown, courageously, using what reason we have, to plan for security and freedom" (Popper 1947, 177).

Chapter 12

Anti-Rumor Campaigns and Conspiracy-Baiting as Propaganda

David Coady

1. INTRODUCTION

The scholarly treatments of rumors and of conspiracy theories have much in common. In both cases, it is usually assumed that the phenomena in question (rumors or conspiracy theories) are bad things that should not be believed. I argue that this is all wrong. Neither rumors nor conspiracy theories deserve to have a bad reputation. I also argue that rumors and conspiracy theories have a bad reputation because of a certain kind of propaganda. Not all propaganda is objectionable, but this kind of propaganda is objectionable, because it is anti-democratic propaganda.

2. RUMOR

The standard arguments against rumor are epistemic arguments, since they claim that rumors cannot be a genuine source of knowledge or justified belief. They are also, in effect, moral arguments, which imply that we have an obligation not to believe or spread rumors. Hence my epistemic defense of rumors will also be a moral defense of rumor-mongers (i.e., those who start and/or spread rumors). This does not of course imply that all rumors should be believed or that spreading or starting rumors (i.e., being a rumor-monger) is always ethically defensible. It is merely an argument that the epistemic presumption against believing rumors and the corresponding moral presumption against spreading, starting, or believing them is unfounded.

2.1 Four Arguments Against Rumors

Argument One: The Spread of Rumors

Probably the most common argument against rumor is based on the idea that rumors are essentially things that spread. This distinguishes rumor from another informal mode of communication (or testimony, to use the philosophical jargon) with which it is sometimes conflated, namely gossip. Unlike gossip, rumor cannot be firsthand. No eyewitness account can *be* a rumor[1], and I don't think a second-hand account can be one either. For a communication to be a rumor it must *by definition* have spread through a large number of informants (henceforth, rumor-mongers); the further it has spread the more fully it deserves the name "rumor."

This feature of rumors is central to Gordon Allport and Leo Postman's influential book *The Psychology of Rumor* (1947), which purports to study rumors experimentally. In their experiments, a volunteer was asked to describe a picture as accurately as possible to a second volunteer, who had not seen the picture; the second volunteer was asked to repeat what he was told to a third volunteer, and so on. Allport and Postman observed that as these "rumors" spread they tended to become increasingly inaccurate. This will come as no surprise to anyone familiar with the children's game known as "Chinese Whispers" or "Telephone." Like the children's game, the Allport and Postman experiments are set up in such a way that each time a message is transmitted, there is a significant chance of accidental or deliberate distortion, and no chance of correction. Hence it is virtually inevitable that a message will become increasingly inaccurate as it is passed on. Allport and Postman thought that this kind of inaccuracy is characteristic of rumors generally, and concluded "that it is never under any circumstances safe to accept rumor as a valid guide for belief and conduct" (1947, 148).

This model of rumor is intuitively appealing, but deeply misguided. There are several important differences between real rumors and the "rumors" of the Allport and Postman experiments. Those spreading real rumors often have the opportunity to cross-examine their informants, and often have prior knowledge of the subject matter of the rumor. Furthermore, rumors don't necessarily spread in a unilinear fashion, hence rumor-mongers can hear different versions of a rumor from different people. Most importantly, those spreading real rumors, unlike the participants in the Allport/Postman experiments, are spreading them because they choose to, not because they have entered into an agreement to do so. Hence they can decide not to pass on a rumor if they think it is unlikely to be true.

Each of the above points show that rumor-mongers have resources available to them to do more than merely produce an inferior version of what they have heard. They are able to use these resources to get the story straight in their own mind, and minimize distortion. They can also evaluate the internal consistency of the rumor, as well as its consistency with other things they already know. This in turn can put them in a position to reject part or all of a rumor if it is unlikely to be true, modify parts of it that are unlikely to be wholly true, and alter the content of the rumor on the basis of plausible hypotheses about how it came to be modified as it spread. All this means that, not only is it not inevitable that rumors will become increasingly inaccurate as they spread, it is possible for them to become *more accurate* as they spread.[2] What is more, even if a rumor doesn't become more accurate as it spreads, the very fact that it has spread can be evidence that it's accurate.

This is not just a theoretical possibility. There is empirical evidence that, in certain circumstances, rumors that survive and spread are more likely to be true, either because they were true all along, or because they became true (or truer) as they spread. During World War II, the U.S. military tried to limit the spread of rumors among troops. It was worried, not because the rumors tended to be false, but because they tended to be true, and there was a danger they might spread to the enemy, giving them important military intelligence, especially about planned troop deployments. The military tackled this problem by regularly redeploying troops, to break up the channels along which rumors passed. Theodore Caplow (1947), who studied these anti-rumor campaigns, found that although this strategy didn't prevent rumors, it did have the desirable effect (desirable, that is, from the military's point of view) of making rumors less accurate. Caplow accounts for this in the following passage:

> Distortion in terms of wishes and avoidance seems to be an individual rather than a group characteristic. As channels solidified, this phenomenon became comparatively rare, because of the exclusion of persons associated with previous invalidity. When they were broken up, wish fulfilment again became conspicuous. (1947, 301)

So the survival and reproductive success of these rumors was partly dependent on their being spread by people with a reputation for reliability. Judgment about the reliability of one's source is part of an overall judgment of the plausibility of what one is told. Caplow uncovered empirical evidence that rumor-mongers can make such judgments and make them quite well. He cited numerous examples of rumors becoming increasingly accurate as they spread, and found "a positive and unmistakeable relation between the survival of a rumor, in terms of both time and diffusion, and its veracity" (1947, 302).

It should be clear then that the fact that rumors spread is no reason for skepticism about them. On the contrary, the fact that they have survived a lengthy process of peer review (to put the matter in academic terms) is *prima facie* evidence that they are true.

Argument Two: Rumors as Unofficial Communications

Robert Knapp, a doctoral student of Allport, defined rumor as "a proposition for belief of topical reference disseminated without official verification" (1944, 22). This is another common theme in the rumor literature, according to which rumors are essentially unofficial things. On this view, if a rumor is officially confirmed, it ceases to be a rumor.

Elsewhere I have argued that to describe a communication as "official" is to say that it has been endorsed by an institution with significant power over what is believed at a particular time and place (2007, 200). Statements by government officials acting in their official capacity are one clear kind of official communication. To characterize rumors as unofficial communications then is to say that they lack this kind of institutional endorsement. Does this feature of rumors imply that we should adopt an attitude of *prima facie* skepticism toward them? Knapp clearly thought so; he claimed that "rumors are more subject than formal modes of transmission to inaccuracy" (1944, 22–23). But this is at best a contingent truth. In some societies, rumors are much more accurate than formal modes of transmission. For example, in the Soviet Union in 1953, R. A. Bauer and D. B. Gleicher found that the majority of people believed that official information was less reliable than "word-of-mouth communication" (1953, 307), and that this belief was particularly widespread among the better-educated classes. These findings are hardly surprising, because at this time and place rumor would have been more reliable than official information.

Of course, Stalin's Soviet Union is a fairly extreme example, and most readers in the West are probably justified in having higher levels of trust in official information. Does that mean that, in our societies at least, we should agree with Knapp, and other critics of rumor, that rumor is less reliable than official information? It seems to me that this view both exaggerates the reliability of official information and underestimates the reliability of rumor.

Neil Levy has argued that it is "almost always rational" to accept official information, where this is characterized as information "promulgated by the authorities" (2007, 181). But Levy's position seems to trade on an ambiguity. There is a sense in which official information can be identified with information promulgated by authorities, and there is a sense in which it is almost always rational to believe authorities. But they involve two quite different senses of the word "authority." We can call the former sense "institutional authority" and the latter sense "epistemic authority." In the institutional sense, being an authority just means being entitled to speak on behalf of a certain institution, such as a government, a police service, or a university. In the epistemic sense, being an authority means being particularly well informed about a certain subject, in other words it means being an expert. I accept that we should almost always believe epistemic authorities (on the subjects about which they are authoritative). But it does not follow that we should almost always believe institutional authorities (and hence official information).

Indeed the dangers of the view that we should almost always believe institutional authorities should be obvious. Perhaps in an ideal society it would almost always be rational to believe official information, but that is not our society, nor I suspect, is it any society that will ever be. What is more, if there ever were such a society, it would inevitably be unstable, since it would lead to complacency about officialdom that would be exploitable by officials trying to manipulate public opinion to advance their interests. To the extent that the view that we should place our trust in official information, rather than rumor, gains widespread acceptance, official information will be less subject to scrutiny and, as a result, less reliable.

Argument Three: Belief in Rumors as Unjustified by Definition

C. A. J. Coady (2006, 262) suggests that rumor deserves its bad reputation because, by definition, it lacks a "strong justificatory base." He considers a report that reached the American ambassador to Japan in January 1941, according to which the Japanese Navy was planning a surprise attack on Pearl Harbor. The ambassador dismissed the report on the ground that sources in the Peruvian Embassy, from which the report had come, were "not very reliable." Of course, we now know that the report was accurate. Coady considers two things we might say:

> The ambassador could have been right in his assessment of the general reliability of sources in the Peruvian Embassy. On the other hand, it might have been his assessment of their credibility that was at fault and the communication may not have deserved the title "rumor." (2006, 269)

On this view, we can only determine whether a communication is a rumor once we have determined whether it came from a reliable source. If it came from an unreliable source, we may call it a "rumor," otherwise not. This seems unsatisfactory for two reasons.

First, there are many communications which come from unreliable sources, but which are clearly not rumors, for example eyewitness accounts by people with poor eyesight or in poor viewing conditions, or official statements by compulsive liars. If we make rumors unreliable by fiat, we face the challenge of explaining what distinguishes rumor from other unreliable communications in a way that leaves rumor as the interesting and important phenomenon it clearly is. I don't see how that can be done. If it can't be done, then stipulating that rumors are unreliable is entirely ad hoc, and can only be understood as a way of suggesting falsely that communications that spread through many informants and/or have not been officially endorsed should not be believed.

Second, if rumors by definition lack justification, then those who exhort others not to believe rumors are making a purely semantic point. That is not what they usually claim to be doing. They usually claim to be establishing the unreliability of rumor as a substantive fact (even something that can be demonstrated experimentally), not as a trivial definitional one.

Argument Four: Rumors as False by Definition

Another approach rumors' opponents can take is to say, not that belief in rumors is by definition unjustified, but that rumors themselves are by definition false. I don't know of anyone who explicitly says this, nonetheless, it is implicit in a lot of anti-rumor rhetoric. For example, Cass Sunstein's book *On Rumors* (2009) is tellingly subtitled *Why Falsehoods Spread, Why We Believe Them, and What Can Be Done.*[3] Throughout this book Sunstein moves freely between talk of "rumors," "false rumors," and "falsehoods" as if these are just different ways of talking about the same thing (e.g., 57). So although he doesn't explicitly define rumors as false (he explicitly refuses to offer a definition of rumor at all), he does so implicitly. Defining rumors as false, whether implicitly or explicitly, is just as ad hoc as defining belief in them as unjustified. It also makes nonsense of our ordinary concept of a rumor. For example, we think of rumors as things that can be confirmed. But we cannot confirm rumors if they are false by definition.

2.2 Anti-rumor Campaigns as Anti-democratic Propaganda

Sunstein is particularly concerned about the possibility that false rumors may cause people to unjustifiably lose faith in government (2009, 9). This concern is characteristic of most, if not all, anti-rumor rhetoric. Critics of rumor are typically committed to an ideal of official control of information. This is an ideal which is known in Indonesia as "Guided Democracy," according to which the people can be trusted to vote, so long as the information on which they base their vote is controlled by an elite. It should be obvious that guided democracy is not really democracy at all.[4] Sunstein characterizes rumors as a threat to democracy,[5] but rumor is not a threat to democracy; critics of rumor, like Sunstein, who want the state and other powerful institutions to control the flow of information are.

The fact that there is empirical evidence that rumors are reliable in a range of contexts has puzzled many writers. The following passage is fairly typical:

The reputation of the workplace rumor as inaccurate apparently is itself inaccurate! The reason for this disparity is puzzling. If the overwhelming majority of rumors that are recalled were true, why would the overall impression of rumor tend to be not credible? We have noticed this pattern repeatedly: When asked about rumor overall, people classify it as false or low-quality information. When asked to recall specific rumors people tend to report true or high-quality information. (DiFonzo and Bordia 2007, 154)

DiFonzo and Bordia offer several explanations for this disparity, which I won't dwell on, because I think the real explanation is quite straightforward. Those responsible for the dissemination of official information, i.e., institutions with considerable influence over what many people believe, typically have an interest in maintaining or increasing that influence. Hence, they have an interest in giving unofficial information, including rumor, a bad name. Given their influence over what people believe, it should not be surprising that they have been quite successful at this. In short, it seems clear that rumor's bad reputation is a consequence of propaganda, and false propaganda at that.

In the past, governments made little effort to conceal the fact that campaigns against rumor were a form of propaganda. For example, as head of the Division of Propaganda Research in the United States during World War II, Robert Knapp was responsible for setting up "Rumor Clinics." His guidelines for these clinics included the need to "assure good faith in the regular media of communication," the need to "develop confidence and faith in leaders," and the need to "campaign deliberately against rumormongering by showing its harmful effects, its inaccuracies, and the low motives of the originators and liaisons of such tales" (Rosnow and Fine 1976, 121). As we have seen, many U.S. officials at this time were at least as concerned about accurate rumors as they were about inaccurate ones (in fact I think it's clear they were more concerned about the accurate ones). It is understandable that officials seek to control information, both true and false, in times of war. Nonetheless the anti-democratic nature of such aspirations should be clear. Furthermore, these campaigns did not end with the war. Knapp's "Rumor Clinics" developed into "Rumor Control Centers," under the auspices of the Department of Justice (Rosnow and Fine 1976, 120–23). Anti-rumor propaganda continues to be widespread. Cass Sunstein is not just an academic; he was a close advisor to President Obama, and head of "The Office of Information and Regulatory Affairs," where his responsibilities included overseeing policies relating to "information quality."[6] It is not surprising that someone in his position would try to persuade people not to believe communications that lack official endorsement.

3. CONSPIRACY THEORY

I have argued that rumors do not deserve their bad reputation, and that they have this reputation as a result of anti-democratic propaganda; I will now argue that the bad reputation of conspiracy theories is also undeserved and also the result of anti-democratic propaganda. First, however, I want to note a disanalogy between rumors and conspiracy theories. Whereas it is usually reasonably clear what people mean by "rumors" (they mean messages that have spread through many informants and lack official status), it is rarely clear what they mean by "conspiracy theories." The expressions "conspiracy theory" and "conspiracy theorist" (unlike the expressions "rumor" and "rumor-monger") are quite new. These terms first entered popular conscious-ness through the work of Karl Popper, who appears to be responsible for their negative connotations.[7] We have managed to get along without them in the past, and I hope we will learn to do so again. In what follows, I will consider a variety of ways of understanding who conspiracy theorists are and where they go wrong.

3.1 Conspiracy Theorists Are People Who Believe in Conspiracies.

This is a natural first thought. But there cannot be anything wrong with being a conspiracy theorist, if the concept is understood this way. After all, people sometimes conspire.[8] Even Popper acknowledges this (1962, 2:95, 1972, 342), and most of his followers will reluctantly concede the point. Since people conspire, there can't be anything wrong with believing that they do. Hence there can't be anything wrong with being a conspiracy theorist.

3.2 Conspiracy Theorists Are People Who Fail to Recognize that Conspiracies Are Rare.

In *Conjectures and Refutations*, Popper claims that although conspiracies occur, they are "not very frequent" (1972, 342). But Popper is just wrong about this. Conspiracies occur regularly throughout history and across all cultures, a point that has been established very effectively in a series of art-icles by Charles Pigden (1995, 2006, 2007). Prior to Popper, no one seems to have thought otherwise. Indeed, Popper appears to contradict himself, when he says elsewhere that conspiracies are a "typical social phenomena" (1962, 2:95). In other words, there are a lot of them.

3.3 Conspiracy Theorists Are People Who Fail to Recognize that Conspiracies are Unimportant.

Several authors have suggested that conspiracy theorists go wrong, not by overstating the frequency with which conspiracies occur, but by overstating their significance when they do occur. Again, Popper provides some support for this approach, when he claims that conspiracies do not "change the character of social life" and that, were they to cease "*we would still* be faced with fundamentally the *same problems* which *have* always faced us" (1972, 342).

But Popper himself effectively admits that conspiracies are important, when he says that "Lenin's revolution, and especially Hitler's revolution and Hitler's war are, I think, exceptions. These were indeed conspiracies" (1972, 125). With exceptions like these it's hard to put much faith in the rule. Just to be clear, Lenin's revolution was The October Revolution, which created the Soviet Union, Hitler's revolution brought the Nazis to power in Germany, and Hitler's war was the Second World War (or at least the European theatre of that war). All of these conspiracies have had an enormous impact on "the character of social life" in every country in the world ever since. And it's not as if these are isolated exceptions. Those interested in the enormous impact conspiracies have had just on the twentieth century should consult Pigden (2006, 34–36) and Olmsted (2009). So, it is simply not true that we would be faced with "fundamentally the same problems" without conspiracies. We would be faced with quite different problems.

3.4 Conspiracy Theorists Are People Who Don't Recognize that Conspiracies Tend to Fail.

Machiavelli said that "experience demonstrates that there have been many conspiracies, but few have been concluded successfully" (Machiavelli, Chapter 19, 62). Likewise, Popper claimed that few "conspiracies are ultimately successful. Conspirators rarely consummate their conspiracy" (1962, 2:95). Daniel Pipes has run a similar line, claiming that "familiarity with the past shows that most conspiracies fail" (1997, 39). So perhaps the problem with conspiracy theorists is that they are people who fail to recognize that conspiracies are prone to failure. This objection is sometimes conflated with the previous one,[9] but the two objections should be distinguished. A successful conspiracy can be unimportant, and a failed conspiracy can be quite momentous. The failed conspiracy by Soviet generals against Gorbachev in 1991 brought about, or at least hastened, the break-up of the Soviet Union and the failed conspiracy by Richard Nixon and his associates to cover up the Watergate scandal led to his resignation. The collapse of the Soviet Union and the resignation of Richard Nixon are both, by any standards, momentous historical events.

The idea that conspiracies tend to fail is very widespread and seems to be what many people are getting at when they object to conspiracy theories and theorists. Conspiracy theories are often contrasted with cock-up theories, with the suggestion that the latter are always, or typically, preferable to the former.[10] But, popular though it is, this idea is wrong in two ways. First, conspiracies and cock-ups are not incompatible. It is, after all, possible to cock-up a conspiracy. Second, although conspiracies sometimes fail, there is no reason to think that they are more prone to failure than other things people do. Indeed it is hard to see why people would continue to conspire if the historical record really shows that the activity tends to be pointless or counter-productive.

In fact, the historical record shows no such thing. On the contrary, it shows that conspiracies are often successful. The conspiracies to assassinate Julius Caesar, Abraham Lincoln, Archduke Ferdinand, and Anwar Sadat were all successful, as was the conspiracy to attack New York and Washington on September 11, 2001. I could go on at length.

Perhaps the argument is that such conspiracies are not ultimately successful, since they have unintended and unwanted consequences. This may be the line Popper and his followers are running when they accuse conspiracy theorists of ignoring the unintended and/or unwanted consequences of social action. But the fact that conspiracies have unintended and/or unwanted consequences (from the perspective of the conspirators) does not entail that they are particularly prone to failure. For *most* (and perhaps all) human actions have unintended and/or unwanted consequences (from the point of view of the actors), but that surely does not entail that most (or all) human activity is doomed to failure. To suppose it does would be to lose our grip on the distinction between failure and success.

Is there any reason to suppose that conspiracies are more likely to fail than other things people do? You might argue that since secrecy is essential to most definitions of conspiracy,[11] all the conspiracies I have mentioned above have failed, inasmuch as they are not secret (after all I know about them); these examples show that there are conspiracies, indeed that there are lots of them, and that many of them are important, but they also show that conspiracies tend to fail, because they tend to be exposed *in the end*. This seems to be Pete Mandik's reasoning when he denies that the belief that al-Qaeda blew up the World Trade Center is a conspiracy theory on the grounds that it isn't secret (2007, 213–14).

This argument is mistaken in two ways. First, there is no reason to believe the premise is true. Second, the conclusion does not follow from the premise. Why accept the premise that conspiracies always or usually end up being exposed? There is an obvious selection bias at work here. I can't provide you with any examples of conspiracies that are still completely secret, because if they were completely secret (and I wasn't in on them), I wouldn't know about them. But this doesn't support the claim that there are no such conspiracies, or even the claim that there aren't many of them.

Even if it is true that conspiracies tend not to remain secret, the conclusion that they tend to fail wouldn't follow. To suppose that it would would be to interpret the secrecy required for successful conspiracy far too strictly, so strictly that a conspiracy will count as a failure if anyone other than the conspirators ever finds out about it. But the conspirators that we know of typically have much more limited secrecy aims than that. They want to keep their activities secret from some people (usually the targets of the conspiracy and those who might sympathize with them) for some period of time (often only until the deed is done). Indeed many conspiracies *need* to be widely publicized if the conspirators are to succeed in their long-range plans.[12]

It is possible that there are conspiracies whose success requires permanent secrecy from everyone not involved in the conspiracy. But these are not the conspiracies that those who are castigated as conspiracy theorists believe in. They do not believe that the conspiracies they believe in have successfully been kept secret from everyone *including them*. To characterize their position this way would be to suppose that they are straightforwardly inconsistent. And I have never seen any reason to suppose that anyone makes *this* mistake.

3.5 Conspiracy Theorists Are People Who Believe that Western Governments or Their Agents Conspire Often, Successfully, or Significantly.

Just believing in lots of significant and/or successful conspiracies is not *on its own* enough to get you accused of being a conspiracy theorist. Much depends on whom you attribute the conspiracies to. No matter how many conspiracies you believe the North Korean regime is involved in, and no matter how important and successful you believe those conspiracies are, you will not be called a "conspiracy theorist," unless you also think Western governments or their agents are involved. So perhaps the error of conspiracy theorists is that they fail to recognize that neither Western governments nor their agents conspire, or that they rarely do, or that it doesn't much matter when they do, or that they rarely achieve their aims when they do.

The United States is the most important Western government, and it is typically someone's belief in conspiracies by American governments or their agents that leads him or her to be accused of being a conspiracy theorist. So we will use the United States as a case study. Robert Anton Wilson, who is a fairly typical and widely cited conspiracy-baiter, begins his book *Everything*

Is Under Control: Conspiracies, Cults and Cover-ups by citing a survey according to which 74 percent of Americans "believe that the U.S. government regularly engages in conspiratorial and clandestine operations." He says that this statistic is significant, because it means that most Americans "now believe what only embittered left-wing radicals believed a century ago" (1998, 1).[13] The rest of his book is premised on the assumption that his readers are among the 26 percent who don't believe their government is regularly conspiring and that no argument for this position is required. It is simply assumed that the majority of Americans have become susceptible to "strange" and "paranoid" conspiracy theories.

The statistic Wilson cites is disturbing, but not for the reason he thinks. It is an indictment of the American media and educational system that 26 percent of Americans—over a quarter of them—appear to be unaware that their government regularly engages in conspiratorial and clandestine operations. They have obviously never heard of the CIA or the NSA, or perhaps they think that they are fictional entities regularly used as plot devices on television. Anyone familiar with U.S. history and politics will be aware that U.S. governments and their agents engage in conspiratorial and clandestine activities on a regular basis. Not that they are alone in this. Conspiring is, and always has been, an important part of politics. The only thing that makes the U.S. government special in this respect is that it is exceptionally powerful. As a result, its conspiracies tend to be more important than conspiracies by other governments.

3.6 Conspiracy Theory and the Open Society

Despite the variety of uses of the expressions "conspiracy theory," "conspiracy theorist," "conspiracism," etc., they are standardly used to deride those in Western countries who believe their governments, or other powerful institutions in their society, are engaged in conspiracies (or many conspiracies, or important conspiracies or successful conspiracies, etc.). This usage serves to intimidate and silence such people, whether or not their beliefs are justified, and whether or not they are true. Hence, this usage makes it less likely that such conspiracies will be exposed (or exposed in a timely manner), and more likely that the perpetrators of conspiracies will get away with them. Hence, there is reason to think that the fact that these expressions have pejorative connotations causes our society to be less open than it otherwise would be. There is a sad irony in the fact that Popper, the author of *The Open Society and Its Enemies* (1962), should have started a practice (i.e., conspiracy baiting) which has made it easier for conspiracy to thrive at the expense of openness.

In fact the term *conspiracy theorist* has evolved to the point where it is little more than a label for people who believe, or are interested in investigating, any proposition which conflicts with an officially sanctioned or orthodox belief. Indeed, the expression is sometimes used of such people, even when their so-called conspiracy theory does not involve a conspiracy at all (e.g., David Coady (2006d, 125)). The expressions "conspiracy theory" and "conspiracy theorist" are the respectable modern equivalents of "heresy" and "heretic" respectively; these expressions serve to castigate and marginalize anyone who rejects or even questions orthodox or officially endorsed beliefs.

Understood in this way, the relationship between conspiracy theories and officialdom is like the relationship between rumors and officialdom, with the difference that rumors are defined as merely lacking official endorsement, whereas conspiracy theories, on this way of understanding them, must actually contradict some official version of events. What if we accepted a definition of "conspiracy theory" along these lines? Would that justify adopting a dismissive attitude toward conspiracy theories? No. As we saw during our discussion of rumor, to say that a version of events has official status should be seen as epistemically neutral. Hence, to say that a conspiracy theory by definition contradicts an official version of events is to say nothing about whether it is true, or whether a person who believes it is justified in doing so.

3.7 Conspiracy-baiting as Propaganda

The propagandistic nature of campaigns against conspiracy theories and theorists is at least as evident as the propagandistic nature of campaigns against rumors and rumor-mongers. Both forms of propaganda serve to herd opinion, or at least "respectable opinion," within limits set by governments and other powerful institutions.

Cass Sunstein again provides a good case-study of this propaganda at work. In his 2009 article "Conspiracy Theories: Causes and Cures" (co-written with Adrian Vermeule), conspiracy theory is tentatively defined as *"an effort to explain some event or practice by reference to the machinations of powerful people, who attempt to conceal their role (at least until their aims are accomplished)"* (2009, 205). The authors concede that some conspiracy theories are true (206), and that some are justified (207). Nonetheless, they stipulate, without giving any reason, that they will concentrate on the conspiracy theories that are "false, harmful, and unjustified" (204). Not only do they focus on such "bad conspiracy theories," they repeatedly refer to conspiracy theories as if we could assume that they have some or all of these undesirable characteristics. They claim, for example, that "conspiracy theories are a subset of the larger category of false beliefs" (2009, 206), and that they are a product of "crippled epistemologies" (204). Hence, they not only ignore, but

implicitly define out of existence, conspiracy theories that are true, beneficial, and/or justified. Talking about conspiracy theories as if we could assume
they are false, harmful, and unjustified, is, given their definition, tantamount
to assuming that explanations which posit secretive behavior on the part of
powerful people are false, harmful, and unjustified. As we have seen, many
such explanations are both true and justified.

They may still, of course, be harmful. Sunstein and Vermeule are concerned
that conspiracy theories can "have pernicious effects from the government's
point of view, either by inducing unjustifiably widespread public skepticism
about the government's assertions, or by dampening public mobilization
and participation in government-led efforts, or both" (2009, 220). Sunstein
and Vermeule do not consider any point of view other than that of the government (such as that of the citizen), nor do they consider the possibility
that widespread public skepticism about the government's assertions might
be justified, or that the public might be right not to want to participate in
government-led efforts.

Putting all that aside for the moment, you might have thought that if there
is a problem with people being overly skeptical of government assertions, the
solution would lie in greater honesty and openness on the part of government.
Sunstein and Vermeule adopt a somewhat different approach:

> Our main policy claim here is that government should engage in *cognitive infil-
> tration of the groups that produce conspiracy theories.* (2009, 218)

Of course, it would be self-defeating for governments to be entirely open
about their participation in such programs; hence, Sunstein and Vermeule recommend that "government officials should participate anonymously or even
with false identities" (2009, 225). In other words, Sunstein and Vermeule
recommend that governments should engage in conspiracies[14] in order to
undermine belief in conspiracy theories. Of course, there is a danger that the
targets of these government conspiracies will find out about them. Sunstein
and Vermeule can hardly dismiss this possibility, since they also claim that in
open societies, such as the United States, Britain, and France, "government
action does not usually remain secret for very long" (2009, 208–9). If the
targets of Sunstein and Vermeule's proposed conspiracies were to find out
about them, they would then believe even more conspiracy theories[15] (albeit
true ones). This would be counterproductive, from the government's point of
view (which is the only point of view that gets a look in). It's not absolutely
clear what Sunstein and Vermeule would recommend in these circumstances.
They do say that "as a general rule, true accounts should not be undermined"
(2009, 206). Nonetheless, they regard it as an "interesting question" whether
"it is ever appropriate to undermine true conspiracy theories" (2009, fn 17).

There is a glaring inconsistency between Sunstein and Vermeule's assurances that government can't get away with secrecy in open societies like ours, and their advocacy of government secrecy and deception. Presumably they don't think the cognitive infiltration they recommend is doomed to failure. But this inconsistency is the least of the worries raised by their paper. Shouldn't we be worried by the prospect of government officials secretly and deceptively manipulating public opinion? Shouldn't we be especially worried when powerful government officials like Sunstein recommend that government officials behave that way? Sunstein and Vermeule are reassuring:

> Throughout, we assume a well-motivated government that aims to eliminate conspiracy theories, or draw their poison, if and only if social welfare is improved by doing so. (2009, 219)

But why should we assume government is "well-motivated" or that it will always seek to improve "social welfare," rather than (say) its own welfare? What reason can we have for abandoning the defining insight of liberal political thought that we can't just assume that governments are well-intentioned and will act in our interests rather than their own, especially when it comes to actions that are carried out in secret? All Sunstein and Vermeule have to say in defense of their assumption is that it is "a standard assumption in policy analysis" (2009, 219). It is a standard assumption of a certain kind of policy analysis, the kind known as "state propaganda."

4. CONCLUSION

Rumors and conspiracy theories (along with rumor-mongers and conspiracy theorists) have an undeserved bad reputation. In both cases, this is the product of anti-democratic propaganda, a species of propaganda that thrives wherever people are overly credulous toward formal authority. It is important that people who value democracy and openness, along with those who simply value the truth, recognize this propaganda for what it is.

NOTES

1. It may, of course, later become one.
2. When I speak of rumors becoming more accurate, I mean that they increasingly conform to a pre-existing reality. It is also possible that a rumor could become more accurate, because reality changes to conform to the rumor. Some rumors, for example rumors about stock market collapses or social conflict, are self-fulfilling.

3. Although Sunstein sometimes seems to concede that not all rumors are false, all the rumors he discusses are false, or at any rate they are clearly believed to be false by him.

4. See D. Coady (2012, chap. 3).

5. He describes the marketplace of ideas (i.e., free speech) as an inadequate remedy for the problem (Sunstein 2009, 10–11). Although he eschews "old-style" censorship, he thinks that legal measures may be necessary to stop the spread of false rumors (Sunstein 2009, 12).

6. This information about Sunstein's former position is available at https://obamawhitehouse.archives.gov/omb/oira. Accessed July 14, 2018.

7. According to John Ayto (1999), the expression "conspiracy theory" dates back to 1909, but only acquired its derogatory connotations in the 1960s.

8. You might think that the question of whether or not conspiracies occur depends heavily on how we define the word *conspiracy*. But it actually doesn't matter. There are some controversies over what the word *conspiracy* means, but on all definitions that I am aware of, it is (or at least should be) uncontroversial that conspiracies occur. Unlike the expressions "conspiracy theory" and "conspiracy theorist," the word *conspiracy* is almost univocal. Minor differences over its precise meaning will not matter for the purposes of this paper.

9. Pipes explicitly fails to distinguish these objections.

10. Bernhard Ingham, press secretary to Mrs. Thatcher, is the classical source for this contrast. "Many journalists have fallen for the conspiracy theory of government. I do assure you that they would produce more accurate work if they adhered to the cock-up theory." (Quoted in the *Brisbane Times*, 1/9/09).

11. The *Oxford English Dictionary* lists an archaic usage, which makes no reference to secrecy. According to it, a conspiracy is simply a "[u]nion or combination (of persons or things) for one end or purpose."

12. This is certainly the case with the al-Qaeda conspiracy to blow up the twin towers and the conspiracy to kill Julius Caesar (Plutarch 1999, 356–57). For more on this topic see Dentith and Orr (2017).

13. I doubt whether Wilson is right that a century ago only "embittered left-wing radicals" believed that their government was engaged in regular conspiratorial and covert operations. But if he is right and the majority did have more faith then that their government was open and above-board, then the majority was wrong and the embittered left-wing radicals were right.

14. Sunstein and Vermeule's proposals constitute conspiracies on any definition that I have ever come across. The cognitive infiltration they recommend not only involves secrecy and deception, it is also morally suspect, to put it very mildly, since it involves dishonestly manipulating public opinion. What is more, it appears to be illegal, under statutes that prohibit the government from engaging in "covert propaganda," which is defined as "information which originates from the government but is unattributed and made to appear as though it came from a third party." See http://www.prwatch.org/node/7261, accessed May 5, 2018.

15. To believe that the government is engaged in secretive and deceptive cognitive infiltration is to believe a conspiracy theory, on Sunstein and Vermeule's own definition as well as on every other definition I have ever come across.

Chapter 13

On Some Moral Costs of Conspiracy Theory

Patrick Stokes[1]

1. INTRODUCTION

In a previous chapter, I argued that conspiracy theorizing *as a practice* should be evaluated not simply in terms of its epistemic rationality, but also ethically. This axis of evaluation has been touched on in the literature on conspiracy theory, but fairly briefly, sometimes only as an afterthought, and almost always in consequentialist terms. There have been some suggestions the practice of conspiracy theorizing can promote alienation from political society (Heins 2007) and diminish the welfare of conspiracy theorists by burdening the "double suffering" of imaginary ills on top of their real ones (Räikkä 2009a, 458; Hofstadter 1964, 86). On the whole, however, philosophers have downplayed the harms associated with conspiracy theories. Steve Clarke, for instance, asserts that while most popular conspiracies are "harebrained and lacking in warrant [. . .] few are actually harmful" (2002, 148). The psychologist Jovan Byford has claimed this was a prevalent attitude in cultural studies in the *X-Files*-inflected 1990s, in which conspiracy theory was treated as a form of playful, postmodern ironizing (2011, 146–49). It's certainly true that some conspiracy theories have the appearance of a mere game. This is perhaps most true of those conspiracies that don't have an obviously political dimension, such as the claim that Paul McCartney died in 1966 and was replaced by a look-alike, or that Elvis faked his death in 1977. Some conspiracy theories are deliberately offered as jokes, such as the *Bielefeldverschwörung*, the claim that the German city of Bielefeld doesn't really exist, given nobody seems to even know anyone who's been there. Irony, however, involves a certain suspension or reserve in relation to the propositions one asserts, whereas conspiracy theorists are, on the whole, non-ironically committed to their claims, or at least assert them as live, non-ironic possibilities.

I argued in my previous chapter in this volume that while a generalist dismissal of conspiracy theory as a class of explanation cannot be sustained, we have ethical grounds to be reluctant to participate in conspiracy theorizing as a practice, and indeed to be reticent about entertaining conspiracy theories as possible candidates for the truth. I touched briefly on some of the reasons why conspiracy theory as a social practice can be harmful, particularly in terms of producing or licensing harassment and other forms of abusive behavior (though of course this is neither a necessary consequence of conspiracy theorizing nor unique to it). Hence I think Juha Räikkä is right that "The ethical evaluation of conspiracy theorizing as a cultural phenomenon should be distinguished from the ethical evaluation of particular conspiracy theories" (2009a, 458). Yet our evaluation of the latter may well be conditional upon our evaluation of the former; if the cultural practice of conspiracy theorizing turns out to be ethically problematic, then taking a specific conspiracy theory seriously may likewise turn out to be a morally problematic thing to do. How then might we evaluate conspiracy theorizing as a practice in ethical terms?

Consequentialist considerations, though important, do not get at a deeper cost of conspiracy theorizing. In this chapter I will argue that beyond the negative social costs conspiracy theorizing can (contingently and non-exclusively) produce, engaging in conspiracy theorizing involves a willingness to entertain and multiply accusations, and that such a willingness violates a moral comportment we owe to others. To explicate this, I'll use Clarke's Lakatosian understanding of conspiracy theories to illustrate the distinctive way in which conspiracy theories *qua* research programs defend themselves, and show how this is morally problematic. Conspiracy theories tend to generate what I'll call *auxiliary accusations*: a class of accusation of malfeasance made *purely* to defend a theory from countervailing evidence. Like all accusations, making these accusations comes at a moral cost. And in the case of most conspiracy theories, that cost is, so to speak, generally unrecouped.

Again, this does not furnish a knock-down a priori reason to dismiss any given conspiracy theory; it does not move us from what I called "reluctant particularism" back to generalism. However, it does give us *prima facie* reasons to be wary of taking part in conspiracy theorizing. Conspiracy theories may well turn out to be true, but for beings like us—that is, beings living in society with others, deploying our epistemic resources in contexts of ethically governed social and political relationships—the bar for entertaining them should be considerably higher than epistemologists would have us believe.

2. DEGENERATIVE RESEARCH PROGRAMS

An important challenge to conspiracy theory, raised by Clarke (2002, 136), is that "Conspiracy theories often have the appearance of forming the core of what Imre Lakatos referred to as "degenerating research programmes." Using a Lakatosian framework we can analyze conspiracy theories, like other research programs, as comprising a core set of hypotheses surrounded by a series of auxiliary hypotheses which are posited as a protective "belt" against data that contradict the core hypotheses. While the core hypotheses are integral to the theory—one cannot give up a core hypothesis and have the *same* theory any more—auxiliary hypotheses are dispensable as their function is only secondary. However, research programs where the positing of auxiliary hypotheses strengthens the program—that is, expands its explanatory power or its capacity to make successful predictions and retrodictions—can be said to be progressive programs, while programs where the auxiliary hypotheses offer no such gain can be said to be degenerative. In a degenerative research program, the epistemic cost of adding more and more defensive hypotheses is not offset by a corresponding increase in explanatory or predictive power.

We can add, as a side-benefit of Clarke's application of Lakatos, that this framework also incorporates beliefs we would typically view as conspiracy theories but which do *not* explain a given event in terms of a conspiracy of actors working in secret. Some conspiracies are "born conspiratorial"—they posit a conspiracy as the explanation for some event and work out from there—but others merely posit a conspiracy *defensively* in order to explain away evidence that seems to contradict the theory. In Lakatosian terms, theories of the former type posit a conspiracy as part of their theoretical core, while the latter type only posit a conspiracy as an auxiliary hypothesis. Of course, the former type will also generally include conspiracy explanations in its auxiliary hypotheses too, and conversely it's at least logically possible for a conspiracy theory not to make conspiratorial claims in defending itself.

The infamous "NASA faked the moon landings" theory is a classic example of a "born conspiratorial" theory: it offers conspiracy as its core explanation for a given set of observed events, and without that conspiracy it would no longer be the theory that it is. But it also uses conspiracy explanations defensively, as part of the belt of auxiliary hypotheses it puts in place to defend itself against disconfirmatory data. That is, contradictory data *itself* is posited as an artifact of, and so not evidence against, the posited conspiracy. For example, photographs of the Apollo landing sites taken by lunar orbiters, as became available in 2009, offer fairly stark evidence against the "NASA Faked the Moon Landings" research program. Against this, the program can offer a number of auxiliary hypotheses, all of which involve accusing someone of furthering the conspiracy: the images are fake, hardware was placed on the moon at a later date, and so forth. Note too that none of these auxiliary hypotheses strengthen the explanatory or predictive power of the theory in any way; these accusations, at least for now, function *purely* defensively. That's not necessarily a problem for a research program, conspiratorial or otherwise: Lakatos' framework doesn't compel us to reject a theory merely because it's become degenerative. It merely says we should generally prefer progressive programs to degenerative ones where both are available. A degenerating program might, under some conditions, still be the only game in town.

An example of a purely "defensive" conspiracy theory is the OPV-HIV Hypothesis. In the early days of HIV research, it was proposed that Simian Immunovirus first crossed the species barrier into humans via batches of oral polio vaccine (OPV) that had been made using chimpanzee cells in Africa in the 1950s. This was not a conspiracy theory as defined above; it did not posit the creation of HIV as the outcome of actors working in secret to bring about such an outcome. It was also quickly challenged by a large amount of disconfirmatory data: evidence the relevant OPVs weren't made from chimpanzee cells at all, surviving vaccine stocks testing negative for SIV, computer modeling suggesting that HIV crossed the species barrier decades before the development of OPV, and so on. The OPV-HIV hypothesis was quickly dropped by the relevant scientific community (Worobey et al. 2004). However, the OPV-HIV hypothesis persists, with its supporters insisting that there has been an active cover-up of the truth on the part of scientists. Hence the non-conspiratorial hypothesis became a conspiracy theory in the process of defending itself.

However, the applicability of the Lakatosian framework to conspiracy theory has been subject to important objections. Pigden argues that Clarke has offered no evidence that conspiracy theories typically form the core of degenerating research programs, and that "Given the vast array of conspiracy theories accepted by all competent historians, this is as close to being self-evidently false as such a claim can be" (Pigden 2006, 145 n6). Of course, Pigden's assertion here depends on the particularly formal, and thus capacious, definition of conspiracy given in the epistemological literature (as discussed in my previous chapter). Clarke's claim is more compelling however when applied to conspiracy theory as a recognizable social practice—the offering of conspiracy explanations that tend to involve cryptic yet powerful actors of relatively long duration and stability, manipulating affairs in very comprehensive ways—rather than a formal type of explanation. Most of what are *popularly* discussed under the heading of "conspiracy theories" do indeed appear to be degenerating research programs (The sort of theories I'm thinking of here overlaps, to some extent, with Keeley's (1999) category of "unwarranted conspiracy theories"). The research program that posits a conspiracy to assassinate John F. Kennedy, for example, has made little in the way of substantive progress in the past fifty years, while the Moon Landing Hoax research program is in fairly dire condition. Of course there is a risk of circularity here we need to be careful of: while we can—and I think should—pick out recurring or characteristic features of "conspiracy theories" as the label is popularly used, we can't simply fall back into using "conspiracy theory" as a shorthand for theories about *untrue* conspiracy theories, which will presumably be degenerative. It's worth noting too that there is no evident correlation between how popular a conspiracy theory is and how degenerative its research program has become; for instance, the claim that anthropogenic climate change is a hoax based on manipulated data runs into more and more disconfirmatory data each year, yet continues to be made even by lawmakers.

Even if many conspiracy theories do tend to be degenerating in practice, however, that might in fact not tell us anything about their potential truth-value. If a theory's auxiliary hypotheses make successful predictions or retrodictions, or help explain facts the core theory does not, then the theory's research program can be said to be progressive. What predictions, then, would a conspiracy theory's auxiliary hypotheses make? We might assume they would predict that evidence of conspiratorial activity will appear: eventually, incriminating documents will surface, credible whistleblowers will appear, and so on. Yes this, according to Basham, is precisely what conspiracy theories predict *won't* happen and so precisely why Lakatos' framework with its privileging of progressive research programs over degenerative ones is not applicable to conspiracy theory:

> [W]hile nature does not, presumably, fake the data essential to our physical theories, in the case of our social theories, *people do.* The apparent "degenerate" status of a conspiracy theory—failure to be able to generate a great many new, successful predictions, and reliance on auxiliary hypothesis to maintain the theory—is exactly what a fairly well-constructed conspiracy would eventually leave investigators with: A closed door to additional investigation, and a wealth of false-leads and disinformation produced by the conspirators and those they influence, in order to obscure the conspiracy. (2006, 136)

In other words, a theory's lack of successful predictions doesn't discount the theory if that lack is itself part of what the theory predicts. We might object that if conspiracy theories predict that there will *never* be any evidence of their conspiracy, because the conspirators will always and reliably repress any such evidence, then the theory has simply become unfalsifiable. But both Basham and Keeley argue that unfalsifiability is not a knock-down objection against a conspiracy theory. As Keeley puts it:

[U]nfalsifiability is only a reasonable criterion in cases where we do not have reason to believe that there are powerful agents seeking to steer our investigation away from the truth of the matter. [. . .] Falsifiability is a perfectly fine criterion in the case of natural science when the target of investigation is neutral with respect to our queries, but it seems much less appropriate in the case of the phenomena covered by conspiracy theories. (1999, 121)

In other words, that a conspiracy theory is degenerative does not necessarily count against it. Remembering that progressive vs. degenerative is meant to provide some degree of rational grounding to the choice between competing research programs, this means that conspiracy theories aren't necessarily epistemically non-preferable to "official" narratives simply because they are degenerative. The lack of evidence that makes them degenerative is in fact precisely what those theories predict.

I'll leave it to others to contest or defend that claim; the point I want to make with Lakatos here is a somewhat different point to the one Clarke made. It is, according to Clarke, an epistemic flaw among conspiracy theorists that "they have a tendency to continue to believe in conspiracy theories that are at the core of degenerating research programmes, when those programmes have degenerated past the point where the majority of people would rationally decide to abandon belief in a theory" (Clarke 2007, 169). Still, Lakatos warns us that there is no specific, identifiable moment at which a research program has become self-evidently degenerative, nor any clear threshold point at which it becomes clear we should abandon a degenerative program for a progressive one. Nor do we have any particular reason to think that a degenerative program may not become progressive in the future. Hence the fact that even conspiracy theories as popularly understood tend to form degenerative research programs can only be a defeasible reason for avoiding believing in them. However, as our discussion of defensive conspiracy theories shows, the Lakatosian framework also helps to discern a key feature of conspiracy theorizing that is important to our *moral* evaluation of this practice: the tendency to launch merely defensive accusations for no predictive or explanatory gain. In other words, even if Keeley and Basham are right that program-degeneracy isn't an epistemic flaw for conspiracy theories, the Lakatosian structure may still help us get a grip on moral problems with conspiracy theorizing as a practice.

3. AUXILIARY HYPOTHESES AND
AUXILIARY ACCUSATIONS

As already stated, to posit a conspiracy as an explanation is to necessarily pose an *accusation*. One cannot have a conspiracy without conspirators, and "conspirator" is not, in this context, a compliment. While Jesse Walker (2013) does posit a category of "benevolent" conspiracy theory, the term is generally taken to apply to something inherently sinister, and some (though not all) philosophers working on the epistemology of conspiracy theory have felt the need to build moral disreputability into their definitions of conspiracy theory, so as to exclude things like surprise birthday party planning from being counted as conspiracy theories (Pigden 2006, 157). Dentith (2016b) is prepared to bite that particular bullet and accept that surprise birthday parties are conspiratorial, but in general, conspiracy theories level accusations that can range from the merely venal to the outright murderous. And accusations are not morally neutral.

Here we need to distinguish two different actions: *forming* a suspicion or accusation, and *voicing* a suspicion or accusation. It is one thing to idly wonder if Prince Philip ordered MI6 to assassinate Princess Diana, and another to make that accusation in the public sphere. These are distinct actions, yet both have moral valence: even a private accusation is, arguably, a wrong to the person accused if the accusation is ill-formed or under-supported by evidence. In either case it seems that a reasonably solid norm governing accusation is that we should only accuse others of wrongdoing when we have solid evidence of wrongdoing on their part. Or put differently, we should show a certain reticence about accusing someone of doing something wrong, and only voice the accusation once the weight of evidence compels us to do so. The legal principle of "innocent until proven guilty" has sometimes been defended as a prudential rule for avoiding conviction of the innocent, but it has an analogue in our everyday interactions with others too: given the binary character of accusation (you can accuse someone of *partially doing* something but you cannot *partially accuse them* of doing something) we find ourselves compelled to forbear accusing someone, i.e., believing in or asserting their guilt until impelled to do so, that is, when the evidence has crossed the relevant threshold.

While warrant is clearly an epistemic notion, there is a relevant moral difference here between simply holding an under-warranted or mistaken belief and making an under-warranted or false accusation. The latter activates a different sort of blameworthiness on the part of the accuser. William Kingdon Clifford gives an example of a group who had leveled accusations that turned out to be unfounded. After this, they were considered "not only as persons whose judgment was to be distrusted, but also as no longer to be counted honourable men" (1886, 341). An unwarranted accusation may be made in good faith—indeed it may even turn out to be true—but it nonetheless comes at a moral cost, distinguishable from (if connected to) its epistemic deficiencies. Hence conspiracy theory, a practice in which accusation is unavoidable, is morally risky, as Räikkä notes: "When it comes to political conspiracy theorizing, publishing suspicions can be morally problematic, because harsh claims are made in too early a stage of the investigations" (2009a, 466). Harsh claims sometimes need to be made, but they need to be made from a suitably robust evidence base—a norm that both embeds and entails a corresponding attitude of *reticence*. And we don't need to pin down a precise threshold for justified public accusations to say many published conspiracy theories have not met that moral burden.[2]

The conspiracy theorist can however, and no doubt would, reply that the accusations made *are* justified: the accusation is entailed by the best explanation of the available evidence. Indeed the conspiracy theorist can maintain that their conspiracy explanation is *superior* to the "official" narrative, as it explains more observations than the official story does. As Keeley points out, "This is the beauty of conspiracy theories. They offer wonderfully unified accounts of all the data at hand, both those the official story explains, plus those niggling, overlooked errant data" (1999, 119; see also Clarke 2002, 135). That ultimately counts *against* at least mature conspiracy theories, according to Keeley; these explain more and more data by expanding the scope of their skepticism, but given the inevitable imprecision in our theories, a theory that explains *too* much is thereby suspicious. A conspiracy theorist might reply, however, that we have neither a clear threshold for a theory's being "too" successful, nor any good grounds to prefer a less-successful theory to a hyper-successful one.

The Lakatosian framework, however, draws our attention to the fact that not all accusations made by conspiracy theories are made on the level of the theoretical core. Many are also made defensively, not to explain observations but to defend the theory against disconfirmatory evidence. If I claim that mass-casualty events are false flag operations perpetrated by the U.S. government in order to win public support for new draconian gun laws or security measures, I necessarily accuse the U.S. government. This is a "core" accusation. If I withdraw the accusation, I either cease to have a conspiracy theory, or, if I blame someone else, I have a *different* conspiracy theory. But suppose it's now put to me that the media reportage of these events seems to support the "official" narrative of these events. This appears to be disconfirmatory evidence, requiring me to either abandon my theory, accept an apparent explanatory incompleteness in my theory (which would involve surrendering a large part of its epistemic advantage over the official narrative), or defend it with countervailing auxiliary hypotheses. Given the positing of a conspiracy, the conspiracy theorist might reply that the most reasonable explanation for the media's failure to uncover the conspiracy is that *the media themselves are complicit in the conspiracy*. The principle of "Hanlon's Razor," that one should always accept incompetence as an explanation ahead of deliberate malfeasance, or "cock-up before conspiracy," has been widely taken to be, as Neil Levy puts it, "one of the markers of intellectual seriousness" (2007, 181). Versions of this heuristic have been supported by Pete Mandik (2007) and Clarke, though as Dentith points out, it's not clear how we'd demonstrate empirically that conspiracies are less frequent than cock-ups (2014, 117), while David Coady notes that cock-up and conspiracy aren't incompatible (2012, 116). Moreover, someone who *already* accepts the existence of a large, powerful conspiracy that explains the initial observed state of affairs can say they are being perfectly parsimonious by using that same conspiracy to explain the media's silence. Indeed that sort of reasoning is quite unexceptional in other contexts: when a criminal informant suddenly changes his story on the witness stand, our inference that he's been "gotten to" by the very people he was to inform on seems perfectly reasonable and economical. So why not the inference that the same government that staged the hoax massacre also coerced or corrupted the media not to expose their misdeeds? But the claim is in fact not parsimonious, because it expands the number of conspirators and thereby accuses new actors (the media, putative witnesses, etc.). Of course, it may be true—the media *might* be in on the conspiracy, just as the seemingly non-corrupt guards may have taken bribes to get at the would-be mob supergrass and coerce him into silence. But unless these auxiliary hypotheses lead to fairly rapid verification, they offer no explanatory or predictive gain and remain mere epistemic *and moral* liabilities of the research program. Moreover, these auxiliary hypotheses are themselves subject to potential falsification—save at the cost of defending them by positing yet another auxiliary hypothesis, itself most likely another accusation. Hence, as Keeley puts it, the more people a conspiracy theory has to accuse in order to explain the apparent success of the conspiracy in hiding evidence of its misdeeds, the harder it becomes to believe the theory (1999, 122).

Still, there is nothing essential to the formal structure of conspiracy explanation that compels the conspiracy theorist to multiply accusations in this way. Clarke, responding to Keeley, notes that while conspiracy theorists may often increase the number of claimed conspirators in order to defend their theory, this is, he thinks, "an observation about the fallacious reasoning patterns of some contemporary conspiracy theorists" and is "simply not relevant to the epistemic evaluation of [unwarranted conspiracy theories] as a class" (2002, 141; see also Dentith 2014, 35). Explaining *one* set of observations with reference to a conspiracy doesn't logically entail we have to explain *every* set of observations in that way. A false flag theorist might insist the media are not conspirators, but simply dupes like everyone else (everyone, of course, except the conspiracy theorist herself). Coady claims, along with Pigden, that few if any of the people popularly described as "conspiracy theorists" would subscribe to what Popper called "the conspiracy theory of society," i.e., the claim that *every* event is the outcome of a conspiracy (D. Coady 2012, 212), with the corollary that *every* official narrative is false. It's true that nothing about the epistemic form of conspiracy theories, nor of the tradition or style of Conspiracy Theory, entails an a priori commitment to explaining *every* event as the result of a conspiracy.

Even so, the figure of the "conspiracy theorist" as the term is popularly used is not someone who simply believes in *a* conspiracy theory or even *a number* of discrete conspiracy theories, but someone who frequently or habitually applies this style of explanation. As Emma Jane and Chris Fleming put it, the conspiracy theorist's reasoning is "a tendency to *a priori*-ism: an epistemological orientation whereby the conspiracy theorist always-already knows the meaning of yet-uncovered evidence and awaits it with her or his categories pre-fabricated" (2014, 36). Such a person may not be antecedently committed to the proposition that every event is the outcome of a conspiracy, but may nonetheless interpret many or all events *individually* as being the outcome of conspiracies. They may, in other words, be conspiracist in the same way the Buddha is omnipotent, according to some sources in the Theravada tradition: the Buddha doesn't know everything simultaneously, but all knowledge is effortlessly available to him as he cogitates. The conspiracy theorist doesn't ascribe conspiracy explanations to every individual event simultaneously, but conspiracy explanations are effortlessly available to them as they consider any given event. If a conspiracist doesn't believe a specific event is the outcome of a conspiracy, that may simply mean they haven't gotten around to analyzing it yet.

Effortlessly adding unproductive auxiliary hypotheses to a theory might strike us as a form of epistemic profligacy. The conspiracy theorist takes on more and more evidentiary debt, so to speak, as she enunciates more and more accusations that will at some point need to be "paid for" with evidence. But just as adding auxiliary accusations is more epistemically expensive, so too it is, so to speak, more *morally* expensive. When the OPV-HIV hypothesis "went conspiratorial," it took on board a new and explanatorily inert auxiliary hypothesis (namely, that there was a cover-up within the medical fraternity) with no real evidence in its favor. But it also took on board the moral liability of leveling an accusation. Even if the parties are not specified, a class of persons are nonetheless impugned. And the ethical gravity of this becomes more serious with each defensive move. Dentith claims that the fact we need to level accusations when articulating a conspiracy theory should not be viewed as a reason not to make them, as this might have a "chilling effect" that would provide cover to actual conspirators (2014, 77). This worry is legitimate. However, a style of explanation that legitimates positing more and more accusations could equally be said to have an "over-heating" effect, where morally harmful claims are voiced more freely than norms of justified accusation should allow.

The conspiracy theorist may retort that if they are justified—as they believe themselves to be—in inferring from the initial evidence that a conspiracy has occurred and making a corresponding accusation, then they are likewise justified in making whatever auxiliary accusations as are necessary to defend the structural integrity of their theory. Yet the motive for making an auxiliary accusation is different from the motive for making the initial accusation, and this difference is, I'd suggest, a morally significant one. The auxiliary accusation is not part of the theory's explanatory mechanism, but of its immune system. It is not imposed upon the conspiracy theorist by the evidence as the initial accusation at least notionally is; the impetus for the auxiliary accusation comes entirely from an imperative to sandbag a theory from disconfirmation. As such these accusations violate the precept against making accusations without evidence that has reached a certain threshold. At the risk of sounding overly dramatic, the conspiracy theorist sacrifices the moral status of others in order to save her preferred theory. As such, conspiracy theory as a practice licenses a distinctive kind of standing indifference to others' legitimate claims not to be impugned without overwhelmingly good cause.

At the very least, auxiliary accusations involve taking a significant risk of getting it wrong and causing unjustified harm. Nonetheless, the moral cost of an accusation can be, so to speak, recouped—*if* the accusation turns out to be correct. But here the degenerative character of conspiracy theory becomes relevant: the auxiliary hypotheses of degenerative research programs don't yield additional explanatory or predictive strength. They protect the core of the theory, but only at the cost of bloating it with ad hoc inclusions that do no further epistemic work. These accusations, in short, don't pay off. Even if, as Keeley and Basham argue, that's not a problem *epistemically*—because a lack of evidence is precisely what a theory built around active deception by powerful actors would predict—it *is* a problem when we factor in the moral costs. As more and more time passes, the standing and expanding accusations become more and more morally problematic.

This tendency to accrue greater moral costs over time, and those of a sort that are disconnected from proper grounds of accusation, does not provide a priori grounds for rejecting any given conspiracy theory. Nor, given the findings of epistemologists working on conspiracy theories, should we expect them to do so. What it does provide, however, is one reason (additional to the sort of reasons provided by, e.g., Keeley (1999)) to be suspicious of explanations that are recognizably sourced from the conspiracy tradition of explanation, and to avoid engaging in conspiracy theorizing. This reason is defeasible, and just as well: conspiracies happen, and if we *never* made auxiliary accusations we would no doubt be oblivious to certain classes of genuine harm. Hence, my position is not generalist—that is, it does not *dismiss* any given conspiracy theory out-of-hand *just because* it is a conspiracy theory. But it does give us a strong reason to be deeply suspicious of and reluctant to entertain explanations of the conspiracy style, lest we find ourselves obliged to level accusations out of loyalty to the theory rather than fidelity to the evidence.

4. CONCLUSION

I suspect the above discussion will largely leave many epistemologists cold. Embedded in it are some very fundamental assumptions about the relationship between epistemology and ethics, assumptions it is quite open for someone to doubt or even reject out of hand. That should not, however, surprise us. The literature on conspiracy theory to date has concentrated on showing the epistemic rationality of at least some conspiracy belief, in the face of and opposition to "pathologizing" assumptions about conspiracy theorists in other disciplines and in general discourse. In doing so, perhaps understandably, the focus has been on conspiracy theories as propositional entities, and accusation as a stance taken toward a set of propositions: to accuse is to endorse a series of propositions about the actions of others. But as I've tried to bring out above, accusation is also a stance taken toward another *person*. As a speech act "accusing" behaves more like "insulting," "demeaning," or "objectifying" than "proposing" or "hypothesizing." It's an act that changes the moral status of another.

Differences in these basic assumptions will become more and more salient as the philosophical discussion of conspiracy theory grapples with ethical and political questions. For instance, the erosion of trust is sometimes mentioned in the literature as a consequence of conspiracy theory—but what *sort* of trust is in play here? The philosophical literature on conspiracy theory largely embeds a calculative view of trust. When most philosophers ask "How much should we trust our society's sources of information?" they are asking a question about reliability: "On past performance, how much confidence should we have that these institutions are telling the truth and/ or acting in a way consistent with their stated commitments to acting in our interests?" There is, as Dentith (2014) notes, no way of determining in advance just how conspired the world really is. But nonetheless, it is not *unconspired*—conspiracies occur, and most philosophers working on this topic take conspiracy to be a more pervasive feature of social and political life than we usually assume, and think we should calibrate our suspicions accordingly. David Coady, for instance, explicitly endorses a sort of Aristotelian account of trust, according to which "the intellectual virtue of *realism* is a golden mean between the intellectual vices of *paranoia* and *naivety*" (2006b, 126). Thus our phronetic judgement should aim to be *just suspicious enough*. Alasdair MacIntyre (2007) has offered a similar account of ideal trust as a mean between excessive suspicion and credulity, arrived at through a long process of moral training: learning who to trust, and when, and how much.[3]

Yet trust as an interpersonal and moral phenomenon is not simply a matter of calculating and responding to reliability. For one thing, it involves mutual responsiveness to need, taking the fact the other person knows I am reliant on them to be a reason for them to act consistent with my interests (Jones 2012). We know that not everyone is trustworthy in that sense. Basham tells us that "Human life is conspiratorial. We can face this, embrace it, but if we deny it, we empower it in the worst way" (Basham 2016, 13). People lie, cheat, and steal, and sometimes they conspire in order to do so. But human life is also predicated on foundational, non-calculative trust. When I walk into a room I don't mentally calculate the odds of you trying to kill me, not because I've previously assured myself that the odds are too low to worry about, but because of that default background trust that is a condition for social life. As K. E. Løgstrup (1997) put it, trust is both conceptually and ontogenetically primary, distrust secondary; without that foundational trust the sphere of human life falls apart. Accordingly, our judgments of what to believe of other people are guided by heuristics that are not merely epistemic in character, but also ethical. Giving "the benefit of the doubt" is not, or not typically, merely a judgment about the reliability of the other party, but an expression of that normative default attitude toward others.

This picture of foundational trust sits awkwardly, to say the least, with the standing vigilance required to maintain a democratic polity. There are always good reasons to be suspicious of power of all forms, both overt and covert, explicit and intrinsic. The work of identifying and uncovering power relations is indispensable, and it seems to involve a relentless and remorseless hermeneutics of suspicion. That tension—between foundational trust and vigilance—is a real and seemingly permanent feature of political and social life. What I have called "reluctance" is an expression of that tension, an awareness of being caught between the duty to view others as good faith interlocutors and the duty to uncover wrong-doing. The sort of generalized, eager suspicion involved in entertaining and advancing conspiracy theories abandons that reluctance, and thereby misses that central dimension of human sociality.

Those of us who want to understand what to make of conspiracy theory will need to come to grips with these fundamental ethical issues as well.

NOTES

1. My thanks to audiences at a workshop on the ethics of conspiracy theory at Deakin University, September 2016, and to Lee Basham and an anonymous referee for helpful comments on earlier versions of this paper.

2. Räikkä (2009a, 463–64) holds that the threshold of evidence required to level an accusation is higher if the target of the accusation is a private person rather than a public one—say, the president's secretary instead of the president. I don't see any clear argument for this claim, however. Räikkä links this view to the idea that a public figure has given up a degree of privacy—but even if they have, the link between the right to privacy and the right not to be slandered is, at best, opaque.

3. On MacIntyre's Aristotelian account of trust, which he offers in opposition to Løgstrup's view of trust as foundational, see Stokes (2017b).

Chapter 14

Conspiracy Theories, Deplorables, and Defectibility

A Reply to Patrick Stokes

Charles Pigden

1. A BRAND PLUCKED FROM THE BURNING? THE CASE OF PATRICK STOKES

Patrick Stokes has come a long way. Once a conspiracy theory skeptic of a fairly conventional kind, disposed to the opinion that conspiracy theories *as such* are somehow suspect or unbelievable, he now concedes (as we have seen in chapters 2 and 13) the following claims (on which he thinks there is an emerging philosophical consensus):

(1) When endeavoring to explain historical events, "conspiratorial activity is at least sometimes, perhaps even often, the best available explanation to which to infer." [The basic argument for this derives from two facts, well-attested by both history and the nightly news: (a) that people often conspire, and (b) that since plotters are frequently not impotent, conspiracies are often causally efficacious.]
(2) Given (1) if we define a conspiracy theory as a theory which explains some event as partly due to conspiratorial activity, "there is nothing intrinsically irrational, or even unreasonable, about explanations of [this] form."
(3) If we try to deal with this difficulty by developing a more elaborate conception of "conspiracy theories" (one which matches the usage of Western cultural elites) we wind up with "a blatantly gerrymandered and chauvinistic definition, according to which a conspiracy theory is 'a theory which posits a secret and morally suspect plan *on the part of Western governments or government agencies* to influence events by partly covert means' (Pigden 2006, 164). We have obvious reasons to look askance at any definition of conspiracy theory that entails that conspiracies are something only *other* societies do."[1] Thus "the search for a (non-question-begging) definition of 'conspiracy theory' that would exclude beliefs about these accepted conspiracies, but include those wacky theories we want to dismiss, appears doomed to failure."

(4) Given points (1), (2), and (3), "a return to blithe generalism is unsustainable" where a "blithe generalism" denotes the policy of systematically doubting or dismissing conspiracy theories *as such* simply because they *are* conspiracy theories. Stokes even concedes the claim, that critics of the conventional wisdom such as myself have been arguing for over twenty years, that the "blithe generalism" about conspiracy theories that is common among the political, cultural, and journalistic elites (henceforward the punditocracy) "is sometimes used to provide cover for political actors who don't want the true nature of their actions scrutinized too closely." (He should have said "often" and not "sometimes," but you can't have everything.)

As a longtime proponent of the emerging consensus, all this is music to my ears. I have been arguing for points (1) to (4) for over twenty years and it is good to know that my arguments have had some effect especially on such a culturally influential figure as Patrick Stokes. (Stokes is a winner of the AAP Media Prize, a regular contributor to *The Conversation* and *New Philosopher*, and a media commentator on philosophical matters. This is about as good as it gets for an Australian philosopher who hasn't quite made it into the media big-time of Europe or the United States.) So it seems that I ought to be rejoicing over the conversion of a repentant sinner. But it's not quite time to bring out the fatted calf. For although Stokes admits that a blithe generalism is unsustainable, he can't quite bring himself to accept *particularism*, the idea that the term *conspiracy theory* should be stripped of its pejorative connotations and that conspiracy theories should be considered on their merits. (I remark in passing that particularism is quite compatible with the view that many conspiracy theories can be dismissed in short order as *devoid* of intellectual merit. It is just that they will be dismissed because of their specific deficiencies and *not* because they are conspiracy theories. What is wrong with false, crazy or dangerous conspiracy theories is that they are *false, crazy or dangerous* NOT that they are *conspiracy theories*, since many conspiracy theories are neither dangerous, crazy, nor false.) Instead, what Stokes proposes is that "we" (and I will be returning to that pronoun later) should adopt a "defeasible generalism" or "reluctant particularism." This does not start from the premise that conspiracy theories are always false or irrational, but it would "approach such theories with a certain reticence, given the social practice in which they are embedded, and the moral costs associated with taking part in the conspiracy theory tradition." What is the justification for this reticence? Well, what Stokes thinks is that if we don't treat conspiracy theories with the right kind of reticence, we encourage the spread of conspiracy theorizing, that is, a set of irrational social and intellectual practices with a wide range of pernicious effects. His beef with particularism is that it risks investing these practices with an intellectual respectability that they do not deserve and which it would be dangerous to concede. We should be cautious about postulating conspiracy theories for fear of succumbing—or encouraging others to succumb—to an irrational and dangerous style of thinking, a social practice with severe moral costs.

2. A CONCRETE PRACTICE OR A FAMILY OF PRACTICES?

My first objection is a little pedantic. Stokes insists that "conspiracy theorizing is not merely a formal category of explanation but a concrete and historically and socially conditioned practice." But given his concessions to particularism, this claim is clearly false, at least if we emphasize the "a." For the "a" implies that conspiracy theorizing consists of *one* "concrete and historically and socially conditioned practice." But, on Stokes' own showing, conspiracy theorizing consists in a *multitude* of different practices, corresponding to all the different ways (some sensible, some silly, and some totally insane) that people can arrive at conspiratorial beliefs. This is because one of the things that Stokes has admitted is that if conspiracy theories are defined as theories which postulate a conspiracy, then "we're *all* conspiracy theorists [since] we all believe that conspiracies are the best explanation of many historical events, from the murder of Julius Caesar to Stalin's show trials to Watergate."[2] Since (a) we are all conspiracy theorists; since (b) we arrive at our conspiracy theories in a multitude of different ways; and since (c) to *theorize* about X is to come up with *theories* about X, it follows that conspiracy theorizing is not just *one* "concrete and historically and socially conditioned practice" but a *family* of *diverse* practices. There are as many varieties of conspiracy theorizing as there are ways of arriving at a conspiracy theory. And many of these ways of arriving at conspiracy theories are intellectually kosher.

But perhaps this objection misses the point. What Stokes is really driving at is not that there is just *one* practice of conspiracy theorizing but that a great deal of real-world conspiracy theorizing is not just irrational (relying, for example, on sinister anti-Semitic scripts which are just waiting in our cultural store-house ready to be revived and redeployed) but actively dangerous, since bad conspiracy theorizing often leads people to commit acts of violence and cruelty or to expose their children to the risk of avoidable diseases. Though conspiracy theories and conspiracy theorists *need* not be irrational and dangerous, a great many of them are, and so are the intellectual processes by which the theorists arrive at their theories. Thus what Stokes' thesis boils down to is the claim that we should be reticent about postulating conspiracy theories for fear of encouraging *bad* conspiracy theories, and that we should be cautious about indulging in conspiracy theorizing ourselves for fear of encouraging *bad* conspiracy thinking *mostly* in other people but also, *perhaps*, in ourselves. Although, in Stokes' opinion, conspiracy theories are not necessarily or even usually false or irrational, what he is recommending is that we should treat them *as if* they were usually one or the other.

3. THAT LITTLE WORD *WE*

And this brings me back to that little word *we*. When Stokes suggests that *we* should be reticent about adopting conspiracy theories, what is the group that the "we" is supposed to refer to? No doubt Stokes would ideally like to include everyone within the ambit of his "we," but realistically the people within reach of his argument constitute a much more restricted class. The very best he can hope for (if this book proves to be a best-seller) is that his policy of "defeasible generalism" or "reluctant particularism" will be widely accepted by the saner sections of the world's journalistic, cultural, and political elites with a remote chance that it might just seep down to the *hoi polloi*. If the policy were widely accepted, journalists and pundits (at least in the mainstream media) would be saying things like this: "Though I am reluctant to accept conspiracy theories, the evidence for collusion with Russia during the 2016 presidential campaign is beginning to look overwhelming." "That climate change is a hoax is, of course, a conspiracy theory. Though not all conspiracy theories are false or silly, this one is a real doozy."

Would this be good enough for me? Well, it would be a considerable improvement on the current situation, but it would not be improvement enough. For as I understand it, "conspiracy theory" would still have enough of a pejorative connotation to grease the fallacious slide from "This theory posits a conspiracy" via "This theory is a conspiracy theory" to "This theory is false and/or irrational." And though *bad* conspiracy theorizing is indeed a pernicious practice, the social practice of denying or dismissing true and important conspiracy theories simply because they *are* conspiracy theories (call this "conspiracy denialism") is *also* a pernicious social practice, and to roughly the same degree. And although this practice would be a little less easy under Stokes' suggested regime, it would still be a bit too easy for my taste.

4. DENIALISM AND ITS COSTS

Since Stokes makes a great deal of the pernicious effects of bad conspiracy theorizing, it is perhaps worth saying a little something about the moral costs of conspiracy denialism. It is now reasonably obvious that the Bush regime, aided and abetted by Tony Blair, decided to go to war with Saddam Hussein's

Iraq without an adequate *casus belli*. To deal with this difficulty there was a clearly a conspiracy to *talk up* Saddam's supposed connections with al-Qaeda and to *talk up* the threat of Iraqi weapons of mass destruction. I say *talk up*; I don't say *lie about*. I am sure that there was a fair bit of out-and-out lying during the prolonged PR campaign that justified the war, as well as big dollops of bullshit artistry, lashings of wishful thinking, a substantial dose of doublethink, and perhaps some contribution from the unreal attitude that comes from ceasing to believe in objective truths. As the famous Downing Street Memo of 7/23/02 puts it: "Bush wanted to remove Saddam, through military action justified by the conjunction of terrorism and WMD. But the intelligence and facts were . . . fixed around the policy." People preferred to be told what they wanted to hear and preferred not to hear what they did not want to be told. But I don't suppose anyone said to themselves at the outset of the PR campaign that led to the invasion of Iraq "Of course Saddam does not *really* have any weapons of mass destruction. But we need to pretend that he does in order to justify the war." For to bang on about WMDs in the belief that there were really no such things would be to court a massive loss of credibility (and a huge dose of public hostility) once the lie was ultimately exposed. It is far more likely that the leading actors thought, supposed, or hoped that Saddam had at least *some* WMDs which could be subsequently used to justify the invasion. Nonetheless, there *was* a conspiracy to talk up the threat of weapons of mass destruction and to justify the war, and the conspirators protected themselves from public scrutiny partly by resorting to conspiracy denialism. The upshot was that hundreds of thousands of people (perhaps over a million) died an early death and millions more were reduced to lives of misery, terror, and destitution. Conspiracy denialism was used to help justify a massive war-crime. It does not get much worse than that.[3]

5. THE IMPOTENCE OF RETICENCE AND AN INTERVIEW WITH TRUMP

But I want to suggest another problem for defeasible generalism (or reluctant particularism): It would do nothing to diminish (let alone solve) the problem that bothers Stokes, namely that large segments of the population are prone to patterns of irrational conspiratorial thinking with the result that foolish and pernicious conspiracy theories are widely believed. Remember that the best that Stokes can hope for is that his policy would be accepted by the saner sections of the elite; that is the respectable members of the punditocracy would become defeasible generalists. But the lumpen-punditocracy—the *Fox and Friends* journalists and commentators, the Breitbart talking heads and the political representatives of the rabid right (and in some case the rabid left)—would remain unaffected, as would their benighted followers. After all, there is *currently* a strong presumption in respectable circles that conspiracy theories are somehow *infra dig*—since anti-conspiratorial generalism still rules the intellectual roost despite the best efforts of David Coady (2012), Lee Basham (2018), M R. X. Dentith (2017b) and myself—but conspiracy thinking of the most dangerous and irrational kind continues to flourish on the fringes of respectable opinion—a point that Stokes himself is at pains to prove. Respectable society may be sneering at conspiracies and conspiracy thinking, but the deplorables carry on regardless.

Moreover, a refined attitude of reticence would be utterly impotent in the context of ideological debate. Suppose, *per impossibile,* that Patrick Stokes got to debate with Donald Trump:

> **TRUMP**: The failing *New York Times* and the totally dishonest mainstream media (enemies of our country, but I forgive them) say that there was collusion between my campaign and Russia. (By the way did I tell you how I won the electoral college by the biggest margin in history?) This is FAKE NEWS, a total conspiracy by the haters and losers. As for climate change this is a total hoax, all those scientists lying to line their own pockets. The Mueller investigation is a total WITCH HUNT, thirteen Democrats out to get me. Sad.

> **STOKES**: Mr. President, the right view with respect to conspiracy theories is to take up an attitude of reticence unless the evidence is particularly strong. If you assume that the *New York Times* and the mainstream media are out to get you, you risk succumbing to a style of thinking—indeed a concrete and historically and socially conditioned practice (and as such open to ethical evaluation)—that leads to both error and cruelty. As for climate change, it is surely unreasonable to posit a conspiracy on the part of such a large group of people. If you carry on this way you will end up believing that even evolution is a hoax! As for the idea that the Mueller investigation is a witch hunt (if you mean by this that they are conspiring to frame you with the aid of faked evidence), I would respectfully suggest that the evidence is lacking and that therefore the policy of reluctant particularism dictates that you reject the theory.

> **TRUMP** (playing to the gallery): Little Aussie Patrick says that I should not accept these conspiracy theories because conspiracy theories are bad. But conspiracy theories are NOT bad or not always bad. People tell me that even Patrick thinks that some conspiracies real; so Patrick thinks that some conspiracy theories are not bad. Which is it? If some aren't bad I say mine aren't bad. Fake philosophy! Sad.

Now I don't want to carry the joke too far since it is hard to stage a dialogue between Trump and a philosopher without giving Trump more brains than he appears to have. But I do have a serious point to make. As a weapon in ideological controversy (at least against conspiracy theorists) reluctant particularism is pretty well worthless, since it presupposes a thesis that a real-life opponent could easily deny or evade—that conspiracy theories are often irrational and dangerous. A sufficiently gung-ho conspiracy theorist could simply deny it. A more sophisticated conspiracy theorist would evade it by insisting that whatever may be wrong with *some* conspiracy theories, *his* conspiracy theory is both rationally up to snuff and non-pernicious in its effects. And a reluctant particularist would have absolutely no comeback without getting down to cases and criticizing the theory's specific defects, on which topic reluctant particularism has nothing much to say. The reluctant particularist claims that many conspiracy theories are bad in various ways but he does not have a criterion or a symptomatology to distinguish the bad from the good. Defeasible generalism is thus a philosophical weapon of mass destruction, but it is far too feeble to do any serious damage, at least to its intended targets. An attitude of reticence is not going to refute anyone. (Plus its rather condescending *de haut en bas* tone is likely to cause unnecessary offense and thus discourage conversions.) Meanwhile, by suggesting that conspiracy theories are inherently but defeasibly suspect, it gives aid and comfort to the conspiracy theory denialists who engage in "a concrete and historically and socially conditioned practice" which is roughly as pernicious in its effects as the bad kind of conspiracy thinking.

6. CONCLUSION—AN ALTERNATIVE STRATEGY: PARTICULARISM AND DEFECTIBILITY

I am going to suggest a different strategy. To my mind the right way to go is to adopt a robust particularism while at the same time developing a set of criteria which will help us distinguish between good and bad conspiracy theories, between those it is sensible to believe or investigate, and those which can be dismissed at the outset as unlikely to be true. For the rest of this paper I shall try to develop one such criterion. There is a feature shared by most of the conspiracy theories that Stokes deplores that is *not* shared by most of the theories that he would regard as intellectually respectable:

Defectibility[4]: A conspiracy is defectible if the costs of defection are low and the rewards of defection are high. A theory has defectibility if the conspiracy it postulates is defectible.

This needs a little elucidation. In some conspiracies the costs of defection are high, and the rewards of defection are low. Take a Mafia conspiracy to run a series of highly lucrative protection rackets, illegal gambling dens, and drug-running operations and to protect themselves from legal retribution, by paying off policemen, prosecutors, and judges. The costs of defection from this conspiracy would be enormous. To confess to the Feds that you were part of such a conspiracy would be to own up to a wide range of crimes, to expose yourself at the very least to the threat of long years in jail, and perhaps even to the death penalty. And if the state did not decide to enforce the death penalty, death or something worse (such as the death and/or torture of your family) is what you could expect from your former co-conspirators if they managed to catch you, since, in the words of Ezekiel 25:17, they could be relied on to "strike down with great vengeance and furious anger those who attempt[ed] to poison and destroy [their] brothers." Furthermore, by defecting from the conspiracy you would be giving up on the (often-considerable) profits of an agreeable criminal lifestyle. Thus the costs of defection would be high and the rewards low. Such conspiracies, then, are non-defectible, or have low defectibility. It is for this very reason that Mafiosi and their confederates do not often defect unless they are already under indictment and facing massive amounts of jail-time, and only then if their safety (and that of their families) is guaranteed by a place in a witness protection program. With a non-defectible conspiracy such as this, sentiment, self-interest, and even a concern for others conspire to ensure loyalty to ones' fellow-conspirators.

Consider, by contrast, the highly defectible conspiracy proposed by the Watergate conspirator and real-life comic-book villain G. Gordon Liddy. Liddy pitched a scheme (one of many enterprising schemes) to Nixon's Committee to Re-Elect the President (commonly known as CREEP) that involved hiring a yacht that would be fitted out as a high-class bordello and anchored close to the Democratic Convention Center. Senators, congressmen, and lesser politicos from the Democratic Party would be lured in to sample its delights and whereupon their lust-fueled indiscretions would be recorded on tape to be subsequently used against them for the benefit of the Republican campaign. This scheme would be unlikely to work unless the staff had been primed to coax these lecherous politicos into spilling whatever beans they had access to. Thus the hookers would have had to be in on the deal. Now despite the fanatical loyalty of some Republican women, it is not very likely that the boat could have been staffed by Daughters of the American Revolution prepared to make the supreme sacrifice for the party. (Apart from anything else, amateurs, however enthusiastic, could not have been expected to give the necessary satisfaction.) So Liddy would have had to rely on professionals. And here lies the problem. However much he intended to pay these women, each of them could have gotten a lot more by pocketing her wages and betraying the conspiracy by selling her story to the newspapers. They might even have derived a certain amount of glory as patriotic prostitutes. Any NDAs that Liddy might have tried to apply would have been impossible to enforce in the courts, since they would probably have been judged illegal (plus the court cases would have brought even more discredit to the Republican cause). Thus the rewards for defection would have been high and the costs low to nonexistent. It would have been a highly defectible conspiracy that would have collapsed in a couple of weeks. Furthermore the costs of collapse would have been catastrophic for Nixon's campaign. This is perhaps one reason why (besides the inordinate expense) the scheme was vetoed by Liddy's boss, John Mitchell (then attorney general), who preferred to go with the safer, saner, and less expensive option of the Watergate break-in. (See Wheen 2009, 113 and White 1975, 157.)

To take another example from a perhaps more respectable source, consider the conspiratorial scheme proposed by Cass Sunstein and his intellectual sidekick Adrian Vermeule to deal with the threat of false and pernicious conspiracy theories (2009).[5] Such theories cannot be effectively countered by overt (and honest) government propaganda since the conspiracy theorists in question don't trust the government. They tend to live in Internet and informational bubbles where their conspiratorial prejudices are reinforced by likeminded folk who suffer from the same "crippled epistemologies." They are not exactly irrational (though obviously a lot less rational than sophisticated types such as Sunstein and Vermeule) but their rationality operates under unfavorable conditions leading to unfortunate results. (Their intellects are not crippled, but their epistemologies are.) How are these lost souls to be redeemed from ignorance and error? How are they to be cured of their unfortunate propensities to believe in false and harmful conspiracy theories? The Sunstein solution is that the government should pay covert propagandists, posing initially as ideological sympathizers, to infiltrate these Internet bubbles and to gradually undermine these conspiratorial belief-systems from within. As the bubble-boys of conspiracy are slowly exposed to new information by the covert agents of rationality (and a supposedly virtuous government) their epistemologies would be gently de-crippled and their conspiratorial fantasies gradually dissolved.

Now there are a number of problems with this scheme. To begin with such a program could not be subject to democratic scrutiny without becoming public at least in outline. And once it became public it would be likely to provoke an epidemic of paranoid conspiracy theorizing. No new recruit to a conspiracist cell would be trusted, and every mildly anti-conspiratorial blogger would be suspected of being a government stooge. The government's credibility would plummet, and rightly so. After all the government would be admitting, in effect, that they thought it acceptable to manipulate and lie to at least a subclass of its citizens. *Thus in order to succeed the program would have to be exempt from democratic scrutiny.* But a government whose policies are not subject to democratic scrutiny is not a genuinely democratic government. For in order for a government to express the people's will, a majority of the people must have endorsed its policies (at least in their general outlines) which is not possible if they don't know what the government is doing or what it intends to do. Thus the only government that could successfully implement this policy would be a government that did not comply with Sunstein's methodological assumption: "we assume a *well-motivated* government [my italics] that aims to eliminate conspiracy theories, or draw their poison, if and only if social welfare is improved by doing so. . . . This is a standard assumption in policy analysis" (Sunstein and Vermeule 2009, 219). But a government that is willing to systematically deceive even a subclass of its citizens is *ipso facto not* well-motivated (at least if we assume democratic norms), likewise a government that can only pursue some of its policies successfully if they are exempt from democratic scrutiny. For that is a government that is conspiring to undermine democracy. It is rather as if Sunstein and Vermeule had said "we assume a well-motivated government that aims to send its opponents to concentration camps in cattle-trucks if and only if social welfare is improved by doing so. . . . This is a standard assumption in policy analysis." The contradiction between their methodological assumption and the policy they *actually* propose is less brutal and less blatant than this, but it is a contradiction nonetheless. Governments that develop policies that can only succeed if they are secret (because they involve deceiving sizeable classes of citizens) are not well-motivated by democratic standards. But setting the moral criticisms aside, there is a problem with the *practicality* of the conspiracy that Sunstein and Vermeule want to set in motion. For any government that was not prepared to go the whole authoritarian hog (by viciously punishing whistle-blowing infiltrators), the conspiracy would be highly defectible, and therefore likely to be exposed. However much the government might have intended to pay its infiltrators, each of them could have gotten a lot more by pocketing their wages and betraying the conspiracy by selling their story to the newspapers. They might even have derived a certain amount of glory as patriotic whistleblowers (setting aside the possibility that they might have genuine qualms of conscience). Any NDAs that Sunstein's government might have tried to apply would have been impossible to enforce in the courts since they would probably have been judged illegal (plus the court cases would have brought even more discredit to the government's cause). Thus the rewards for defection would have been high and the costs low to nonexistent. Indeed, there would be a strong incentive for each of Sunstein's infiltrators to be the first defector since the first defector would reap the largest dividends both in terms of a reputation for democratic righteousness and in terms of cold hard cash. Given the impracticality of his scheme, it is perhaps a little surprising that Sunstein has an otherwise well-deserved reputation as a behavioral economist.

Now it is not a coincidence that neither Liddy's conspiracy nor the conspiracy proposed by Sunstein and Vermeule were ever put into practice.[6] Had somebody attempted to implement them, they would both have fallen over in pretty short order. *The more defectible a conspiracy is the less likely it is to remain secret for very long.* And since a reasonable period of successful secrecy is essential to most conspiracies, the more defectible a conspiracy is the more likely it is to fail. This is an important point about conspiracies, but it carries a corollary for conspiracy *theories*. A successfully secret but highly defectible conspiracy is unlikely to be real since it would likely unravel. *Hence conspiracy theories that postulate successfully secret but highly defectible conspiracies are likely to be false.* Indeed, the more defectible the conspiracy alleged by a conspiracy theory is, the less likely the theory is to be true.

Here is why this matters: conspiracy theories can be ranked in terms of the defectibility of the conspiracies that they postulate. The more defectible the alleged conspiracy, the less likely the theory is to be true. And most of the conspiracies postulated by the theories to which Stokes takes exception—the ones he regards as both crazy and pernicious—are defectible in the extreme.

Consider, for example, the idea that Anthropic Global Warming is a hoax propagated by the scientific community both to line their pockets with grants and subsidies and to facilitate a supposed socialist agenda. Now if this conspiracy theory were true the entire scientific community would have to be in on the deal. But to date there have been no defections. Though righteous right-wing pundits have their dark suspicions, so far not a single scientist (out of a total population that probably runs into the millions) has decided to blow the whistle on her colleagues' nefarious schemes. Yet the conspiracy itself is highly defectible. The costs of defection would be low, and the rewards amazingly high. Any scientist who chose to betray her confederates by confessing to the hoax would be on the gravy train for life, as oil companies, coal companies, and right-wing think-tanks fell over themselves to fund her research, not to mention the lucrative speaking engagements on *Fox and Friends* and the gratitude to be expected from wealthy oil sheikhs. She might expect a little hostility from her erstwhile colleagues, but her defection would be likely to start a cascade and she would not be lonely for long. Thus the theory postulates a conspiracy that is (a) successfully secret despite an enormous tally of co-conspirators, and (b) highly defectible. It is therefore almost certainly false.

Take another example, that of the Sandy Hook truthers who believe that the massacre was a false flag operation and that the grieving relatives (sometimes transformed by trauma into zealous gun control advocates) were "crisis actors," playing a pre-arranged part. Here again the alleged conspiracy is successfully secret but highly defectible, since the crisis actors would be lavishly rewarded if they confessed to the NRA. In order to play their parts successfully they must maintain an ordinary middle-class lifestyle for months and/or years without being able to enjoy the massive rewards that would surely be necessary to get anyone to perform such roles. Thus the temptation to get bigger rewards without the trouble and tedium of playing the part would be overwhelming. Yet none of these crisis actors has defected. Thus the conspiracy theory involves a successfully secret but highly defectible conspiracy—strong evidence, this, that it is false.

Now, I am not saying that defectibility is the only criterion for telling good conspiracy theories from bad. But it is at least a start. And it might pave the way for *arguments* with Climate Change Deniers or Sandy Hook Truthers which might actually convince them if they were the epistemically crippled but rational agents that Sunstein takes them to be. Of course that is only true of some of them. No rational argument is likely to convince somebody as dishonest, as stupid, and as sophistical as Donald Trump (if it is not a contradiction in terms to describe him as both stupid and sophistical). But not all his followers are beyond the reach of reason and an argument is more likely to win converts than preaching the virtues of an attitude of suspicion (which is what Stokes' defeasible particularism amounts to).

Thus we do not need to embrace Stokes' reluctant particularism to reject his problematic narratives. When dealing with false and dangerous conspiracy theories, a policy of honest argument seems better than a patronizing attitude of reticence, especially as that reticence is likely to be confined to the intellectual elite.

NOTES

1. Stokes does not mention the further difficulty, that since Western governments or government agencies frequently conspire, and do so in causally efficacious ways, even if we adopt this "blatantly gerrymandered and chauvinistic definition" of conspiracy theories, "there is nothing intrinsically irrational, or even unreasonable, about explanations of [this] form"—that is, explanations of historical events as due in part to the covert machinations of Western governments or government agencies. The same holds, of course, if we extend the definition to cover conspiracies on the part of Western multinational companies.

2. Indeed, we can reinforce this point with a dilemma. Either you think that history and the nightly news are reasonably reliable or you do not. Since history and the nightly news are chock-a-block with conspiracy theories, many of them established beyond reasonable doubt, if you think that history and the nightly news are reasonably reliable you will believe a wide range of conspiracy theories, from which it follows that you are a conspiracy theorist. If, on the other hand, you think that history is bunk and that the nightly news is totally fake, then you presumably believe that persons

or persons unknown conspired to fake them, from which it follows that you too are a conspiracy theorist though of a much more radical and paranoid kind. So whether or not you think that history is bunk and that the news is fake, you will be a conspiracy theorist of one kind or another, though you will be a lot less unhinged if you are a conspiracy theorist of the first kind rather than the second.

3. For the conspiracy to talk up the threats, see Rich (2006), Chilcot (2016), Bower (2016), and Oborne (2016). For the use of denialism to shield this conspiracy, see D. Coady (2006b), Pigden (2006), and Olmsted (2009), especially p. 9.

4. Yes, it really is a word, though it is not commonly employed in the sense that I intend to use it.

5. Sunstein is inclined just to talk about "conspiracy theories" in this connection but he does rather grudgingly admit that conspiracy theories *as such* need not be unreasonable or unwarranted, so it is best to interpret him as worrying about *false and pernicious* conspiracy theories rather than conspiracy theories *tout court*. With a sizeable dollop of charity he can be construed as a defeasible generalist.

6. However, Sunstein managed to incur the costs of his proposed conspiracy without putting it into effect, costs which were largely born by the regime that he served and which may have contributed to the Democrats' disastrous defeats in the 2010 midterms. In 2009, the president nominated Sunstein to the Office of Information and Regulatory Affairs. The word went out from the Right's attack-dogs such as Glenn Beck to dig up the dirt on Sunstein. Their followers may not be all that bright, but most of them know how to read and some of them can use Google. So they turned up his article in the *Journal of Political Philosophy*. Whereupon Glenn Beck and Co. seized upon it, pointing out its anti-democratic subtext and wondering out loud whether the policy Sunstein suggested had been covertly implemented so that even now supposedly independent bloggers were secretly spreading socialistic poisons at the behest of the evil Obama and his cohorts. The accusation was almost certainly false but Sunstein managed to exacerbate the problem that he set out to solve. The blogosphere was more paranoid than ever, absurd anti-government conspiracy theories were more rife, and as for Obama, he had one more cross to bear. Sunstein glories in the hostility of the "populist" right, printing their denunciations on the dust jacket of *Conspiracy Theories and Other Dangerous Ideas*. Given subsequent historical developments I think he should be a bit less smug.

Chapter 15

Taking Conspiracy Theories Seriously and Investigating Them

M R. X. Dentith

1. INTRODUCTION

As my fellow contributors have shown, we should—indeed must—take conspiracy theories seriously. Even the most reluctant among us admit that conspiracies occur, and that some form of the particularist approach to conspiracy theories is justified. Thus, the kind of prescription we find in the *Le Monde* declaration of Bronner et al. (2016) is a cure for a phantom problem. As I argue with Lee Basham in chapter 6, and Martin Orr in chapter 10, the theoretical underpinnings of Bronner et al. (both in their *Le Monde* piece and their subsequent *Social Epistemology Review and Reply Collective* article (Dieguez et al. 2016)) is the product of an unquestioning adherence to generalism, where we keep being told that conspiracy theory and conspiracy theorizing is unwarranted. As David Coady argues in chapter 12, this is mere propaganda, which we must resist.

It is fair to say that there is at least some theoretical antagonism between philosophers and social scientists when it comes to conspiracy theory theory (this antagonism, happily, is not personal, as can be attested by philosophers and social psychologists happily dining and drinking together at conferences on conspiracy theories). Marius Hans Raab, in chapter 11, offers an interesting and timely perspective on the two major research strands which make up psychological research into these things called "conspiracy theories." Raab's analysis of how conspiracy belief research in psychology is in a split-brain state speaks very much to the worries I expressed in an earlier paper, "The Problem of Conspiracism" (2018a) and reiterated elsewhere (with Martin Orr; see Dentith and Orr (2017)); the conspiracist mindset claim endemic to much generalist accounting of belief in conspiracy theories gets the analysis back-to-front. As Kurtis Hagen argues in chapter 9, a little epistemic humility would go a long way here given that the social scientific study of belief in conspiracy theories has pathologized conspiracy theorists unfairly. We need to be attentive to what conspiracy theorists actually say rather than our construals of what is said by them. Take, for instance, one of the examples Ginna Husting uses in chapter 8, the case of Cynthia McKinney, a U.S. politician who, in the immediate wake of 9/11, asked probing questions in Congress about what exactly the government knew about 9/11 before the fact. She was labeled as a "conspiracy theorist" and her questions condemned (in a way which made them out to be almost "un-American," despite being the kind of questions we should expect in a functioning democracy).

The McKinney case calls to mind Stokes' arguments about the ethics of accusation and its relationship to conspiracy theorizing. Lee Basham and I responded to some of these concerns in section 1, while Charles Pigden took Stokes to task in the previous chapter. But I have an especial interest here because—in recent work—I have been working on not just why we should take conspiracy theories seriously but also how we might go about investigating them (2017a, 2018b).

2. INVESTIGATING CONSPIRACY THEORIES

What motivates the investigation of a conspiracy theory (if we are to take them seriously, as the arguments in this volume urge)? The answer is simple: we should be spurred on by the idea that if a particular claim of conspiracy turned out to be warranted, then surely we would be obliged to do something about it! While, as I have argued elsewhere, not all secretive activity is sinister, and some conspiratorial activity might even be permissible (2014), conspiracies are at the least suspicious kinds of activity, and if they are occurring, we ought to know why.

However there are two problems when it comes to the investigation of conspiracy theories: there is not enough time in the day to investigate all of them, and few—if any—of us have the requisite expertise to assess any given particular conspiracy theory fully anyway. That is, it is hard to work out how to apportion the epistemic burden when it comes to treating conspiracy theories seriously, let alone start investigating them. This is, of course, a natural outcome if we treat our epistemic inquiries as individual efforts. But if we analyze conspiracy theories through the lens of social epistemology we can investigate them in a manner which proves to be more fruitful.

A community of inquiry (the label comes from both the work of John Dewey (1938) and C. S. Pierce (1958)) presents not just the best-case scenario for investigating conspiracy theories, but also a model as to how we can distribute said epistemic burden when it comes to the discussion and analysis of such theories. Not just that, but a properly constituted and functioning community of inquiry can investigate conspiracy theories without engaging in the kind of accusations which motivates Stokes' "reluctant" particularism.

Such a community investigates problems in a democratic and participatory fashion: by working together through a problem multiple viewpoints and differing levels of expertise combine to produce investigations which distribute the epistemic load.[1] This last point cannot be overstated: consider the wide variety of conspiracy theories cited in this volume alone. Coming to grips with the minutiae of just one of these theories is hard, let alone clusters or groups of them. Most of us do not have enough time in the day to devote to just the most mundane of our activities, let alone start investigating and resolving all the complex problems (some of which will be conspiracy theories) that we encounter. But by working in a democratic and participatory fashion we can share the epistemic load, and thus make the process of investigation easier on all concerned.

Potential members of such a community of inquiry might include interested members of the lay public, journalists (both professional and citizen), the police, the judiciary, and politicians. Although these members will, in many cases, turn out to be members of institutions, the diversity of members, and the lack of a central institution which governs them, should soothe the concerns of certain conspiracy theorists who worry that the experts who weigh in on conspiracy theories might well be involved in a conspiracy against them. That is, a community made up of diverse members is less likely to be conspired than a group of experts associated with a single institution.[2] Such communities of inquiry can also be transnational or international in scope. Thus worries that certain views might be impermissible socially or politically in one society or context can be counteracted by those views being expressible elsewhere; a diverse community will have diverse views, a point we will return to.

By working as a group we can solve, then, the issue of not having enough time in the day. No longer are we required to personally solve every issue. Rather, by distributing the burden of the investigation across a community we can participate in such investigations without those investigations taking up all our available time. The community of inquiry model also speaks to another way in which we can share the epistemic burden: some of us have certain skills or expertise others lack, and thus we can step in to fill the void (so to speak), knowing that in other situations, where we lack said skills or expertise, someone else qualified to do so will step up. As such, communities of inquiry both solve the epistemic issue of not having enough time in the day and also of distributing expertise where necessary.

The question of expertise here is interesting. In some cases it is easy to point toward specific expertise on a subject, but in some cases there may not be some expert (or set of experts) with respect to how we resolve a problem. In such cases the community can work together, pooling their resources and sharing the epistemic burden in cases where you simply cannot go to a subject matter authority for an expert opinion. This is of particular interest to the investigation of conspiracy theories, because it is plausible to claim it is a domain with only *improvised* knowledge, rather than one which has accredited experts.[3]

Why say there may be no experts or set of experts with regard to conspiracy theories? After all, this volume is a testament to expertise on conspiracy theory theory. But therein lies the rub: we are experts about conspiracy *theory* rather than experts in conspiracy theories. That is, if we are working with some kind of institutional theory of expertise, then there is no institution which accredits (or is recognized as accrediting) conspiracy theorists. Expertise about conspiracy theories is, in this sense, improvised. But we can compensate for a lack of conspiracy theory expertise in this broad sense by sharing the epistemic burden across a suitably constituted community; the community of inquiry model allows us to talk about expertise in a social or community way. It is also important to note that though there may not be accredited experts with regards to conspiracy theories *now*, there might be one day. The institutions we typically associate with accredited expertise now are, after all, typically the product of past communities of inquiry, codified (or, in some cases, commodified) over time.

This also has an added feature: for the conspiracy theorist of a certain stripe, appeals to expertise or authority which are used to dismiss some conspiracy theory will be problematic. Such conspiracy theorists will be worried—rightly or wrongly—that the institutions which accredit expertise or confer authority might themselves be conspired, and thus part of the conspiracy to engender doubt about the conspiracy theory. This concern cuts both ways: the arch skeptic of conspiracy theories will also be concerned about investigations which are only made up of people who already assume the existence of the conspiracies they are investigating.

A good example of such a community of inquiry approach into a particular claim of conspiracy comes from Dewey himself, given his involvement (and organization) of the Commission of Inquiry into the Charges Made against Leon Trotsky in the Moscow Trials (aka the Dewey Commission) in the 1930s. This investigation uncovered a conspiracy by the Soviets to engineer guilty verdicts against Stalin's purported enemies ("purported" because the dissidents were largely the product of Stalin's paranoia). As such, I am not really suggesting anything novel by advocating for a community of inquiry approach into conspiracy theories, as such inquiries have occurred in the past, albeit in a piecemeal and less than systematic fashion.

Which leads to the next point: you might be forgiven for thinking that I am advocating for a model which is already a dismal failure. Though we can point to the report on the Moscow Trials, or maybe the debunking of the "Weapons of Mass Destruction" narrative that supposedly justified the invasion of Iraq in 2003, these are but a few scattered successes compared to a significant number of failures: this is surely a worrying sign. After all, there are communities which discuss and dissect the "Lone Gunman" theory about the assassination of JFK, and it seems for every person who claims it's "Case Closed!" there is someone else who will claim that they have seen compelling evidence there really were people on the grassy knoll back in November of 1963. Given that Kennedy was assassinated over half a century ago, the various communities investigating these theories seem to have led to a greater diversity of views on the matter, rather than the emergence of a single, widely believed narrative. When we look at the theories surrounding the September 11th Attacks of 2001 (aka 9/11) there continue to persist various investigatory communities looking into the MIHOP (Made It Happen On Purpose) or LIHOP (Let It Happen On Purpose) theories, which rival the official (conspiracy) theory of the event.[4] The results of these investigations are contentious and, despite claims from both sides that the case is settled, the various competing theories persist.

Now, such disagreements might just be for appearance, which is to say that such disagreements could be construed as insincere. Maybe one side has a particular agenda they want to advance, and thus promote a theory not on the basis of the evidence but, rather, because of politics or pragmatics. This may be the case in certain situations: it certainly seems that the theory the Iraqi Regime in 2003 was producing Weapons of Mass Destruction was a thesis held to for political, rather than epistemic, ends. However, I think we can also point the finger toward the thesis of generalism, which still has sway in the discourse around these things called "conspiracy theories." We are often told (or, perhaps better put, informed by unquestioning research in the social sciences) that belief in conspiracy theories is irrational. Our putative investigations are, then, typically set up in diametric opposition to one another, a "she said/they said" approach to dealing with conspiracy theories. What we typically find in public discourse concerning such theories bifurcates along the lines of "These conspiracy theorists are just irrational!" and "No, you're ignoring the elephant in the room!" We all too often form our communities with the assumption we know the answer, and thus are looking for evidence to confirm it.

These failures to come to consensus, then, may well be due to the respective investigating communities being badly constituted. After all, any community of inquiry into a particular conspiracy theory needs to be made up of not just diverse people with respect to things like expertise, but also with regard to their attitudes toward conspiracy theories. More often than not, however, investigations into claims like 9/11, the vaccination conspiracy theories, and the like are designed (presumably unwittingly) from the outset to either prove or disprove some conspiracy theory, rather than take it seriously, investigate it, and see where the results of such an investigation lead.

A diversity of views on conspiracy theories should work to root out insincerity in the community as a whole. It will also make it harder for dogmatic proponents of one theory or another to deny the results of such an inquiry. Sure, people will reject the results for factors other than arguments and evidence. But if a diverse group comes to consensus on the warrant or lack of warrant of a particular conspiracy theory, then that is evidence that the results of the investigation have been and need to be treated seriously. In the case where there is dissent, those who disagree with the majority view should always be able to explain their minority view; the community's findings will be more akin to a judicial decision than a jury decision. As such, a properly constituted community should, then, not just be a salve to the conspiracy theorist, but also the conspiracy theory skeptic. That is, for us to take conspiracy theories there must be some people in our communities of inquiry who are willing to ask "But why should we take this seriously?"

3. CONSPIRACY THEORIZING AS A SOCIAL PRACTICE

To take conspiracy theories seriously and investigate them entails engaging in the practice of conspiracy theorizing. However, Stokes argues that we do not reason in a vacuum but, rather, in a world freighted with pre-existing moral and political meanings. Given this, and the fact the practice of theorizing about conspiracy involves making accusations—sometimes at an early stage of investigation—Stokes takes it that conspiracy theorizing as a social practice entails harm. He writes in chapter 2:

> The very act of entertaining a conspiracy theory as a *worthwhile hypothesis for investigation* may come at a serious moral cost, both in licensing socially harmful practices and in violating the attitude of trust that is, I argue, a precondition of ethical life.

Stokes argues that because of this we are morally obliged to reject some theories, even at the risk of occasionally being wrong.

Now, it is true that certain conspiracy theories are associated with known harms: anti-Semitic conspiracy theories have a long and terrible history of associated violence aimed at the Jewish people. Anti-vaccine conspiracy theories have led to a decrease in the immunization rate in some countries, and thus an uptick in early childhood diseases that were—a generation ago—almost on the edge of extinction. As such, I understand the motivation behind Stokes' reluctance to endorse particularism *sans* some ethical filter. Conspiracy theories that claim the Jewish people are behind the world's various calamities are indeed the kind of claim we do not need to treat seriously. As I argued in chapter 4, part of the evidence as to why we do not take some of these *particular* conspiracy theories seriously is because we have good anthropological, sociological, and related theories as evidence to how these narratives first emerged. Some of this evidence strongly suggests that the appellation "conspiracy" in these cases was insincerely fomented by agents who wanted to blame the Jewish people in order to make them scapegoats. As such, our suspicion of these theories is rooted in a particularist understanding of them.

Diversity is the key here: even if some members do happen to embrace certain tropes, in a properly constituted community of inquiry others will question them. After all, the constitution of these communities should be diverse not just with respect to gender, ideology, class, and the like, but also their attitude to conspiracy theory; we might think of this as being a "Devil's Advocate" condition.[5] Given this, it is fair, I think, to say that members of any given community of inquiry will end up being explicitly cognizant of certain conspiracy narratives or tropes, without necessarily having to in any way endorse them. They will not theorize in a vacuum. If they investigate some alleged banking conspiracy theory (which are often accused of being crypto anti-Semitic in nature), they will do it with the knowledge of systemic racism, a familiarity with tropes, and an eye on new, and compelling evidence. It may also mean that investigators must do work that other (more ordinary) epistemic agents are not obliged to do. Some of that work might even be dirty. But—and I hope this speaks to Stokes' concern here—our investigators, the members of our communities of inquiry, will not only be cognizant of conspiracy narratives, but that some of their putative work might entail passing wrongs. Thus they will only be motivated to investigate when there are compelling reasons to do so.

Our communities of inquiry need not perform their investigations publicly either: the members might work behind closed doors, only going public once an investigation has concluded. Advocating secret investigations into particular conspiracy theories is, on the face of it, a problematic move. The worry about private investigations is that they might be hiding something. Yet we now live in a world in which the worry about such investigations can be fixed by technology; mechanisms can be put in place to ensure that the results of private investigations will not just be publicly accessible, but the materials used in the investigation will also be made public. From numbering systems which serialize lodged documents in order to provide a safeguard against

evidence tampering, automated release systems which ensure that after a set
time evidence is released to the public, to automatic redaction technology
which ensures people only tangentially associated with the investigation can
keep their privacy when documents are released, we have already existing
mechanisms which allow for private investigations to eventually be reviewed
publicly. So, the question now is whether we are solely concerned with open
practices, or open and accessible *results*?

Indeed, we can even know that conspiracy theories are being investigated
without needing to know the exact details of the investigation if we have
systems in place to ensure the results of said investigation will be made
public. That is, we can—in some cases—run our investigations in total secret.
Then, once we have our findings, we can publish *all* the data, and give a full
accounting of our investigative methods. As such, we can circumvent the
problems associated with secretive investigations while also ensuring that
harmful public accusations are not made too early on in an investigation.

4. CONCLUSION

Taking conspiracy theories seriously and investigating them does not tell us
that a given community of inquiry will end up endorsing any particular conspiracy theory. It simply tells us that they might. Thus, when someone alleges
a conspiracy we ought to ensure there is some investigation of that claim. Yet
given the limits of reason from the point of everyday living—given we have
finite time and energy to devote to our epistemic pursuits—the best and most
comprehensive way to take conspiracy theories seriously and investigate
them is to form communities of inquiry. Through careful composition and
then analysis, even the most complex conspiracy theory can be investigated
via a community of inquiry. In some cases those investigations will reveal
nothing of interest, and thus we will know our polities are safe. But sometimes those investigations will reveal the existence of a conspiracy, one which
may well be a threat to the polis. We ought to know whether conspiracies are
occurring, and also why. That is why we must take conspiracy theory seriously, not just as a field of study, but also as a set of theories which make
claims about the world. As this text ably demonstrates, the costs are high if
we ignore conspiracy theories, while the benefits of taking them seriously are
enormous.

NOTES

1. The community of inquiry approach has become popular in certain pedagogical frameworks, as its use in the classroom encourages students to work together, rather than rely on a teacher as the source of knowledge.

2. While there will always be the worry a really competent conspiracy can plan the outcome of a conspiracy, such "superconspiracies" (to use a term from Michael Barkun (2003)) cannot really be protected against.

3. See Dentith and Keeley (2018) for more on this.

4. No matter what you believe about the events of 9/11, you likely believe some theory about a conspiracy, given that all accounts make reference to an event best explained by a group of people working together in secret.

5. One thing which might prove to be troubling no matter how well we construct our communities of inquiry is a curious aspect of contemporary public debate, where passion of any kind (whether anger, joy, or sadness) is oft taken to be a reason to dismiss someone's argument. For example, the marginalized person of color, or the trans individual, say, who gets angry about some policy debate or discussion of institutional prejudice which directly affects them is typically taken to not be arguing properly. Instead, they are asked to be dispassionate, as if separating their lived experience from their discourse is somehow a good thing. It is easy to be dispassionate about events which do not directly affect you, but it is very cruel indeed to ask those who are directly affected to be dispassionate about those very same events. Given our communities of inquiry will be moored in social mores concerning how debates and investigations are meant to be run, this issue—that of requiring people to be dispassionate—may well be a recurrent issue for the community of inquiry model. Unfortunately, without rethinking what we might term the standards of "public epistemology," this is an issue which will have to be dealt with on a case-by-case basis.

Bibliography

Abalakina-Paap, M., W. G. Stephan, T. Craig, and W. L. Gregory. 1999. "Beliefs in Conspiracies." *Political Psychology* 20 (3): 637–47. https://doi.org/10.1111/0162-895x.00160.

Ahmed, Sara. 2004a. "Affective Economies." *Social Text* 79 (22): 117–39.

———. 2004b. *Cultural Politics of Emotion*. New York: Routledge.

Aistrope, Tim. 2016. "The Muslim Paranoia Narrative in Counter-Radicalisation Policy." *Critical Studies on Terrorism* 9 (2): 182–204.

Allport, Gordon W., and Leo Postman. 1947. *The Psychology of Rumor*. New York: Henry Holt.

Altheide, David. 2002. *Creating Fear: News and the Construction of Crisis*. New York: Aldine de Gruyter.

Arendt, Hannah. 1998. *The Human Condition*. Chicago: The University of Chicago Press.

Arnold, Gordon B. 2008. *Conspiracy Theory in Film, Television and Politics*. Westport, CT: Praeger.

Ashworth, Michael. 2017. "Affective Governmentality: Governing Through Disgust in Uganda." *Social & Legal Studies* 26 (20): 188–207.

Ayto, John. 1999. *Twentieth Century Words*. Oxford: Oxford University Press.

Bale, Jeffrey M. 2007. "Political Paranoia v. Political Realism: On Distinguishing between Bogus Conspiracy Theories and Genuine Conspiratorial Politics." *Patterns of Prejudice* 41: 45–60.

Barkun, Michael. 2003. *A Culture of Conspiracy: Apocalyptic Visions in Contemporary America*. Berkeley: University of California Press.

Basham, Lee. 2003. "Malevolent Global Conspiracy." *Journal of Social Philosophy* 34: 91–103.

———. 2006. *Afterthoughts on Conspiracy Theory: Resilience and Ubiquity*. Edited by David Coady. Hampshire, UK: Ashgate.

———. 2011. *Conspiracy Theory and Rationality*. Edited by Carl Jensen and Rom Harré. Newcastle on Tyne: Cambridge Scholars Publishing.

———. 2016. "Between Two Generalisms: A Reply to Stokes." *Social Epistemology Review and Reply Collective* 5: 4–14.

———. 2017. "Pathologizing Open Societies: A Reply to the *Le Monde* Social Scientists." *Social Epistemology Review and Reply Collective* 6 (2): 59–68.

———. 2018. "Joining the Conspiracy." *Argumenta* 3 (2): 271–90. https://doi. org/10.23811/55.arg2017.bas.

Basham, Lee, and M R. X. Dentith. 2015. *Bad Thinkers? Don't Be so Gullible!* Edited by S. Abbas Raza. http://www.3quarksdaily.com/3quarksdaily/2015/08/ bad-thinkers-dont-be-so-gullible.html.

———. 2016. "Social Science's Conspiracy-Theory Panic: Now They Want to Cure Everyone." *Social Epistemology Review and Reply Collective* 5: 12–19.

Basham, Lee, and Juha Räikkä. in press. "Conspiracy Theory Phobia." In *Conspiracy Theories and the People Who Believe Them*, edited by Joe Uscinski. Oxford: Oxford University Press, forthcoming 2018.

Bauer, R. A., and D. B. Gleicher. 1953. "Word-of-Mouth Communication in the Soviet Union." *Public Opinion Quarterly* 17: 297–310.

Bell, Macalester. 2005. "A Woman's Scorn: Toward a Feminist Defense of Contempt as a Moral Emotion." *Hypatia* 20 (4): 80–93.

Berinsky, Adam J., Gregory A. Huber, and Gabriel S. Lenz. 2012. "Evaluating Online Labor Markets for Experimental Research: Amazon.com's Mechanical Turk." *Political Analysis* 20 (03): 351–68. https://doi.org/10.1093/pan/mpr057.

Bessi, Alessandro. 2016. "Personality Traits and Echo Chambers on Facebook." *Computers in Human Behavior* 65 (December): 319–24. https://doi.org/10.1016/j. chb.2016.08.016.

Bjerg, Ole, and Thomas Presskorn-Thygesen. 2016. "Conspiracy Theory: Truth Claim or Language Game?" *Theory, Culture & Society* 34: 137–59. https://doi. org/10.1177/0263276416657880.

Blencowe, Claire. 2010. "Foucault's and Arendt's 'Insider View' of Biopolitics: A Critique of Agamben." *History of the Human Sciences* 23 (5): 113–30.

Bonobo. 2009. "Soylent Green Is Made Out of People!!!" *Democratic Underground* (blog). October 16, 2009.

Bost, Preston R., and Stephen G. Prunier. 2013. "Rationality in Conspiracy Beliefs: The Role of Perceived Motive." *Psychological Reports: Sociocultural Issues in Psychology* 113: 118–28. https://doi.org/10.2466/17.04.PR0.113x17z0.

Bower, Tom. 2016. *Broken Vows: Tony Blair and the Tragedy of Power*. London: Faber and Faber.

Bratich, Jack Z. 2008. *Conspiracy Panics: Political Rationality and Popular Culture*. New York: State University of New York Press.

Braun, Kathrin. 2007. "Biopolitics and Temporality in Arendt and Foucault." *Time & Society*, 5–23.

Bronner, Gérald, Véronique Campion-Vincent, Sylvain Delouvée, Sebastian Dieguez, Karen Douglas, Nicolas Gauvrit, Anthony Lantian, and Pascal Wagner-Egger. 2016. "Luttons Efficacement Contre Les Théories Du Complot." *Le Monde*, June, 29.

Brotherton, R., C. C. French, and A. D. Pickering. 2013. "Measuring Belief in Conspiracy Theories: The Generic Conspiracist Beliefs Scale." *Frontiers in Psychology* 4. https://doi.org/10.3389/fpsyg.2013.00279.

Brotherton, Robert, and Christopher C. French. 2014. "Belief in Conspiracy Theories and Susceptibility to the Conjunction Fallacy." *Applied Cognitive Psychology* 28: 238–48. https://doi.org/10.1002/acp.2995.

Bruder, Martin, Peter Haffke, Nick Neave, Nina Nouripanah, and Roland Imhoff. 2013. "Measuring Individual Differences in Generic Beliefs in Conspiracy Theories across Cultures: The Conspiracy Mentality Questionnaire (CMQ)." *Frontiers in Psychology* 4. https://doi.org/10.3389/fpsyg.2013.00225.

Buenting, Joel, and Jason Taylor. 2010. "Conspiracy Theories and Fortuitous Data." *Philosophy of the Social Sciences* 40: 567–78. https://doi.org/10.1177/004839310 9350750.

Buhrmester, Michael D., Sanaz Talaifar, and Samuel D. Gosling. 2018. "An Evaluation of Amazon's Mechanical Turk, Its Rapid Rise, and Its Effective Use." *Perspectives on Psychological Science* 13 (2): 149–54. https://doi.org/10.1177/1745691617706516.

Buhrmester, Michael, Tracy Kwang, and Samuel D. Gosling. 2011. "Amazon's Mechanical Turk: A New Source of Inexpensive, Yet High-Quality, Data?" *Perspectives on Psychological Science* 6 (1): 3–5. https://doi.org/10.1177/1745691 610393980.

Butter, Michael, and Peter Knight. 2016. "Bridging the Great Divide: Conspiracy Theory Research for the 21st Century." *Diogenes*. https://doi.org/10.1177/0392192 116669289.

Byford, Jovan. 2011. *Conspiracy Theories: A Critical Introduction*. London: Palgrave Macmillan.

Campbell, Elaine. 2010. "The Emotional Life of Governmental Power." *Foucault Studies* 9: 35–53.

Caplow, Theodore. 1947. "Rumors in War." *Social Forces* 25: 298–302.

Cardindale, Matthew. 2008. "Politics US: Taking on the Two-Party Monopoly." *Inter Press Service*, April.

Cassam, Quassim. 2015. *Bad Thinkers*. Edited by Brigid Hains. http://aeon.co/magazine/philosophy/intellectual-character-of-conspiracy-theorists/.

———. 2016. "Vice Epistemology." *The Monist* 99: 159–80. https://doi.org/10.1093/monist/onv034.

Castanho Silva, Bruno, Federico Vegetti, and Levente Littvay. 2017. "The Elite Is Up to Something: Exploring the Relation Between Populism and Belief in Conspiracy Theories." *Swiss Political Science Review* 23 (4): 423–43. https://doi.org/10.1111/spsr.12270.

Champion, Jack. 2004. "Paranoid Shift or By Their Fruits, You Shall Know Them." *Democratic Underground* (blog). March 14, 2004. http://www.democraticunderground.com/discuss/duboard.php?az=view_all&address=104x1217989.

Chigwedere, Pride, G. R. Seage, S. Gruskin, T. H. Lee, and M. Essex. 2008. "Estimating the Lost Benefits of Antiretroviral Drug Use in South Africa."

JAIDS: Journal of Acquired Immune Deficiency Syndromes 49 (4): 410–15. https://doi.org/10.1097/QAI.0b013e31818a6cd5.

Chilcot, Sir John. 2016. *The Report of the Iraq Inquiry: Executive Summary.* London: Her Majesty's Stationery Office.

Clarke, Steve. 2002. "Conspiracy Theories and Conspiracy Theorizing." *Philosophy of the Social Sciences* 32: 131–50.

———. 2006. *Appealing to the Fundamental Attribution Error: Was It All a Big Mistake?* Edited by David Coady. Hampshire, UK: Ashgate.

———. 2007. "Conspiracy Theories and the Internet—Controlled Demolition and Arrested Development." *Episteme* 4: 167–80.

Clifford, William Kingdon. 1886. *Lectures and Essays by the Late William Kingdon Clifford.* London: Macmillan.

Coady, C. A. J. 2006. *Pathologies of Testimony.* Edited by Jennifer Lackey and Ernest Sosa. Oxford: Oxford University Press.

Coady, David. 2006a. "An Introduction to the Philosophical Debate about Conspiracy Theories." In *Conspiracy Theories: The Philosophical Debate*, edited by David Coady, 1–12. Hampshire, UK: Ashgate.

———, ed. 2006b. *Conspiracy Theories and Official Stories.* Hampshire, UK: Ashgate.

———, ed. 2006c. Conspiracy Theories: The Philosophical Debate. Hampshire, UK: Ashgate.

———, ed. 2006d. *The Pragmatic Rejection of Conspiracy Theories.* Hampshire, UK: Ashgate.

———. 2007. "Are Conspiracy Theorists Irrational?" *Episteme* 4: 193–204.

———. 2012. *What to Believe Now : Applying Epistemology to Contemporary Issues.* Chichester, West Sussex, UK: Wiley-Blackwell.

Conan Doyle, Arthur. 1891. "A Scandal in Bohemia." *The Strand*, June.

Costa, P. T., and R. R. McCrae. 1992. *Revised NEO Personality Inventory and NEO Five Factor Professional Manual.* Odessa, FL: Psychological Assessment Resources.

Craft, Stephanie, Seth Ashley, and Adam Maksl. 2017. "News Media Literacy and Conspiracy Theory Endorsement." *Communication and the Public* 2 (4): 388–401. https://doi.org/10.1177/2057047317725539.

Darwin, Hannah, Nick Neave, and Joni Holmes. 2011. "Belief in Conspiracy Theories: The Role of Paranormal Belief, Paranoid Ideation and Schizotypy." *Personality and Individual Differences* 50: 1289–93. https://doi.org/10.1016/j.paid.2011.02.027.

Dean, Jodi. 1998. *Aliens in America : Conspiracy Cultures from Outerspace to Cyberspace.* Ithaca, NY: Cornell University Press.

deHaven-Smith, Lance. 2013. *Conspiracy Theory in America.* Austin: University of Texas Press.

deHaven-Smith, Lance, and Matthew T. Witt. 2013. "Conspiracy Theory Reconsidered Responding to Mass Suspicions of Political Criminality in High Office." *Administration & Society*, October. https://doi.org/10.1177/0095399712459727.

Delaval, Craig. 2003. "Cocaine, Conspiracy Theories & the CIA in Central America." *FrontLine*.

Democratic Underground. 2006. "Question I Need Help." *Democratic Underground* (blog). 2006. https://upload.democraticunderground.com/discuss/duboard. php?az=view_all&address=364x2309.

———. 2008. "Emotionalism." *Democratic Underground* (blog). 2008. http:// www.democraticunderground.com/discuss/duboard.php?az=show_mesg&forum= 125&topic_id=66024&mesg_id=66243.

———. 2011. "Comment in 'Conspiracy Theories' That Were Really True." 2011. https://www.democraticunderground.com/discuss/duboard.php?az= view_all&address=439x1235256.

Dentith, M R. X.. 2014. *The Philosophy of Conspiracy Theories*. London: Palgrave Macmillan. https://doi.org/10.1057/9781137363169.

———. 2016a. "In Defence of Particularism: A Reply to Stokes." *Social Epistemology Review and Reply Collective* 5: 27–33.

———. 2016b. "When Inferring to a Conspiracy Might Be the Best Explanation." *Social Epistemology* 30 (5–6): 572–91. https://doi.org/10.1080/02691728.2016.11 72362.

———. 2017a. "Conspiracy Theories and Their Investigator(s)." *Social Epistemology Review and Reply Collective* 6 (4): 4–11.

———. 2017b. "Conspiracy Theories on the Basis of the Evidence." *Synthese*. https://doi.org/10.1007/s11229-017-1532-7.

———. 2018a. "The Problem of Conspiracism." *Argumenta* 3 (2): 327–43. https:// doi.org/10.23811/58.arg2017.den.

———. 2018b. "Expertise and Conspiracy Theories." *Social Epistemology*. https:// doi.org/10.1080/02691728.2018.1440021.

Dentith, M R. X., and Brian L. Keeley. 2018. *The Applied Epistemology of Conspiracy Theories*. Edited by David Coady and James Chase. London: Routledge.

Dentith, M R. X., and Martin Orr. 2017a. "Secrecy and Conspiracy." *Episteme*. https://doi.org/10.1017/epi.2017.9.

———. 2017b. "Clearing Up Some Conceptual Confusions About Conspiracy Theory Theorising." *Social Epistemology Review and Reply Collective* 6 (1): 9–16.

Dewey, John. 1938. *Logic: The Theory of Inquiry*. New York: Holt.

Dieguez, Sebastian, Gérald Bronner, Véronique Campion-Vincent, Sylvain Delouvée, Nicolas Gauvrit, Anthony Lantian, and Pascal Wagner-Egger. 2016. "'They' Respond: Comments on Basham et al.'s 'Social Science's Conspiracy-Theory Panic: Now They Want to Cure Everyone.'" *Social Epistemology Review and Reply Collective*, 20–39.

DiFonzo, Nicholas, and Prashant Bordia. 2007. *Rumor Psychology: Social and Organizational Approaches*. Washington, DC: American Psychological Association.

Douglas, Karen M., Robbie M. Sutton, and Aleksandra Cichocka. 2017. "The Psychology of Conspiracy Theories." *Current Directions in Psychological Science* 26: 538–42.

Draper, Eric. 2006. "Two Months Before 9/11, an Urgent Warning to Rice." *Washington Post*, October 6, 2006. http://www.washingtonpost.com/wp-dyn/content/article/2006/09/30/AR2006093000282.html.

Drok, Nico, and Liesbeth Hermans. 2016. "Is There a Future for Slow Journalism? The Perspective of Younger Users." *Journalism Practice* 10: 539–54.

Eilperin, Juliet. 2002. "Democrat Implies September 11 Administration Plot." *New York Times*, March, A16.

Embretson, Susan E., and Steven Paul Reise. 2000. *Item Response Theory for Psychologists*. Multivariate Applications Book Series. Mahwah, NJ: L. Erlbaum Associates.

Feldman, Susan. 2011. "Counterfact Conspiracy Theories." *International Journal of Applied Philosophy* 25: 15–24.

Fenster, Mark. 2008. *Conspiracy Theories: Secrecy and Power in American Culture*. 2nd edition. Minneapolis: University of Minnesota Press.

Ferguson, Galit. 2010. "The Family on Reality Television: Who's Shaming Whom?" *Television & New Media* 11: 87–104.

Fetzer, James, and Mike Palecek, eds. 2015. *Nobody Died at Sandy Hook*. n.p.: Moon Rock Books.

Foucault, Michel. 1988. "Technologies of the Self." In *Technologies of the Self*, edited by L. H. Martin, H. Gutman, and P. H. Hutton, 16–49. Amherst: University of Massachusetts Press.

———. 2010. *The Birth of Biopolitics: Lectures at the College de France (1978–9)*. Edited by Michael Senellart. Translated by Graham Burchell. New York: Palgrave Macmillan.

Franks, Bradley, Adrian Bangerter, Martin W. Bauer, Matthew Hall, and Mark C. Noort. 2017. "Beyond 'Monologicality'? Exploring Conspiracist Worldviews." *Frontiers in Psychology* 8 (June). https://doi.org/10.3389/fpsyg.2017.00861.

Frohn, Dominic. 2013. "Subjektive Theorien von Lesbischen, Schwulen Und Bisexuellen Bzw. Transidenten Beschäftigten Zum Umgang Mit Ihrer Sexuellen Bzw. Ihrer Geschlechtsidentität Im Kontext Ihrer Beruflichen Tätigkeit—Eine Explorative Qualitative Studie." *Forum: Qualitative Social Research* 14 (3). http://nbn-resolving.de/urn:nbn:de:0114-fqs130368.

Frontiers in Psychology Editorial Office. 2014. "Retraction: Recursive Fury: Conspiracist Ideation in the Blogosphere in Response to Research on Conspiracist Ideation." *Frontiers in Psychology* 5 (March). https://doi.org/10.3389/fpsyg.2014.00293.

Gadenne, Volker. 1984. *Theorie Und Erfahrung in Der Psychologischen Forschung*. Vol. 36. Die Einheit Der Gesellschaftswissenschaften. Heidelberg, Germany: Mohr Siebeck.

Galliker, Mark. 2016. *Ist Die Psychologie Eine Wissenschaft? Ihre Krisen Und Kontroversen von Den Anfängen Bis Zur Gegenwart*. Wiesbaden, Germany: Springer.

Ganser, Daniele. 2006. "The 'Strategy of Tension' in the Cold War Period." In *9/11 and American Empire, Volume 1: Intellectuals Speak Out*, edited by David Ray Griffin and Peter Dale Scott, 79–100. Northampton, MA: Interlink Pub Group.

Goertzel, Ted. 1994. "Belief in Conspiracy Theories." *Political Psychology* 15 (4): 731–42.

Goffman, Erving. 1963. *Stigma: Notes on the Management of Spoiled Identity.* Englewood Cliffs, NJ: Prentice-Hall.

Golden, Tim. 1996. "Though Evidence Is Thin, Tale of CIA and Drugs Has a Life of Its Own." *New York Times,* October 21, 1996.

Goldstein, Sasha. 2014. "Sandy Hook 'Truther' Caught in Virginia with Signs Stolen from Playgrounds Built for Newtown Victims: Police." *New York Daily News,* May 30, 2014.

Guaranteed. 2004. "Fun with Tinfoil: What Really Happened with the Egyptian Airliner Crash?" *Democratic Underground* (blog). January 3, 2004. http://www.democraticunderground.com/discuss/duboard.php? az=view_all&address=104x981730.

Gutsche, Robert. 2017. *Media Control: News as an Institution of Power and Social Control.* New York: Bloomsbury.

Hagen, Kurtis. 2011. "Conspiracy Theories and Stylized Facts." *Journal for Peace and Justice Studies* 21: 3–22.

———. 2017. "What Are They Really Up To? Activist Social Scientists Backpedal on Conspiracy Theory Agenda." *Social Epistemology Review and Reply Collective* 6 (3): 89–95.

———. 2018a. "Conspiracy Theories and Monological Belief Systems." *Argumenta* 3 (2): 303–26. https://doi.org/10.23811/57.arg2017.hag.

———. 2018b. "Conspiracy Theories and the Paranoid Style: Do Conspiracy Theories Posit Implausibly Vast and Evil Conspiracies?" *Social Epistemology* 32 (1): 24–40. https://doi.org/10.1080/02691728.2017.1352625.

Harambam, Jaron, and Stef Aupers. 2014. "Contesting Epistemic Authority: Conspiracy Theories on the Boundaries of Science." *Public Understanding of Science* 24: 466–80. https://doi.org/10.1177/0963662514559891.

Heins, Volker. 2007. "Critical Theory and the Traps of Conspiracy Thinking." *Philosophy Social Criticism* 33: 787–801. https://doi.org/10.1177/0191453707081675.

Hofstadter, Richard. 1964. "The Paranoid Style in American Politics." *Harper's Magazine.*

———. 1965. *The Paranoid Style in American Politics, and Other Essays.* 1st edition. New York: Knopf.

Holtz, Peter, Nicole Kronberger, and Wolfgang Wagner. 2012. "Analyzing Internet Forums: A Practical Guide." *Journal of Media Psychology* 24 (2): 55–66. https://doi.org/10.1027/1864-1105/a000062.

Honig, Bonnie. 1995. "Toward an Agonistic Feminism: Hannah Arendt and the Politics of Identity." In *Feminist Interpretations of Hannah Arendt,* edited by Bonnie Honig. University Park, PA: Penn State University Press.

Husting, Ginna, and Martin Orr. 2007. "Dangerous Machinery: 'Conspiracy Theorist' as a Transpersonal Strategy of Exclusion." *Symbolic Interaction* 30: 127–50. https://doi.org/10.1525/si.2007.30.2.127.

Illouz, Eva. 2007. *Cold Intimacies: The Making of Emotional Capitalism*. New York: Polity Press.

Iraq Family Health Survey Study Group. 2008. "Violence-Related Mortality in Iraq from 2002–2006." *New England Journal of Medicine*, no. 358: 484–93.

Jane, Emma, and Chris Fleming. 2014. *Modern Conspiracy: The Importance of Being Paranoid*. London: Bloomsbury.

Jolley, D., and K. M. Douglas. 2014. "The Effects of Anti-Vaccine Conspiracy Theories on Vaccination Intentions." *PLOS ONE* 9 (2): e89177. https://doi.org/10. 1371/journal.pone.0089177.

Jones, Karen. 2012. "Trustworthiness." *Ethics* 123 (1): 61–85.

Keeley, Brian L. 1999. "Of Conspiracy Theories." *Journal of Philosophy* 96: 109–26.

———. 2007. "God as the Ultimate Conspiracy Theorist." *Episteme* 4: 135–49.

Keller, Bill. 2011a. "Dealing with Assange and the Wikileaks Secrets." *New York Times Sunday Magazine*, January 30, 2011.

———. 2011b. "Let Me Take Off My Tinfoil Hat for a Moment." *New York Times Sunday Magazine*, June 5, 2011.

Kelman, Ari. 2009. "Rumors of Levee Sabotage in New Orleans's Lower 9th Ward." *Journal of Urban History* 35.

Knapp, Robert H. 1944. "A Psychology of Rumor." *Public Opinion Quarterly* 8 (1): 22–37.

Knight, Peter. 2000. *Conspiracy Culture: From the Kennedy Assassination to The X-Files*. London: Routledge.

Kosinski, M., D. Stillwell, and D. Graepel. 2013. "Private Traits and Attributes Are Predictable from Digital Records of Human Behavior." *Proceedings of the National Academy of Sciences (PNAS)* 110 (15): 5802–5. https://doi.org/10.1073/ pnas.1218772110.

Kumar, Deepa. 2006. "Media, War, and Propaganda: Strategies of Information Management During the 2003 Iraq War." *Communication and Critical/Cultural Studies* 3 (1): 48–69.

Lantian, A., D. Muller, C. Nurra, and K. M. Douglas. 2016. "Measuring Belief in Conspiracy Theories: Validation of a French and English Single-Item Scale." *International Review of Social Psychology* 29 (1): 1–14. https://doi.org/10.5334/ irsp.8.

Lantian, Anthony, Dominique Muller, Cécile Nurra, and Karen Douglas. 2017. "'I Know Things They Don't Know!' The Role of Need for Uniqueness in Belief in Conspiracy Theories." *Social Psychology* 48 (3): 160–73. https://doi. org/10.1027/1864-9335/a000306.

Leman, Patrick John, and Marco Cinnirella. 2013. "Beliefs in Conspiracy Theories and the Need for Cognitive Closure." *Frontiers in Psychology* 4. https://doi. org/10.3389/fpsyg.2013.00378.

Lemke, Thomas. 2009. *Foucault, Governmentality and Critique*. Boulder, CO: Paradigm Publishers.

Levy, Neil. 2007. "Radically Socialized Knowledge and Conspiracy Theories." *Episteme* 4: 181–92.

Lewandowsky, S., John Cook, Klaus Oberauer, and Michael Marriott. 2013. "Recursive Fury: Conspiracist Ideation in the Blogosphere in Response to Research on Conspiracist Ideation." *Frontiers in Psychology* 4. https://doi.org/10.3389/fpsyg.2013.00073.

Lewandowsky, S., K. Oberauer, and G. E. Gignac. 2013. "NASA Faked the Moon Landing—Therefore, (Climate) Science Is a Hoax : An Anatomy of the Motivated Rejection of Science." *Psychological Science* 24 (5): 622–33. https://doi.org/10.1177/0956797612457686.

Lipton, Peter. 2004. *Inference to the Best Explanation*. 2nd edition. London: Routledge.

Løgstrup, K. E. 1997. *The Ethical Demand*. Notre Dame, IN: University of Notre Dame Press.

MacIntyre, Alasdair. 2007. "Human Nature and Human Dependence: What Might a Thomist Learn from Reading Løgstrup?" In *Concern for the Other: Perspectives on the Ethics of K. E. Løgstrup*, edited by Svend Andersen and Kees van Kooten Niekerk, 147–66. Notre Dame, IN: University of Notre Dame Press.

———. 2016. *Ethics in the Conflicts of Modernity: An Essay on Desire, Practical Reasoning, and Narrative*. Cambridge: Cambridge University Press.

Mairesse, Francois, Marilyn A. Walker, Matthias R. Mehl, and Roger K. Moore. 2007. "Using Linguistic Cues for the Automatic Recognition of Personality in Conversation and Text." *Journal of Artificial Intelligence Research* 30 (1): 457–500.

Mandik, Peter. 2007. "Shit Happens." *Episteme* 4: 205–18.

Martin, Brian. 1997. *Suppression Stories*. Wollongong NSW: Fund for Intellectual Dissent.

———. 2015. "On the Suppression of Vaccination Dissent." *Science & Engineering Ethics* 21 (1): 143–57. https://doi.org/10.1007/s11948-014-9530-3.

Mason, Michelle. 2003. "Contempt as a Moral Attitude." *Ethics* 113: 234–72.

McKinney, Cynthia. 2002. "Some Thoughts on Our War against Terrorism." 2002. http://www.globalresearch.ca/articles/MCK204A.html.

McPhate, Mike. 2015. "University in Florida Seeks to Fire Newtown Conspiracy Theorist." *New York Times*, December 18, 2015.

Melnick, Joseph, and Sonia March Nevis. 2010. "Contempt." *Gestalt Review*, 3.

Michell, Joel. 1999. *Measurement in Psychology: Critical History of a Methodological Concept*. Ideas in Context. New York: Cambridge University Press.

Mill, John Stuart. 2008. *On Liberty*. Edited by Alan S. Kahan. Boston: Bedford St. Martins.

Miller, Ian. 1997. *The Anatomy of Disgust*. Cambridge, MA: Harvard University Press.

Miller, Joanne M., Kyle L. Saunders, and Christina E. Farhart. 2015. "Conspiracy Endorsement as Motivated Reasoning: The Moderating Roles of Political Knowledge and Trust." *American Journal of Political Science* 60 (4): 824–44. https://doi.org/10.1111/ajps.12234.

Mills, C. Wright. 1959. *The Sociological Imagination*. New York: Oxford University Press.

Nied, A. Conrad, Leo Stewart, Emma Spiro, and Kate Starbird. 2017. "Alternative Narratives of Crisis Events: Communities and Social Botnets Engaged on Social

Media." In *Companion of the 2017 ACM Conference on Computer Supported Cooperative Work and Social Computing*, 263–66. CSCW '17 Companion. New York: ACM. https://doi.org/10.1145/3022198.3026307.

NNN0LHI. 2007. "Why You Conspiracy Theorist, You." *Democratic Underground* (blog). 2007.

Nussbaum, Martha C. 2010. *From Disgust to Humanity: Sexual Orientation and Constitutional Law*. Oxford: Oxford University Press.

Oborne, Peter. 2016. *Not the Chilcot Report*. London: Head of Zeus.

Ohnuma, Keiko. 2008. "'Aloha Spirit' and the Cultural Politics of Sentiment as National Belonging." *Contemporary Pacific* 20 (2): 365–94.

Olmsted, Kathryn S. 2009. *Real Enemies: Conspiracy Theories and American Democracy, World War I to 9/11*. New York: Oxford University Press.

Owen, Robert. 2016. *The Litvinenko Inquiry: Report into the Death of Alexander Litvinenko*. London: The Stationery Office.

Pierce, C. S. 1958. *The Fixation of Belief*. Edited by Philip Wiener. New York: Dover Publications.

Pigden, Charles. 1995. "Popper Revisited, or What Is Wrong with Conspiracy Theories?" *Philosophy of the Social Sciences* 25 (March): 3–34. https://doi.org/10.1177/004839319502500101.

———. 2006. "Complots of Mischief." In *Conspiracy Theories: The Philosophical Debate*, edited by David Coady. Hampshire, UK: Ashgate.

———. 2007. "Conspiracy Theories and the Conventional Wisdom." *Episteme* 4: 219–32.

———. 2016. "Are Conspiracy Theorists Epistemically Vicious?" In *A Companion to Applied Philosophy*, edited by David Coady, Kimberley Brownlee, and Kasper Lipper-Rasmussen. Hoboken, NJ: Wiley-Blackwell. https://doi.org/10.1002/9781118869109.ch9.

———. in press. "Conspiracy Theories and the Conventional Wisdom Revisited." In *Secrets and Conspiracies*, edited by Olli Loukola. Amsterdam: Rodopi.

Pipes, Daniel. 1997. *Conspiracy: How the Paranoid Style Flourishes and Where It Comes From*. New York: Free Press.

Plutarch. 1999. *Roman Lives*. Translated by R. Waterfield. Oxford: Oxford University Press.

Popper, Karl Raimond. 1947. *The Open Society and Its Enemies—The Spell of Plato*. London: Routledge & Sons.

———. 1962. *The Open Society and Its Enemies —The High Tide of Prophecy: Hegel Marx and the Aftermath*. 4th edition. Volume 2. London and Henley: Routledge and Kegan Paul.

———. 1969. *The Open Society and Its Enemies*. 5th edition. Volume 2. London and Henley: Routledge and Kegan Paul.

———. 1972. *Conjectures and Refutations*. 4th edition. London: Routledge and Kegan Paul.

———. 2012. *The Open Society and Its Enemies*. Abingdon, Oxford: Routledge.

Quattrociocchi, Walter, Antonio Scala, and Cass R. Sunstein. 2016. "Echo Chambers on Facebook." *SSRN Electronic Journal*. https://doi.org/10.2139/ssrn.2795110.

Quine, W. V. 1951. "Two Dogmas of Empiricism." *Philosophical Review* 60: 20–43.

Raab, M. H., N. Auer, S. A. Ortlieb, and C. C. Carbon. 2013. "The Sarrazin Effect: The Presence of Absurd Statements in Conspiracy Theories Makes Canonical Information Less Plausible." *Frontiers in Psychology* 4. https://doi.org/10.3389/fpsyg.2013.00453.

Raab, M. H., S. Ortlieb, N. Auer, K. Guthmann, and C. C. Carbon. 2013. "Thirty Shades of Truth: Conspiracy Theories as Stories of Individuation, Not of Pathological Delusion." *Frontiers in Psychology* 4. https://doi.org/10.3389/fpsyg.2013.00406.

Räikkä, Juha. 2009a. "The Ethics of Conspiracy Theorizing." *Journal of Value Inquiry* 43: 457–68. https://doi.org/10.1007/s10790-009-9189-1.

———. 2009b. "On Political Conspiracy Theories." *Journal of Political Philosophy* 17 (June): 185–201. https://doi.org/10.1111/j.1467-9760.2007.00300.x.

Reitman, Ivan. 1984. *Ghostbusters*. Comedy. RCA/Columbia Pictures.

Rich, Frank. 2006. *The Greatest Story Ever Sold*. New York: Penguin.

Rosnow, Ralph L., and Gary A. Fine. 1976. *Rumor and Gossip: The Social Psychology of Hearsay*. New York: Elsevier.

Samrai, Y. 2017. "Students Debate Being 'Guinea Pigs' for PSYCH 1 Requirement." December 4, 2017. https://www.stanforddaily.com/2017/12/02/students-question-psych-1s-experimental-participation-requirement/.

Sassen, Saskia. 2006. *Territory, Authority, Rights: From Medieval to Global Assemblage*. Princeton, NJ: Princeton University Press.

Sauer, Birgit, and Otto Penz. 2017. In *Gender, Governance and Feminist Analysis: Missing in Action*, edited by Christine M. Hudson, Malin Rönnblom, and Katherine Teghtsoonian, 39–58. Abingdon, UK: Taylor & Francis.

Scheele, Brigitte, and Norbert Groeben. 1986. "Methodological Aspects of Illustrating the Cognitive-Reflective Function of Aesthetic Communication. Employing a Structure-Formation Technique with Readers of (Positive) Literary Utopias." *Poetics*, no. 15: 527–54.

———. 1988. *Dialog-Konsens-Methoden Zur Rekonstruktion Subjektiver Theorien: Die Heidelberger Struktur-Lege-Technik (SLT), Konsensuale Ziel-Mittel-Argumentation Und Kommunikative Flussdiagramm-Beschreibung von Handlungen*. Tübingen, Germany: A. Francke.

Schou, Nick. 2006. "The Truth in 'Dark Alliance.'" *Los Angeles Times*, August 18, 2006. http://articles.latimes.com/2006/aug/18/opinion/oe-schou18.

Seitz-Wald, Alex. 2013. "This Man Helped Save Six Children, Is Now Getting Harassed for It." *Salon*, January 15, 2013. http://www.salon.com/2013/01/15/this_man_helped_save_six_children_is_now_getting_harassed_for_it.

Shore, R. 2016. "The Problem with Human Guinea Pigs." January 28, 2016. http://www.vancouversun.com/health/problem+with+human+guinea+pigs/11680820/story.html.

Simmons, William Paul, and Sharon Parsons. 2005. "Beliefs in Conspiracy Theories Among African Americans: A Comparison of Elites and Masses." *Social Science Quarterly* 86: 582–98.

Stokes, Patrick. 2016. "Between Generalism and Particularism about Conspiracy Theory: A Response to Basham and Dentith." *Social Epistemology Review and Reply Collective* 5: 34–39.

———. 2017a. "Reluctance and Suspicion: Reply to Basham and Dentith." *Social Epistemology Review and Reply Collective* 6: 48–58.

———. 2017b. "Spontaneity and Perfection: MacIntyre vs. Løgstrup." In *What Is Ethically Demanded? K. E. Løgstrup's Philosophy of Moral Life*, edited by Hans Fink and Robert Stern, 275–99. Notre Dame, IN: University of Notre Dame Press.

Sunstein, Cass R. 2009. *On Rumors*. New York: Farrar, Strauss and Giroux.

———. 2015. *Conspiracy Theories and Other Dangerous Ideas*. New York: Simon & Schuster.

Sunstein, Cass R., and Adrian Vermeule. 2009. "Conspiracy Theories: Causes and Cures." *Journal of Political Philosophy* 17 (June): 202–27. https://doi.org/10.1111/j.1467-9760.2008.00325.x.

Swami, V., David Barron, Laura Weis, Martin Voracek, Stefan Stieger, and Adrian Furnham. 2017. "An Examination of the Factorial and Convergent Validity of Four Measures of Conspiracist Ideation, with Recommendations for Researchers." *PLoS ONE* 12 (2): e0172617. https://doi.org/10.1371/journal.pone.0172617.

Swami, V., T. Chamorro-Premuzic, and A. Furnham. 2010. "Unanswered Questions: A Preliminary Investigation of Personality and Individual Difference Predictors of 9/11 Conspiracist Beliefs." *Applied Cognitive Psychology* 24: 749–61. https://doi.org/10.1002/acp.1583.

Swami, V., R. Coles, S. Stieger, J. Pietschnig, A. Furnham, S. Rehim, and M. Voracek. 2011. "Conspiracist Ideation in Britain and Austria: Evidence of a Monological Belief System and Associations between Individual Psychological Differences and Real-World and Fictitious Conspiracy Theories." *British Journal of Psychology* 102: 443–63. https://doi.org/10.1111/j.2044-8295.2010.02004.x.

Swire, Briony, Adam J. Berinsky, Stephan Lewandowsky, and Ullrich K. H. Ecker. 2017. "Processing Political Misinformation: Comprehending the Trump Phenomenon." *Royal Society Open Science* 4 (3): 160802. https://doi.org/10.1098/rsos.160802.

T_i_B. 2007. "The Troof Is Out There." *Democratic Underground* (blog). September 17, 2007. http://www.democraticunderground.com/discuss/duboard.php?az=view_all&address=103x308133.

Tierney, Peter. 2015. "The Despicable Cruelty of the Awful Anti-Vaccination Movement— Updated." April 12, 2015. https://reasonablehank.com/2015/04/12/the-despicable-cruelty-of-the-awful-anti-vaccination-movement/.

———. 2016. "The Mobbing of Riley Hughes' Family by Anti-Vaccination Thugs." January 15, 2016. https://reasonablehank.com/2016/01/15/the-mobbing-of-riley-hughes-family-by-anti-vaccination-thugs/.

Tolley, Erin. 2015. *Framed: Media and the Coverage of Race in Canadian Politics*. Vancouver: UBC Press.

Tourangeau, Roger, Lance J. Rips, and Kenneth A. Rasinski. 2000. *The Psychology of Survey Response*. Cambridge: Cambridge University Press.

Tversky, A., and D. Kahneman. 1974. "Judgment under Uncertainty: Heuristics and Biases." *Science* 185 (4157): 1124–31. https://doi.org/10.1126/science.185. 4157.1124.

van der Linden, Sander. 2015. *The Surprising Power of Conspiracy Theories*. Edited by Kaja Perina. https://www.psychologytoday.com/blog/socially-relevant/201508/ the-surprising-power-conspiracy-theories.

van Prooijen, Jan-Willem, and Michele Acker. 2015. "The Influence of Control on Belief in Conspiracy Theories: Conceptual and Applied Extensions." *Applied Cognitive Psychology* 29 (5): 753–61. https://doi.org/10.1002/acp.3161.

Vincent, Cédric. 2006. "Mapping the Invisible: Notes on the Reason of Conspiracy Theories." *Sarai Reader 06: Turbulence*, 41–48.

Vrasti, Wanda. 2011. "Caring Capitalism and the Duplicity of Critique." *Theory and Event* 14 (4).

Wagner-Egger, Pascal, and Pascal Gygax. 2017. "Diana Was Not Involved in the 9/11 Terrorist Attacks! Or Was She? Newspaper Headlines and the Boomerang Effect." *Swiss Journal of Psychology* 77 (1): 15–22.

Walker, Jesse. 2013. *The United States of Paranoia: A Conspiracy Theory*. New York: Harper.

Webb, Gary. 1998. *Dark Alliance: The CIA, the Contras, and the Crack Cocaine Explosion*. Seven Stories Press.

Wheen, Francis. 2009. *Strange Days Indeed*. London: Fourth Estate.

White, Theodore H. 1975. *Breach of Faith: The Fall of Richard Nixon*. New York: Readers Digest Press.

Williams, Bernard. 2015. *Ethics and the Limits of Philosophy*. London: Routledge.

Wilson, Robert Anton. 1998. *Everything Is Under Control: Conspiracies, Cults and Cover-Ups*. New York: Harper Paperbacks.

Wood, Michael J. 2016. "Some Dare Call It Conspiracy: Labeling Something a Conspiracy Theory Does Not Reduce Belief in It." *Political Psychology* 37: 695–705. https://doi.org/10.1111/pops.12285.

———. 2017. "Conspiracy Suspicions as a Proxy for Beliefs in Conspiracy Theories: Implications for Theory and Measurement." *British Journal of Psychology* 108 (3): 507–27. https://doi.org/10.1111/bjop.12231.

Wood, Michael J., and Karen M. Douglas. 2013. "'What about Building 7?' A Social Psychological Study of Online Discussion of 9/11 Conspiracy Theories." *Frontiers in Psychology* 4 (July): 1–9. https://doi.org/10.3389/fpsyg.2013.00409.

———. 2015. "Online Communication as a Window to Conspiracist Worldviews." *Frontiers in Psychology* 6. https://doi.org/10.3389/fpsyg.2015.00836.

Wood, Michael J., Karen M. Douglas, and Robbie M. Sutton. 2012. "Dead and Alive: Beliefs in Contradictory Conspiracy Theories." *Social Psychological and Personality Science* 3: 767–73. https://doi.org/10.1177/1948550611434786.

Worobey, Michael, Mario L. Santiago, Brandon F. Keele, Jean-Bosco N. Ndjango, Jeffrey B. Joy, Bernard L. Labama, Benoît D. Dhed'a, et al. 2004. "Origin of AIDS: Contaminated Polio Vaccine Theory Refuted." *Nature* 428 (6985): 820.

Zelizer, Barbie, and Stuart Allen. 2004. *Journalism after September 11*. New York: Routledge.

Zinoviev, Dmitry. 2017. "Network Analysis of Conspiracy Theories and Pseudosciences." International Conference on Computational Social Science, Cologne, Germany.

Zucca, Costanza, and Fred Fenter. 2014. "Retraction of Recursive Fury: A Statement." *Frontiers Blog* (blog). April 4, 2014. https://blog.frontiersin.org/2014/04/04/retraction-of-recursive-fury-a-statement/.

Index

About the Contributors

M R. X. Dentith is the author of *The Philosophy of Conspiracy Theories* (2014), the first single author, book-length treatment of the epistemological issues surrounding belief in conspiracy theories. They received their PhD in philosophy from the University of Auckland, and have been both a fellow in the Institute for Research in the Humanities (ICUB-IRH) and the New Europe College in Bucharest, where they have worked on their solo research projects, "The Ethics of Investigation: When Are We Obliged to Take Conspiracy Theories Seriously?" and "Towards an Epistemology of Secrecy."

Patrick Stokes is senior lecturer in philosophy at Deakin University, Australia. He is the author of *The Naked Self: Kierkegaard and Personal Identity* (2015) and *Kierkegaard's Mirrors: Interest, Self, and Moral Vision* (2010) and works on issues of personal identity, moral psychology, temporality, and death. He is also a media commentator on philosophy and writes for outlets including *New Philosopher* and *The Conversation*.

Lee Basham is the author of several articles on the epistemology of conspiracy theories and has given a number of talks on the subject. He is among the first philosophers to offer a broad defense of the rational and epistemic legitimacy of conspiracy theorizing. He teaches philosophy at South Texas College and the University of Texas Rio Grande Valley.

Ginna Husting is professor in the Department of Sociology and director of Gender Studies at Boise State University. She earned her PhD in sociology from the University of Illinois at Urbana-Champaign. Her research spans sociology, cultural studies, and feminist theories. Her most recent work examines how the phrase "conspiracy theorist" works in the context of political speech as a means of interactional degradation and exclusion from the sphere of "reasonable interlocutors." She has published articles with Leslie King of Smith College on French and American nationalism in the context of abortion-related protest and RU-486. Her other work focuses on media representations of social protest and their implications for democratic political action.

Kurtis Hagen, former associate professor and chair of the Philosophy Department at SUNY Plattsburgh, is now an independent scholar. His publications include "Is Infiltration of 'Extremist Groups' Justified?" (2010), "Conspiracy Theories and Stylized Facts" (2011), "Project for a New Confucian Century" (2016), and "Would Early Confucians Really Support Humanitarian Interventions?" (2016), as well as many articles on early Chinese philosophy and one book, *The Philosophy of Xunzi: A Reconstruction* (2007).

Martin Orr is professor of sociology at Boise State University. He received his PhD from the University of Oregon in 1992. His research and teaching interests include social inequality, political sociology, social movements, mass media, and the environment. In addition to work on anti-globalization movements and on the social context of sociological theories of race and ethnicity, he is coauthor, with Ginna Husting, of "Dangerous Machinery: 'Conspiracy Theorist' as a Transpersonal Strategy of Exclusion" (2007), and coauthor, with M R. X. Dentith, of "Secrecy and Conspiracy" (2017).

Marius Hans Raab is a research scientist in the Department of General Psychology and Methodology, University of Bamberg, Germany. In his PhD thesis, he developed and discussed empirical approaches for a better understanding of conspiracy theories. He has published several peer-reviewed articles, given popular scientific talks on the topic and is first author of the German popular science book *Am Anfang war die Verschwörungstheorie* [In the Beginning Was the Conspiracy Theory] (2017). Other research interests are dynamics of aesthetic experience and visual perception as well as psychological aspects of marketing and innovation for small and medium-sized businesses.

David Coady's research covers a wide variety of philosophical topics. Most of his current work is on applied philosophy, especially applied epistemology. He has published on rumor, conspiracy theory, the blogosphere, expertise, and democratic theory. He has also published on the metaphysics of causation, the philosophy of law, climate change, cricket ethics, police ethics, and the ethics of horror films. He is the author of *What to Believe Now: Applying Epistemology to Contemporary Issues* (2012), the co-author of *The Climate Change Debate: An Epistemic and Ethical Enquiry* (2013), the editor of *Conspiracy Theories: the Philosophical Debate* (2006) and the co-editor of *A Companion to Applied Philosophy* (2016).

Charles Pigden is a graduate of King's College Cambridge (1979) and did his doctorate (as a Commonwealth Scholar) at La Trobe University, Melbourne, Australia. Since 1988 he has taught philosophy at the University of Otago, New Zealand. He has published on a wide range of subjects including Bertrand Russell's ethics, Hume on Is and Ought, the philosophy of mathematics, and Jane Austen's Mr. Elliot. He has had a longstanding interest in conspiratorial themes, since the publication of his paper "Popper Revisited: What Is Wrong with Conspiracy Theories?" in 1995.

CPSIA information can be obtained
at www.ICGtesting.com
Printed in the USA
LVHW041336180723
752728LV00005B/48

9 781786 608291